Language, Education, and Ideology

Recent Titles in
Contemporary Language Education
Terry A. Osborn, Series Adviser

Foreign Language Program Articulation: Current Practice and Future Prospects
Carolyn Gascoigne Lally, editor

The Future of Foreign Language Education in the United States
Terry A. Osborn, editor

Lasting Change in Foreign Language Education: A Historical Case for Change in National Policy
John L. Watzke

The Reasons We Speak: Cognition and Discourse in the Second Language Classroom
Miguel Mantero

Language, Education, and Ideology

Mapping the Linguistic Landscape of U.S. Schools

Timothy Reagan

Contemporary Language Education
Terry A. Osborn, Series Adviser

Westport, Connecticut
London

Library of Congress Cataloging-in-Publication Data

Reagan, Timothy G.
Language, education, and ideology : mapping the linguistic landscape of U.S. schools / Timothy Reagan.
p. cm.—(Contemporary language education, ISSN 1531–1449)
Includes bibliographical references and index.
ISBN 0–89789–752–8 (alk. paper)
1. Language and education—United States. 2. Language and languages—Study and teaching—United States. 3. Multiculturalism—United States. 4. Language awareness — United States. I. Title. II. Contemporary language education (Praeger (Westport, Conn.))
P40.85.U6R43 2002
418'.0071'073—dc21 2002067302

British Library Cataloguing in Publication Data is available.

Library of Congress Catalog Card Number: 2002067302
ISBN: 0–89789–752–8
ISSN: 1531–1449

First published in 2002

Praeger Publishers, 88 Post Road West, Westport, CT 06881
An imprint of Greenwood Publishing Group, Inc.
www.praeger.com

Printed in the United States of America

The paper used in this book complies with the Permanent Paper Standard issued by the National Information Standards Organization (Z39.48–1984).

10 9 8 7 6 5 4 3 2 1

Copyright Acknowledgments

The author and publisher gratefully acknowledge permission for use of the following material:

Excerpts from T. Reagan, "Toward a political economy of the less commonly taught languages in American public schools," in *The future of foreign language in education in the United States*, edited by Terry A. Osborn. Westport, CT: Bergin and Garvey, 2002. Reprinted by permission of the Greenwood Publishing Group, Inc.

Excerpts from Neil Bermal and Olga Kagan, "The maintenance of written Russian in heritage speakers," in *The learning and teaching of Slavic languages and cultures*, edited by O. Kagan and B. Rifkin. Bloomington, IN: Slavica, 2000. Reprinted by permission of Slavica and Olga Kagan and Neil Bermal.

Dedicated to the memory of
Jane A. Freiberg, M.D.

Contents

Preface

In January 1982, I defended my doctoral dissertation at the University of Illinois, Champaign-Urbana. The dissertation, titled, "Language, Ideology, and Education," was an attempt to address a number of issues related to the controversies about bilingual education and Black English in the U.S. context from an interdisciplinary perspective. This book, in spite of the similarity of title, is in fact a very different work, one informed by twenty years of scholarship and life experience. However, it does share many elements with that dissertation: it is concerned with the interface of language and education and with the political and ideological aspects of that interface. It also deals with these matters from the perspective of a foreign language educator, which the dissertation did not attempt to do, and includes insights from my work on sign language and deafness, language and education in South Africa, and linguistic human rights—all issues about which I knew virtually nothing when I wrote my dissertation.

The target audience for this book is, first and foremost, foreign language educators, but it also includes other educators interested or involved in the teaching and learning of languages. Included in this group are not only those whose professional identification is that of a language educator—foreign language, ESL , bilingual, and English teachers in particular—but also of any educator dealing with any child in a classroom setting. There is an old adage, "Every teacher is an English teacher." I think that, although dated, this adage is still very true, and further, that every teacher must also be something of an applied linguist. The issues addressed in this book are not just issues of concern for language educators; they touch on the very core of what it means to be an advocate for all children.

This book is decidedly and deliberately political in nature. P.W. Botha, as State President of South Africa, once commented at an opening session of Parliament, "Effective meaningful education is possible only if politics are excluded from it" (30 January 1987). In fact, I believe that just the reverse is true: effective, meaningful education is possible only when we recognize the fundamentally political and ideological nature of schooling. Education is not, cannot, and should not be apolitical. This does not mean that indoctrination is acceptable; indeed, only by helping students recognize the political and ideological underpinnings of contemporary social and educational institutions can we prepare them to make their own informed political decisions. This, I believe, should be one of the central goals of all schooling in a democratic society.

Language, Education, and Ideology, as its subtitle suggests, is in essence an effort to "map" the linguistic landscape of contemporary U.S. education. It therefore deals not only with issues of immediate and direct concern for the language educator but also with broader matters that are at the teacher, student, and language nexus. This book is not a "how to" manual; in my view, we already have a more than sufficient supply of books that seek to make important educational issues merely technical problems to be solved. The life of the teacher (and of the student) is far too complex for such an approach, and it is only by allowing ourselves critically to explore what we are doing, and why we are doing it, that we can really hope to improve teaching and learning in the classroom.

In writing this book, I have benefited immensely from interactions with a number of friends and colleagues. I am grateful to Christine Brown, Tom DeFranco, Eva Díaz, Barbara Lindsey, Ceil Lucas, Rose Morris, Daniel Mulcahy, Frank Nuessel, Claire Penn, Xaé Reyes, Sandra Schreffler, Tove Skutnabb-Kangas, Cheryl Spaulding, Humphrey Tonkin, and Jan Vorster for their interest and support. My colleagues in the Neag School of Education at the University of Connecticut are as wonderful a group of committed and caring educators as one would find anywhere, and I want to take this opportunity to thank all of them. I am especially grateful to my friend and colleague Terry Osborn for his insights, criticisms, and good humor. Finally, Jo Ann, Joshua, Bryan, and Kimberly have, as always, been there when I needed them most.

Chapter 1

Language and Power in School and Society: *Cui bono*?

This book, as its title suggests, is about language. It is also about language education in society and about the role of ideology in language education. This means that we will be discussing a broad range of social, cultural, political, and linguistic topics. However, at heart, this book is really about power. It is about the ways in which language establishes, reflects, reinforces, and challenges power and power relations in society. Almost any time that we look at issues of power in society we are concerned, among other things, with answering the question, "*Cui bono?*"—that is, in determining who benefits from particular practices, structures, organizations, attitudes, and so on.

It is hardly radical to suggest that social policies and practices benefit different individuals and groups disproportionately.[1] Indeed, this is really what politics and social organization are all about. For instance, while we may believe that everyone in society benefits from having a well-educated population, that does not mean that everyone benefits equally from expenditures for public schooling. Children and their parents, obviously, benefit more directly (and disproportionately) from such spending than do others in society. Everyone in society benefits to some degree from having a well-developed transportation infrastructure, but drivers benefit more immediately from the presence and maintenance of a good public transportation infrastructure than do nondrivers. Many benefits of this sort are not only necessary for the good of the social order as a whole, but also quite reasonably and appropriately benefit some groups and individuals more than others at any given point in time. As members of a common society, we understand and accept this. One may not be enrolled in a public school or have children in a public school at the moment, but still recognize the value of public education and be willing to invest in it for one's own good, the good of the community, and the likelihood that it will benefit each of us (both directly and indirectly) at other points in one's life.

Although many social benefits of the type discussed here are clearly defensible, others may be less so. The right to vote, for instance, is a social benefit that has been denied to many groups and individuals in our own society and in other societies for a wide array of different reasons—including gender, race, wealth, ownership of property, and educational level. Most of us today would reject the idea that voting should be restricted to white males; the rationale for such a restriction is simply not compelling. At the same time, the rationale for restricting voting rights to legal adults may be compelling. The fundamental issue at stake with respect to the distribution of social benefits is whether the restrictions on benefits are reasonable, appropriate, and just.

Language often plays a number of key roles in the distribution of social benefits. It is the foremost means by which benefits are distributed, it is the communicative glue that holds society together, and it also often functions as a marker of social class and ethnic identity. The idea that the language variety we speak affects others' perceptions and expectations of us is well documented empirically, but, even more, is generally recognized by people in society in all sorts of everyday contexts. For instance, at the beginning of the movie *My Fair Lady*, Professor Henry Higgins, commenting on Eliza's speech, observes to another gentleman, "If you spoke as she does, sir, instead of the way you do, why, you might be selling flowers, too." One's language use is among the clearest indicators in our society of social class and educational level, and while it is not a perfect predictor of these things, it is nevertheless a powerful one. It is, in short, preferable to "speak like the man on the six o'clock news" than to sound like Eliza Doolittle—not because there is anything intrinsically wrong with how Eliza spoke, but rather, simply because of social attitudes and expectations.

LANGUAGE AND POWER

There is an old Spanish proverb, "Saber es poder," which is generally translated "Knowledge is power." There is no question that knowledge can be empowering, just as the lack of knowledge can often disempower. Precisely the same argument applies to language: knowledge of a language can be empowering, and the lack of knowledge of a language can be disempowering. Further, just as it is the case that some knowledge is of greater social value than other knowledge, so too are various languages and language varieties of different value in different social contexts. For example, in the European context, a knowledge of French or German would arguably be of greater utility and value than a knowledge of

Spanish (though this would not, of course, be true in Spain or Portugal). Similarly, in Latin America, a knowledge of Spanish is obviously likely to prove far more useful and valuable than a knowledge of French. In Hong Kong, a knowledge of Chinese would be of significant value, just as in Nairobi a knowledge of Swahili would be useful. These local variations notwithstanding, though, neither Chinese nor Swahili is of the same general value and utility as French or Spanish would be. In other words, some languages are far more useful and valuable internationally than others.

A relatively small number of languages, called "languages of wider communication," dominate contemporary international communication (see Eastman, 1983, pp. 54–59, 125–127; Edwards, 1994, pp. 39–41; Phillipson, 1992, pp. 82–83). These languages of wider communication are not necessarily those languages with the largest numbers of native speakers; rather, they are the languages that are widely used as second or additional languages. Included as languages of wider communication are Spanish, French, Russian, Portuguese, and, of course, English. The economic return to the individual for learning these languages as second or additional languages tends to be significantly greater than for learning other languages (see Kaplan & Baldauf, 1997, pp. 153–192; see also Reagan, 1983). Even more important, these languages often serve a gatekeeping function in society. They are the most common and widely used languages of commerce, education, science, technology, and even politics; competence in at least one of them is essential in most societies if one wishes to succeed in any of these fields. Although these languages are characterized by extensive technical lexicons (especially in areas such as business, science, and research), it is important to note that the languages of wider communication have gained their significance not because of the size of their lexicons, or for any other intrinsic reason, but rather as a result of past (and often continuing) colonial and imperialist endeavors, as well as related pressures brought about by market forces. The fact that the languages of wider communication have experienced extensive lexical development is, in short, more a result of their international status than its cause.

The languages of wider communication provide their users (both native and nonnative) with economic, social, political and educational advantages, as well as conferring status and, of course, power (see, for instance, Fairclough, 1989; Pennycook, 1994, 1998; Phillipson, 1992, 2000; Skutnabb-Kangas, 2000a). If competence in a language of wider communication serves to empower individuals and groups in this way, the lack of competence in a language of wider communication all too often ensures just the reverse—linguistic disempowerment. Further, native speakers of languages of wider communication have a huge advantage over nonnative speakers in their communicative interactions, just as native speakers of more prestigious varieties of the languages of wider communication are disproportionately advantaged over speakers of non-prestigious varieties. The language that an individual speaks, to a considerable extent, determines how he or she is perceived by others. Consciously and unconsciously, we all make judgments about others based in large part on their use of language—judgments about social class, about intelligence, about education, and so on. Indeed, there are actually vocabulary development programs that promise to provide the client with the "vocabulary of a Harvard graduate" as a means of improving others' perceptions of them. These judgments, in turn, tend to reinforce existing power relationships in our society. As David Corson has explained,

> Rather than a privilege that an individual person possesses, power is a network of relations constantly in tension and ever-present in discursive activity. It is exercised through the production, accumulation, and functioning of various discourses. Discourse here is the fickle, uncontrollable "object" of human conflict, although no one is outside it completely, or sufficiently independent of discourses to manage them effectively. The conflict that takes place, however, over and around discourse, can be one-sided if the balance of power consistently favours some groups over others. So the study of power is best located at the point where the dominating activities of the powerful are played out in real and effective practices. For Foucault, the development of particular forms of language meets the needs of the powerful but, as often as not, it meets those needs without any direct exercise of discursive influence by the powerful. (2001, p. 17)

An important theme in this book is not merely that there is a connection between language and power relationships; rather, it is that educators in general, and foreign/second language educators in particular, need to be consciously aware of and sensitive to this connection.[2] Further, we need to help others—colleagues, students, and the general public—to become more critically aware of this connection and more knowledgeable about the nature of language and language diversity (see Blackledge, 2000; Corson, 2001). As Lourdes Ortega has noted,

> The field of foreign language teaching [has failed] to recognize the fact that both societal attitudes towards languages and power struggles resulting from ownership of a language and culture by particular groups are inextricably embedded in the definition of goals for language education. . . . Foreign language education and the foreign language teaching profession need to be reconceptualized in light of socio-cultural, political, and professional forces that affect the realities and potentials of foreign language teaching communities. (1999, p. 243)

One important aspect of this consciousness and sensitivity is learning to be careful about the terminology that we employ in discussing language and linguistic issues. For example, a common distinction made in linguistics is that between standard and non-standard language varieties. In a linguistic context, these labels carry no judgment about the nature or quality of the language variety being discussed. However, in everyday language, there is often an implicit and unarticulated assumption that a standard variety is in some way "better" than a nonstandard one. For this reason, in this book I have chosen to use the term "mainstream" rather than "standard" to refer to the socially dominant and preferred variety of a language, as a way of emphasizing that no intrinsic linguistic superiority is involved. In fact, the use of the term "standard" to refer to a single variety (albeit the socially dominant variety) can itself be taken to be a manifestation of what Deborah Cameron has labeled the "ideology of standardization" (1995, pp. 38–39; see also Lippi-Green, 1997, pp. 53–62), a problem to which we will return later in this book.

LANGUAGE IN THE SCHOOL: "SCHOOL ENGLISH"

The language employed in classrooms across the country is not merely mainstream English, or even a collection of related mainstream Englishes. It is, in fact, a special kind of mainstream English in which the lexicon, syntax, and pragmatics of language are distinct from those of the surrounding variety of mainstream English (see Heath, 1983; Lippi-Green, 1997, pp. 104–132). For virtually all children, entrance into the public school system entails learning a somewhat different linguistic system than that with which they are familiar. For some, of course, the difference is greater than for others, but for most the school presents a linguistic challenge that is often unrecognized by the adults in their lives, both in the school and at home. The specific characteristics of the "School English" that children learn are not themselves all that important, but the fact that they are recognized (both in and out of school) as in some sense "better" than other language usages is very important. These characteristics are not only generally somewhat more formal than typical everyday language use but are also more often artificial in nature, based on prescriptive rules of language use that do not actually reflect real language use. As the writer George Ade indicated in mocking a character's speech, "'Whom are you?' said he, for he had been to night school" (quoted in Muir, 1976, p. 94). The related ideas that the task of English teachers is to "fix" their students' language and that "every teacher is an English teacher" both involve an implicit recognition of this prescriptive linguistic function of schooling. As Ronald Wardhaugh has argued,

> There can hardly be another subject in the school curriculum in North America on which so many hours have been spent with such poor results as teaching about the English language. In reading instruction, grammatical study, or composition, this teaching has been so filled with error and misunderstanding that, as often

as not, it has harmed rather than helped learners. Teaching about language is undoubtedly one of the leading causes of people not being interested in language. . . . Much of the language teaching we have experienced has bred nothing but uncertainty and doubt about language. (1999, pp. 167–168)

This is not to say that there is no legitimate function for the English teacher. Indeed, quite the contrary is true. The role of the English teacher and, indeed, of every teacher—since every teacher does in fact model language use and language attitudes—is to help students acquire a critical understanding of language, language use, and language difference. Such a critical understanding would certainly include the ability to shift between different registers and styles of language use—not for reasons of correctness but rather for reasons of social acceptability (see, for instance, Achard, 1993; L. Andrews, 1998). Beyond this, the function of native language instruction is to provide the student with an understanding of the social and cultural roles played by language, including providing him or her with a broad introduction to the literature and literary tradition of the language (and, indeed, to all human languages to some extent). An especially powerful way to achieve this goal in the case of English is to include the study of the history of the development of modern English. Unfortunately, as Wardhaugh has noted, it is precisely such knowledge that is all too often absent in the education of future English teachers:

We might expect teachers of English at the secondary level . . . and professors of English to know something about what they profess, the English language. They are usually the products of our college and university departments of English and should be well informed on language matters. However, that is also often not the case. The one subject we can be almost sure that is not studied in depth in many such departments is the English language; it actually gets short shrift in many such places. There may be some study of Old English and Middle English so that a favored few can read *Beowulf* and Chaucer. There may be a course on the history of the English language but it is likely to concentrate on superficial matters. (1999, p. 170)

Such oversight need not be the case. The history of the development of modern English is in fact a fascinating study in its own right, as numerous classic and recent works attest (see, e.g., Jones, 1953), just as is the study of the incredible diversity present in contemporary English (see Bamgbose, Banjo & Thomas, 1997; Cheshire, 1991; Crystal, 1997b; Kachru, 1982; McArthur, 1998; Schmied, 1991; Trudgill & Hannah, 1994). It is important for students to understand that early in its development, modern English was seen as a lexically poor and generally inadequate language. As Sir Thomas Elyot, a gifted and compelling writer of English himself, described the problem, there was an "insufficiencie of our owne langage" that others called the "barrenness of the tongue in some parts" (quoted in Jones, 1953, pp. 70–71). Similar criticisms are commonly offered of other languages today, especially when compared to English. There is an irony here that is both powerful and painful.

In any event, the teaching of English can and should play a central role in public education in our society, but it needs to do so as a truly critical undertaking designed to help students understand the nature, purposes, functions, and evolution of language. Merely learning rules about ending sentences with prepositions, splitting infinitives, and the shall/will distinction is not only useless, it is counterproductive.

THE FOREIGN/SECOND LANGUAGE CONTEXT

Turning to the foreign/second language context, the picture is arguably even more bleak than with respect to the teaching of English. Bowers and Flinders have argued that "the language processes of the class can be understood as an ecology of power that advantages certain groups of students over others" (1990, p. 26), and nowhere is this more apparent than in the foreign/second language classroom. While all teachers are empowered to some extent by their presumed expertise (just as students are essentially disempowered by their lack of expertise in the subject matter being studied), in the case of the foreign/second-language teacher, not only is content at issue but so too is the ability to communicate in what is in essence the language of the classroom. This difference alone makes the foreign/second language class different from others and implies a different and even more significant power differential between foreign/second language educators and their students. As Barbara Craig has noted,

> Traditionally, the [foreign/second language] teacher's role has been seen as that of an authoritative expert. This view is based on the conception of knowledge as a quantifiable intellectual commodity. The teacher, as an expert in a field of inquiry or as an expert speaker of a language, has more of this knowledge than his or her students have. Because this knowledge has a separate existence outside of its knowers, it can be given, or taught, to the learners by the teacher-expert. (1995, p. 41)

The teacher of foreign/second languages occupies a unique position in the context of public education. S/he often is called upon to be the school's unofficial translator/interpreter for foreign documents as well as to deal with non-English-speaking parents and visitors.[3] Furthermore, since most administrators and supervisors do not possess the language skills to assess a teacher's proficiency, often the evaluation of such teachers is more limited in nature than might be the case in other subject areas. In fact, foreign language teachers have sometimes been known to use code switching (changing from one language to another) as a strategy to increase the difficulty an administrator may have when observing a lesson. The hope, as it is sometimes expressed, is that observers will assume that since they hear a foreign language being used, sound and effective instruction must be taking place. Such an assumption is hardly justifiable. The use of the target language is obviously a necessary condition for effective second language teaching, but it is far from sufficient.

A foreign language teacher's own language proficiency is rarely evaluated—and then usually in a fairly perfunctory manner. This is, interestingly enough, especially true in the case of the less commonly taught languages, where the teacher is likely to be the sole speaker of the target language in the school. Where there are other speakers of the language on staff, as is sometimes the case with bilingual education teachers, it is not uncommon to find foreign/second-language teachers engaged in subtle disputes about relative language competence, especially where other speakers of the language may speak a less prestigious or nonmainstream variety of the language. In some school districts, foreign/second language teachers replace guidance counselors in the context of placement adviser with respect to foreign/second-language classes and have been known to use this power to guide native speakers into "independent study" courses, thus isolating the student and protecting the teacher from any challenge to her/his linguistic authority in the classroom. Finally, the foreign/second language teacher not only controls, to a significant extent, the content of the foreign language curriculum but also serves as the arbitrator of what counts as "correct" and "incorrect" use in the target language and preferred lexical and grammatical choices. In addition, the teacher has the opportunity to employ what could be called the "official code switch." The foreign/second language teacher decides when classroom conversation should be in English, and when it must be in the target language, thus effectively controlling classroom discourse (see Gee, 1996; Heath, 1983; Hymes, 1996).

An additional problem in this regard is posed by the native speaker of the target language in the foreign/second-language classroom. It is not uncommon for native speakers of Spanish, for instance, to have difficulties in basic Spanish foreign/second-language classes, largely because of the differences between the normative language employed in the classroom and the language variety of the native speaker (see Ruíz, 1991; Valdés, Lozano & García-Moya, 1981). My point here is a simple one: it is not necessarily the native-speaking student who should be seen as the problem but the attitudes and values related to language held by the school and teachers (including foreign-language teachers). As Valdés notes,

> [I]t is a fact that a surprising number of Spanish-speaking students . . . are still being placed in beginning Spanish classes for non-speakers to help them "unlearn" their "bad" habits and begin anew as foreign speakers. It matters not that

> the student is fluent and has internalized every single grammar rule that the teacher may hope to present. If he says *traiba* for *traía,* many schools will make him "begin from the beginning" . . . every day teachers of Spanish casually enroll native Spanish-speaking students in beginning Spanish classes for non-speakers, in which the materials used have been designed exclusively for teaching English-speaking students. The students are expected, in the process, to acquire the standard Spanish dialect as opposed to that normally used in their own speech communities. (1981, p. 7)

THE OBJECTIFICATION OF LANGUAGE

Underlying many of the problems discussed thus far in this chapter is the tendency to objectify not only language but concepts related to language. In other words, instead of recognizing the incredible complexity of the issues under discussion, there is often an understandable tendency to simplify linguistic concepts in educational and social discourse. Take, for instance, the core term "language" itself. We all know exactly what language is, or at least we believe that we do. The devil, as the old adage goes, is in the details. We need to begin by establishing criteria that allow us to distinguish communicative behavior of various sorts from language. Pointing, for instance, may well suffice in some settings to communicate meaning effectively, but it would not, presumably, count as language. My cat is certainly capable of communicating many things: hunger, anger, affection, interest. He is not, though, capable of utilizing language. As far as we know at the present time, only human beings naturally utilize language—but that claim, of course, presupposes a shared understanding of what counts as language. Apes have been taught to communicate using signs, though they have not, popular claims notwithstanding, really learned sign language—but this, again, only begs the question of what ought to count as language (see Wallman, 1992). From a linguistic perspective, there are a number of characteristics that we use to distinguish language (or at least human language) from other forms of communication. Among these characteristics, each of which constitutes, from a linguistic perspective, a necessary condition for a communication system to constitute a language, are the following:

- Language is productive. The number of sentences that can be made is infinite, and new messages on any topic can be produced at any time.
- Language has ways of showing the relationship between symbols.
- Language has mechanisms for introducing new symbols.
- Language can be used for an unrestricted number of domains.
- The symbols of language can be broken down into smaller parts.
- More than one meaning can be conveyed by a symbol or a group of symbols.

- Language can refer to the past, the future, and non-immediate situations; it is not restricted to the present and the immediate.
- Language changes across time.
- Language can be used interchangeably among speakers.
- Language users monitor their use.
- Parts of the system must be learned from other users.
- Language users can learn other variants of the same language.
- Language users can use the language to discuss the language. (Valli & Lucas, 2001, pp. 8–13)

Such a list is very useful, but still leaves other questions unanswered. In fact, every individual speaker uses what linguists would call an idiolect, which means that no two human beings speak exactly the same language in exactly the same manner. In short, even the idea of a particular language—such as English, French, Spanish, Russian, Chinese, or Zulu—is something of a fiction. There is no single thing called English; rather, there are millions of idiolects, varying in all kinds of ways, that are identified by their users as "English." Most may well be mutually intelligible, but others are most certainly not. Decisions about the boundaries of languages are, in fact, social and political rather than linguistic in nature.

A related issue with respect to the concept of "language" is the idea that language is simply the sum of its parts—that is, that Spanish is simply a collection of lexical items and morphological and syntactic rules. The problem is that lists of lexical items and grammatical rules are really ex post facto in nature and that language is inevitably more than merely what is in a textbook or even a comprehensive grammar and dictionary. Language is a profoundly human construct, as the list of characteristics identified above would lead one to expect. Precisely the same observation, of course, is also true of the concept of "culture," which is almost universally objectified in misleading ways in foreign language classes (see Pérez, 1998).

Just as the concept "language" is somewhat of a fiction, so too are many of the other common terms and concepts used in discussions of language. Among the more potentially problematic terms in this regard are "grammar," "dialect," and even "native speaker." These are all, to some extent, like unicorns in that we are fully capable of describing, defining, and even using each term in the abstract (as I did in the earlier section in discussing the native speaker in the foreign language classroom), but when faced with the complexities and uncertainties of the real world, we are really unable to identify any such object in a clear and meaningful way.

THE MYTHOLOGY OF LANGUAGE

Not only is discourse about language impeded by the objectification of the key terminology necessary to discuss such matters, it is subject to an immense amount of folk wisdom, distorted understandings of important linguistic constructs, and misinformation galore. Many common "language myths" have been identified and compellingly critiqued by the authors in Laurie Bauer and Peter Trudgill's (1998) edited volume *Language Myths*. For instance, among the "language myths" addressed in that volume are the ideas that the meanings of words should be "fixed" and not allowed to change (and that change in meaning is a bad thing), that some languages are intrinsically better than others, that some languages are more or less logical than others, that prescriptive grammar should guide language use, that speakers of non-mainstream language varieties are linguistically deprived, that the quality of both written and spoken language in our society are declining, and so on

Not only do such myths about language per se abound, but so too do myths about language learning. With respect to second language learning, for instance, Barry McLaughlin has identified five important misconceptions about language learning that are common among teachers, parents, and the general public. These second language learning myths include:

- Children learn second languages quickly and easily.
- The younger the child, the more skilled in acquiring a second language.
- The more time students spend in a second language context, the quicker they learn the language.
- Children have acquired a second language once they can speak it.
- All children learn a second language in the same way. (1992, pp. 1–9)

A similar list of myths and misconceptions about second language learning is provided by Susan Dicker, who includes such popular, albeit erroneous, beliefs as:

- Children acquire their first language quickly and effortlessly.
- Age is a disadvantage in second language learning; younger learners are better at acquiring a second language than older learners.
- Second languages should be learned in the same way as first languages by being used in natural, everyday situations.
- People who fail to learn a second language well have only themselves to blame; they just aren't trying hard enough.
- It is necessary for someone learning a second language to use it as soon as possible and to be exposed to as much of it as possible.
- When children learn a second language at the same time that they learn their first language, they will confuse the two and don't learn either one well.
- Children who come into the American school system with little or no literacy

in their first languages should be plunged directly into an all-English education.

- Bilingual programs should be short-term and the first language should be phased out as quickly as possible. (1996, pp. 75–99)

These myths, and many like them related to the teaching and learning of languages, continue to influence policy and educational debates in spite of the fact that the reality is demonstrably more complex than these simplistic myths would lead one to believe (see Corson, 1999; Samway & McKeon, 1999). Dicker contextualizes the importance of such myths by noting that

> With the growing population of language minorities in American public schools and colleges, knowledge about the process of language learning should no longer be limited to experts who speak only to each other. Everyone, especially those involved in public education, needs information that is clear and unbiased. Misconceptions about language learning are spread widely in the press and are used by those who have political motives for attacking programs which might benefit non-native speakers of English. (1996, p. 75)

Such myths are often problematic not because they are completely wrong, but because they are wrong in important ways in particular contexts. The real problem, as H. L. Mencken once observed, is that "There is always a well-known solution to every human problem—neat, plausible, and wrong." Issues of language are inherently complex, and efforts to simplify them inevitably do far more harm than good.

CONCLUSION

Language is fundamentally a social activity. Indeed, on some accounts, a language ceases to be a living language not when its last speaker dies, but rather, when its next-to-last speaker dies (Crystal, 2000, p. 2). In other words, a language can no longer be considered to be alive when it can no longer be used to perform communicative functions. Language not only functions in a social context and performs social functions, it represents, reflects, and reinforces power relations in society. Most often, language is utilized to maintain existing power structures and relations, but this need not be the case. As individuals and groups learn more about the nature and functions of language, they become increasingly empowered to respond to linguistic domination. The key, for classroom teachers, is to help their students understand the realities of language, language oppression, and language domination. To do so, as Blair has argued, requires that teachers:

- learn to appreciate non-standard varieties as assets rather than hindrances in the acquisition of the standard (variety).
- extend the range of children's skills by showing them that in certain situations it is appropriate to use certain forms of language, while others suit other contexts.
- teach the features of the standard (variety) that do not exist in the children's variety, looking at genuine communicative needs rather than teaching isolated features artificially.
- pay attention to differences in the rules of interaction between the children's community environment and in the more formal environments where the standard (variety) is used.
- learn as much as possible about the children's cultural and linguistic traditions.
- avoid testing procedures that favour the standard (variety) since these may not reveal genuine ability, only a knowledge of the standard variety. (Quoted in Corson, 2001, p. 96)

Many of us would argue, of course, that this list is merely a subset of what good teaching itself is all about, but, as common sense is most noted for often not being terribly common, so good teaching all too often remains something of a rarity. The intention and focus of this book are to help teachers and others involved in education learn to engage themselves, their colleagues, and their students in critical reflection upon language and language use.

QUESTIONS FOR REFLECTION AND DISCUSSION

1. There are a wide array of myths about language and language acquisition discussed in this chapter. Can you identify other "myths" about language, language teaching, and language learning that you have come across? What characteristics do these myths typically share?
2. The author deliberately chooses to use the term "mainstream" rather than "standard" to describe the socially dominant and preferred variety of a language. What, in your view, is the difference between these two labels? What are the educational implications of this difference?
3. Given what is suggested in this chapter about the relative status and power of the languages of wider communication, do you believe that there is any compelling reason for a student to study a non-language of wider communication? On what grounds might a decision to study such a language be justified?
4. How does "School English" differ from "mainstream" English? Can you provide specific examples of language use that would be acceptable in "mainstream" settings, but not necessarily in school settings? How can this be explained?
5. Why is the objectification of language problematic in the context of foreign language education? How can such objectification, in your view, be minimized or avoided altogether?

FURTHER READING

There are a number of excellent books currently available that discuss many of the issues raised in this chapter. Among the best are Larry Andrews' *Language Exploration and Awareness* (1998), Laurier Bauer and Peter Trudgill's *Language Myths* (1998), and Ronald Wardhaugh's *Proper English: Myths and Misunderstandings about Language* (1999).

NOTES

1. What is really at issue here is the question, in Donna Kerr's terms, of the public of any particular policy. The public of a policy includes not only direct beneficiaries of the policy, however, but also the indirect beneficiaries—who often constitute the far larger and more significant group (see Kerr, 1976, pp. 76–78).
2. I would suggest that this sensitivity and awareness are essential both with respect to the students' native language (generally English in the U.S. context) and the target language of the classroom.
3. This is in fact the reality in which many foreign language educators find themselves; I do not mean to suggest that this is an appropriate role, merely that it is a common one.

Chapter 2

"French isn't a real class": The Marginalization of Foreign Language Education

Recently I asked my son how he was doing in school. He reported that he was doing very well and went on to tell me about his achievements in mathematics, English, social studies, and science, all of which seemed to be going quite well. I then asked him about French, and he looked at me somewhat askance and said, "OK, but French isn't a real class." Puzzled, I asked him what he meant, and he replied, "Look, in real classes like English and math, they give us grades, but in French, we only get S's. If it really mattered, they'd grade us." I am sure that the school's decision to use essentially a pass/fail grading system in the first year of French was well intended. My guess is that it was a way of attempting to minimize student anxiety and make the foreign language learning experience a more positive and effective one. Unfortunately, as my son's comment makes clear, the decision also sent a powerful and unintended message to students. The message, unfortunately, also reflects the reality of the place of foreign language education in U.S. education. Such classes are all too often viewed—not only by students but also by many teachers, administrators, and parents—as non-core, optional, and really relatively unimportant when compared to "real" subjects like English, mathematics, history, and science.

This marginalization of foreign language education is, of course, by no means unique. It is an experience shared by art and music education, among others, and reflects widely held social and cultural values and beliefs. What does make the case of foreign language education unusual is the ideological aspect of its marginalization, and it is with the exploration of this ideological aspect of the marginalization of foreign language education that we will be concerned in this chapter.

ASSUMPTIONS ABOUT LINGUISTIC AND POLITICAL REALITY

A good place to begin an examination of the ideological aspect of the marginalization of foreign language education is with what Dell Hymes has identified as the six core assumptions about language in the United States. Hymes suggests that these core, and generally tacit, assumptions include the following:

- Everyone in the United States speaks only English, or should.
- Bilingualism is inherently unstable, probably injurious, and possibly unnatural.
- Foreign literary languages can be respectively studied, but not foreign languages in their domestic varieties (it is one thing to study the French spoken in Paris, another to study the French spoken in Louisiana).
- Most everyone else in the world is learning English anyway, and that, together with American military and economic power, makes it unnecessary to worry about knowing the language of a country in which one has business, bases, or hostages.
- Differences in language are essentially of two kinds, right and wrong.
- Verbal fluency and noticeable style are suspicious, except as entertainment (it's what you mean that counts). (1996, pp. 84–85).

Each of these assumptions is fundamentally flawed. The list as a whole is grounded in a lack of understanding of the nature of language, confuses historical mythology with historical fact, and is replete with both factual and normative errors. This having been said, Hymes's list nevertheless does fairly accurately reflect commonly held beliefs about language in the United States. To be sure, not everyone accepts these core assumptions, but they do appear often to have significant impact on educational and social policy and thought. In this chapter, we shall explore five broad issues related to these assumptions about foreign language in the United States: the presumption of a monolingual norm in contemporary U.S. society, the role and place of English in the global community, the treatment of foreign languages in the media, the "foreignness agenda" in education, and last, the incredibility of the arguments most commonly used to defend and promote the study of foreign languages in the U.S. context.

THE "MONOLINGUAL NORM"

One of the most powerful ways in which dominance is expressed and maintained in society is through the establishment and maintenance of a "normative" default position (see Cummins, 1996, 2000; Sleeter & McLaren, 1995; Spring, 2000a). In other words, what counts as "normal" functions also to determine what is "not normal." Although this process is by no means deliberate much of the time, it is quite real, and the identification and critique of the implicit dominance in such normativization are important aspects of empowerment. For instance, in contemporary U.S. society, the dominant perceived "norm" in racial terms is white; other racial identities are simply "Other." Such norms are significant because they in effect legitimize one group over others (see Sleeter, 2001). As McLaren and Muñoz have argued,

> Our attention has been drawn to the fact that the term *ethnic* is rarely applied to populations commonly described as "white." If you are white you occupy a space that seemingly transcends ethnicity. Whiteness miraculously becomes the "oneness" without which otherness could not exist—the primogenitor of identity, the marker against which otherness defines itself. Whiteness functions as a frozen state—a dead zone where "traits" associated with skin color, phenotype, race, class, and gender characteristics historically associated with Anglo-Europeans are held to be perpetually raceless. Whiteness has been positioned as the backdrop against which alternative or unconventional social practices and cultural formations are judged, thus ascribing an unprecedented degree of authority and power to its membership and its ethnocentric cultural, social, and ideological expressions, while at the same time repositioning the "other" as deviant. Whiteness has become the laboratory where ethnicities are given defining characteristics, assembled, and categorized. Schools are the clinics which "treat" these ethnic groups, police their behavior, and assimilate them. (2000, pp. 32–33).

This process is especially disempowering when it takes place with groups that have been historically disadvantaged—whether on the basis of race, ethnicity, gender, sexual preference, age, language, disability, or whatever (see Hollings, 1996; Larson & Ovando, 2001; Sleeter & McLaren, 1995). As Lennard Davis has commented in his seminal work on disability studies,

> We live in a world of norms. Each of us endeavors to be normal or else deliberately tries to avoid that state. We consider what the average person does, thinks, earns, or consumes. We rank our intelligence, our cholesterol level, our weight, height, sex drive, bodily dimensions along some conceptual line from subnormal to above-average. We consume a daily balance of vitamins and nutrients based on what an average human should consume. Our children are ranked in school and tested to determine where they fit into a normal curve of learning, of intelligence. Doctors measure and weigh them to see if they are above or below average on the height and weight curves. There is probably no area of contemporary life in which some idea of a norm, mean, or average has not been calculated. . . . To understand the disabled body, one must return to the concept of the norm, the normal body. (1995, p. 23; see also Charlton, 1998; Davis, 1997; Linton, 1998)

In the case of language, the common assumption in our society is that monolingualism is both typical and "normal." Thus, bilingualism or multilingualism are atypical and, in some sense, "not normal." However, as John Edwards has noted,

> To be bilingual or multilingual is not the aberration supposed by many (particularly, perhaps, by people in Europe and North America who speak a "big" language); it is, rather, a normal and unremarkable necessity for the majority in the world today. A monolingual perspective is often, unfortunately, a consequence of possession of a powerful "language of wider communication," as English, French, German, Spanish and other such languages are sometimes styled. This linguistic myopia is sometimes accompanied by a narrow cultural awareness and is reinforced by state policies which, in the main, elevate only one language to official status. (1994, p. 1)

There is an additional aspect of normative monolingualism in contemporary U.S. society that needs to be noted here as well, and that is the overlap of assumptions about social class and monolingualism. Although there is some expectation that very well-educated individuals may have a least a limited knowledge of a second language (almost always another language of wider communication), in fact bilingualism and multilingualism are most commonly associated with groups and individuals at the lower end of the socioeconomic continuum. This association, in turn, simply reinforces the idea that bilingualism and multilingualism are problematic.

In other words, assumptions about the "normalcy" of monolingualism are in fact often the result of historical power relations. The idea that competence in more than one language is non-normative contradicts significant aspects of the human experience. Especially pernicious in this regard are beliefs about the cognitive, psychological and even moral costs of bilingualism and multilingualism. For instance, Dr. Piet Meyer, one-time head of South African Broadcasting Corporation and a leading member of the Afrikaner Broederbond,[1] argued in 1945 that

> all researchers in this field are agreed that bilingual children show backwardness in development as compared with monolingual children . . . bilingualism leads to moral relativism which reaches right into the religious life of the individual. It is definitely certain that Godlessness is more prevalent among bilingual people than among monolinguals. (quoted in Reagan, 1987a, p. 136)

Such claims notwithstanding, the evidence on the effects of bilingualism and multilingualism are in fact far from negative—indeed, early childhood bilingualism and multilingualism appear to provide a number of significant cognitive benefits (see Cenoz & Genesee, 1998; Cunningham-Andersson & Andersson, 1999; Elgin, 2000; Tokuhama-Espinosa, 2001).

ENGLISH IN THE GLOBAL COMMUNITY

The idea that English is becoming, or even has already become, the common global language of our age is a powerful one (see Wallraff, 2000). David Crystal (1997b) has argued not only that "World English exists as a political and cultural reality" (p. ix) but that "there has never been a language so widely spread or spoken by so many people as English" (p. 139). The spread of English, especially as a second language, has indeed been unprecedented in world history. Earlier languages, to be sure, functioned as *lingue franche* for large numbers of people in geographically broad areas for long periods of time, but none have come close to the current status of English.[2] As Charles Ferguson has noted,

> It is a familiar phenomenon for one language to serve as a lingua franca or language of special functions (religious, commercial) over a large area of many languages: Sanskrit, Greek, Latin, Arabic, and French are examples at various periods and in different parts of the world. But there has never before been a single language which spread for such purposes over *most* of the world, as English has done in this century. The importance of this fact is often overlooked in discussions of the characteristic features of this age. The spread of English is as significant in its way as is the modern use of computers. (1982, p. ix)

A knowledge of English has in fact become, in many parts of the world, a necessary condition for being an "educated person." As Burchfield commented,

> English has also become a lingua franca to the point that any literate educated person is in a very real sense deprived if he [*sic*] does not know English. Poverty, famine, and disease are instantly recognized as the cruelest and least excusable forms of deprivation. Linguistic deprivation is a less easily noticed condition, but one nevertheless of great significance. (1985, p. 160)

The spread of English, especially among educated persons, has led many speakers of English to assume that "everyone speaks English" and that there is, therefore, no compelling reason for native speakers of English to study other languages. Certainly there can be no question of the immense status of English. As Crystal has noted,

> English is used as an official or semi-official language in over 60 countries, and has a prominent place in a further 20. It is either dominant or well established in all six continents. It is the main language of books, newspapers, airports and air-traffic control, international business and academic conferences, science, technology, medicine, diplomacy, sports, international competitions, pop music, and advertising. Over two-thirds of the world's scientists write in English. Three-quarters of the world's mail is written in English. Of all the information in the world's electronic retrieval systems, 80% is stored in English. People communicate on the Internet largely in English. English radio programmes are received by 150 million in 120 countries. Over 50 million children study English as an additional language at primary level; over 80 million study it at secondary level (these figures exclude China). (1997a, p. 360)

While it is certainly true that English can be used in many settings around the world, the idea that "everyone" speaks English is nevertheless demonstrably false and, further, is potentially dangerous (see Tonkin, 2001). It is notoriously difficult to estimate the number of individuals who speak any given language, but the most generous estimates for English suggest that there are around 427 million native speakers and an additional 800 million second or additional language speakers of English around the world (see Crystal, 1997a, p. 289). Even if all of these individuals spoke English fluently (a most unlikely scenario), given a total population of more than seven billion, this would mean that fewer than 18% of humanity can speak English. Not only is this percentage relatively low for a language claiming the label "global," but it is also demographically skewed, since the people most likely to speak English are also those, as a rule, who are most westernized—which of course helps to explain Crystal's claims. To assume that we can gain insight into the beliefs, values, and ideas of the world's population only through English, though, is to ensure that we miss out on most of humanity's diversity. In addition, as David Graddol has pointed out, the current status of English is subject to change.

> The likelihood . . . is that the future for English will be a complex and plural one. The language will grow in usage and variety, yet simultaneously diminish in relative global importance. We may find the hegemony of English replaced by an oligarchy of languages. . . . To put it in economic terms, the size of the global market for the English language may increase in absolute terms, but its market share will probably fall. (1997, p. 3)

The future of English aside, the idea that "English is enough" has already become especially damaging in the academic community in the United States, and this in turn has had a negative impact on the study of foreign languages. There was a time when it would have been inconceivable for a person to complete successfully a Ph.D. program without demonstrating at least reading competence in one (or more often, more than one) foreign language (Osborn, 2001). The assumption was that the scholar needed to be able to access publications in his/her discipline in a variety of languages. It has now become commonly assumed by many, perhaps most, in the academic community that this is no longer necessary, since anything important will be published in English. The problem is that this is not necessarily the case; in many disciplines, there are interesting and exciting developments that are not, at least initially, available in English. Even in the sciences, a huge chasm exists between the knowledge base of scientists in the former Soviet Union (which is grounded in work published primarily in Russian) and in the west. Simply to dismiss as unimportant or irrelevant work not published in English is—apart from its social, political and ideological problems—intellectually indefensible, and yet it continues; indeed, it continues as fairly typical academic practice in many fields of study.

Thus far, we have focused on the issue of English as a global language from the perspective of native English speakers. There are, however, other perspectives on the spread of English that are also useful to consider. In recent years, a growing literature has emerged critiquing linguistic imperialism in general and in English in particular (see Hall & Eggington, 2000; Holborow, 1999; Mazrui, 2000; Pennycook, 1994, 1998; Phillipson, 1992; Skutnabb-Kangas, 2000a, 2000b). Linguistic imperialism, as Robert Phillipson has forcefully articulated it, is:

> a distinct type of imperialism. . . . Linguistic imperialism permeates all the types of imperialism, for two reasons. The first has to do with form (language as a medium for transmitting ideas), the second with content. As regards the first, language is the primary medium of communication for links in all fields—indeed language is a precondition for most forms of contact other than brute force. Communication presupposes mutual understanding on the basis of a shared code. It is hardly surprising that it is the Centre's [as opposed to the periphery's] language which is used. Secondly, linguistic imperialism dovetails with other types of imperialism and is an integral part of them. Linguistic imperialism is a primary component of cultural imperialism. . . . [it] is also central to social imperialism, which relates to the transmission of the norms and behavior of a model social structure, and these are embedded in language. . . . It also occurs wherever English plays a major role in the education system of an underdeveloped country and transmits social values. (1992, pp. 53–54)

In practice, what this means is that the spread of English has been closely linked to the colonial and imperialist agendas first of Britain and more recently of the United States, and that it is not infrequently perceived in this way by others. As Chris Searle has argued somewhat polemically,

> Let us be clear that the English language has been a monumental force and institution of oppression and rabid exploitation throughout 400 years of imperialist history. It attacked the black person with its racist images and imperialist message, it battered the worker who toiled as its words expressed the parameters of his misery and the subjection of entire peoples in all the continents of the world. It was made to scorn the languages it sought to replace, and told the colonised peoples that mimicry of its primacy among languages was a necessary badge for their social mobility as well as their continued humiliation and subjugation. Thus, when we talk of "mastery" of the Standard language, we must be conscious of the terrible irony of the word, that the English language itself was the language of the master, the carrier of his arrogance and brutality. (1983, p. 68)

Such a critical view of English comes as a surprise to many native speakers of the language, but is in fact very common in many parts of the world (see Cheshire, 1991; Kachru, 1982). Among the places where the role and place of the English language have proven to be politically controversial are virtually all of so-called "anglophone" Africa (see Bamgbose, Banjo & Thomas, 1997; Mazrui & Mazrui, 1998; Schmied, 1991), the Indian subcontinent (see Agnihotri & Khanna, 1997; Krishnaswamy & Burde, 1998; Mansoor, 1993; Rahman, 1998), Hong Kong (see Poon, 2000), Singapore (see Afrendras & Kuo, 1980), and even in Canada and the United States (see Ricento & Burnaby, 1998). Not only is English a potentially controversial political issue, its growth and perceived (albeit unreal) ubiquity can also constitute a religious challenge in many settings (see Schiffman, 1996, pp. 55–74). As Clammer has pointed out, of

> all the manifestations of human culture, language and religion are two of the most basic, the most universal, and the most important for understanding the world view and motivations of any group of people. It should not therefore be too surprising an idea to suggest that the two sets of phenomena are interconnected, and that the exploration of this interconnectedness is a highly fruitful way of reaching the heart of a people's culture. (Quoted in Karmani, 1995, p. 12)

Religious controversy related to the status of English has been especially significant in the Muslim world (see Karmani, 1995; Kazmi, 1997), due at least in part to the role of Arabic as the sacred language sine qua non of Islam (see Chejne, 1969; Reagan, 2000c, pp. 189–190).

FOREIGN LANGUAGES AND THE MEDIA

Media depictions often provide us with invaluable insights into cultural beliefs and practices. This is especially true with respect to issues of language. In most parts of the world, advertisers utilize foreign languages (and especially English) as a way of promoting products. By associating a particular product with English, the hope is that consumers will also associate the product with such virtues as being modern, up-to-date, cutting-edge, sophisticated, and so on. In the U.S. context, however, for the most part advertisers avoid the use of languages other than English—and in the instances in which other languages are used, they are employed to send very different kinds of messages. In fact, the message sent is almost always one that presupposes the "exotic" nature of the other language, as well as usually tacitly suggesting the monolingual norm in our own context. For instance, a recent advertisement for a U.S.-made luxury car featured a picture of the Earth seen from space. North America was centrally located, and superimposed over the eastern coast of the United States was the Mercedes logo, captioned with the German expression, "Stuttgart, wir haben ein Problem." This advertisement is interesting because it emphasizes the foreignness, and in fact the "Otherness," of Mercedes, while at the same time using a German expression that would be understood by virtually any speaker of English. Another advertisement, this one for an outdoor educational program, proudly notes, "In our school, 'I can't' is a foreign language." A seeming exception to this trend is presented by Volkswagen, which has very successfully marketed in products using the German slogan, *Fahrvergnügen* (driving pleasure).[3] On careful inspection, though, one again recognizes that the tacit message has to do with "Otherness," albeit this time in a more positive light. In any event, it is clear that the use of languages other than English in U.S. advertising remains atypical and, where it does occur, is deeply embedded in ideological and social assumptions about language and language diversity.

THE "FOREIGNNESS AGENDA"

There are a number of other issues that arise in the foreign language curriculum, as it is generally articulated and implemented in the U.S. context, that reflect both subtle bias and internal contradictions. Most blatant in this regard, perhaps, is the label "foreign" itself—a clear identification of the target language of the classroom as "Other" (see National Standards in Foreign Language Education Project, 1996, p. 23; Osborn, 1998, 2002). As such, the target language inevitably becomes something of an object of apathy at best and of suspicion, or even rejection, at worst. Recent efforts to change the nomenclature, utilizing the term "world languages" in place of "foreign languages," to some extent addresses such concerns, but only at the level of what might be termed articulated bias. Regardless of what they are called, in U.S. schools languages other than English are in fact perceived, by both adults and students, as profoundly foreign. This perception is in fact only strengthened by encouraging the use of what is seen as a politically correct label (i.e., "world languages"). The risk with such word games, as Michael Apple has noted, is that "historically outmoded, and socially and politically conservative (and often educationally disastrous) practices are not only continued, but are made to sound as if they were actually more enlightened and ethically responsive ways of dealing with children" (1979, p. 144).

THE INCREDIBILITY OF FOREIGN LANGUAGE ADVOCACY ARGUMENTS

Perhaps somewhat surprisingly, among the factors that work against the credibility of foreign language education in contemporary U.S. society are some of the arguments the foreign language community itself puts forward to support foreign language learning. Public justifications for the study of languages other than English include three distinct types of arguments: cognitive arguments, cultural arguments, and pragmatic arguments. Cognitive arguments tend to emphasize the effectiveness of language study in promoting critical thinking, providing mental discipline, increasing mental flexibility and creativity, and improving cognitive functioning (see Jarvis, 1980; Met & Galloway, 1992). Myriam Met and Vicki Galloway, for instance, have pointed out that

> Research indicates that students who take a foreign language demonstrate enhanced cognitive functioning in the areas of divergent thinking, cognitive flexibility, and metalinguistic awareness. . . . Similarly, several studies of elementary school students who took a foreign language have shown that such students make greater gains on standardized tests of reading/language arts and, on occasion, mathematics than those who do not. . . . Secondary students who take a foreign language attain higher scores on the verbal section of the Scholastic Aptitude Test (SAT) than those who do not; the longer the sequence of foreign language study, the stronger the relationship with increased SAT scores. Indeed, 5 years of foreign language study has been shown to be associated with higher verbal SAT scores than 5 years of any other academic subject in the secondary curriculum. (1992, pp. 853–854)

Although the evidence for such benefits is, I believe, quite compelling, it is not at all clear that these arguments have any more than rhetorical force in the arena of educational policy making. The cultural arguments used to support foreign language study are less strong and tend to rely largely on personal experience and anecdotal evidence. Beyond this, it is also evident that bilingualism all too often accompanies bicultural chauvinism rather than broad cultural tolerance and understanding. Pragmatic arguments, which are grounded in concerns about national security, the economic needs of U.S. society, and the consequences of foreign language study for employment, tend to be the most compelling in the public sphere (see Simon, 1980). Typical of pragmatic arguments is the following passage:

> With a language skill added to your other skills, you might double the chances of getting the job you want. There are openings for an auto mechanic who also speaks Arabic, an electronic radio expert who knows Japanese, a chef (even a woman chef) who understands French. It even could be a foreign language would be more useful to you during the next ten years than a college diploma. . . . You should weigh the judgment of one executive: "A person who speaks two languages is worth two people." Language is, in fact, your hidden job insurance. (Quoted in Jarvis, 1980, pp. 31–32)

The basic problem with this type of argument is that while it may have a certain degree of face validity for foreign language educators and our allies, it is not in fact compatible with the life experiences of most students (or, for that matter, with the life experiences of their parents). The United States, regardless of how one personally feels about it, is in fact a profoundly monolingual society ideologically if not empirically, and relatively few students (or parents, teachers or policy makers, for that matter) really believe that second language skills are necessary for the marketplace. Claims about language skills being job insurance are viewed with considerable scepticism in a society in which monolingualism in English is seen as the norm. A final problem with such pragmatic arguments is the issue of competence: the level of language competence required in those jobs that do require language skills is far beyond what students can be expected to learn in a typical foreign language program at the secondary level. Even if a student had been fortunate enough to study Arabic for two or three years at the high school level, for instance, and had also had the benefit of appropriate automotive training, it is hardly likely that s/he would be able to function as an Arabic-speaking auto mechanic.

CONCLUSION

If the justifications commonly offered for studying a foreign language in secondary school are not compelling, then why do students do so? Are they wasting their time? Are they simply ignorant of their own self-interest? The answer is really quite simple: taking (and passing) foreign language classes often functions as a necessary condition for admission to college. In other words, "getting through" a couple of years of foreign language classes (generally evidenced by little more than simply meeting a "seat time" requirement) is simply one of the hurdles one must endure to get into higher education (which, in turn, is a hurdle that is, for the most part, required for social class maintenance and upward mobility). It is this function, rarely articulated publicly but commonly recognized by both students and others, that in actual fact would seem to be served by secondary level foreign language classes. When we rely on arguments that are in fact counterintuitive for students and their parents, we essentially ignore this reality and contribute both to public perceptions that we are out of touch and to our own marginalization.

QUESTIONS FOR REFLECTION AND DISCUSSION

1. How is normative monolingualism reflected in, and encouraged by, public educational practice in the United States? To what extent can the practices that

encourage normative monolingualism be successfully challenged in the school context? How can this be done?

2. To what extent, and in what ways, do you believe that English can be labeled a "Christian" or a "Judeo-Christian" language? What are the implications of such a label? Can you provide evidence that might help to refute this charge?
3. Some people have argued that since a knowledge of English has become, in many parts of the world, a necessary condition for being an "educated person," this in fact removes any need for the educated native speaker of English to study or learn any other language. Why is such an argument not compelling? What are some of the relevant justifications for native speakers of English studying other languages?
4. Chris Searle is quoted in this chapter arguing, "Let us be clear that the English language has been a monumental force and institution of oppression and rabid exploitation throughout 400 years of imperialist history." Do you believe that this claim is fair and accurate? Why or why not?
5. When David Graddol looks at the future of English in the world, he suggests that "the future for English will be a complex and plural one." What are the important educational implications of this expectation, in terms of the education of both native speakers of English and those studying English as a second or foreign language?

FURTHER READING

The future of English, which is one of the central themes of this chapter, has been the focus of considerable work in recent years. Among the better references in this regard are David Crystal's *English as a Global Language* (1997), Tom McArthur's *The English Languages* (1998), and David Graddol's *The Future of English?* (1997). Also of interest here are works that deal with the complex questions of linguistic imperialism, especially with respect to the role of English in the modern world. See, for instance, Alastair Pennycook's *The Cultural Politics of English as an International Language* (1994) and *English and the Discourses of Colonialism* (1998), as well as Robert Phillipson's *Linguistic Imperialism* (1992).

NOTES

1. The Afrikaner Broederbond was a "cohesive, shadowy secret society" (Rotberg, 1987, p. 79) that functioned as an extralegal body to ensure loyalty and obedience to the Afrikaans' political hierarchy, as well as to stifle dissent and promote conformity, within the Afrikaans community. The Broederbond played a key role in the ethnic mobilization of the early twentieth century in South Africa (see Giliomee & Adam, 1981, pp. 117–118).

2. Among the languages that have functioned as *lingue franche* historically are Sanskrit, Greek, Latin, Arabic, and French. Detailed discussions of the roles and functions of each of these languages are widely available; for Sanskrit, see

Cardona (1990) and Shapiro & Schiffman (1981); for Greek, see Horrocks (1997); for Latin, see Farrell (2001) and Waquet (2001); for Arabic, see Ayalon (1987), Chejne (1969), and Kaye (1990); and for French, see Walter (1994).

3. The use of the term *-vergnügen* as a productive suffix is quite interesting in this regard. I am told, for instance, that a video store has used the word *Video-vergnügen* in its advertising.

Chapter 3

Failure As Success: Language and Ideology in U.S. Foreign Language Education

The marginalization of foreign languages and foreign language education in the United States is, as we saw in the preceding chapter, a fairly complex process that has a number of distinct, albeit overlapping, features. Holding all of the features together, however, is ideology. Ideology is a particularly complex and difficult concept to grasp, and so a brief discussion of what we mean by the term may be helpful. The philosopher of education Richard Pratte began his examination of the relationship between ideology and education by noting,

> What is ideology? It is a much-bandied-about term that has been thoroughly muddied by diverse uses, and yet it is central to many present-day discussions concerning economic and political programs as well as being basic to the understanding of the role and future of American public education. . . . Whatever ideology is or is not, above all else it is a patterning of ideas or beliefs that characterize someone's thoughts. . . . any ideology is a form of thought with a special, intimate relationship to social, political, or economic action. Performing the function of providing individuals with the means of organization for social experience—experience comprehensible only in the content of interrelated society . . . the importance of ideology cannot be underestimated. (1977, pp. 15–16)

More to the point, when we talk about ideology we are most often concerned with a particular subset of ideological beliefs: those of the dominant ideology in society. As Lippi-Green has defined it, ideology is "the promotion of the needs and interests of a dominant group or class at the expense of marginalized groups, by means of disinformation and misrepresentation of those non-dominant groups" (1997, p. 64). This focus on dominance is important, since it allows us to focus our attention on the ways in which the mainstream society both legitimizes and reproduces itself. The German philosopher Jürgen Habermas (1968, 1970, 1971, 1984) argued that domination is embedded in society and social organization and, furthermore, that in the contemporary world, "The domination of science and technology as ideology hides the power of technical control; it assumes the function of legitimating political power as manipulation" (Baldwin, 1987, p. 16). In the context of public schooling, this means that ideology functions to promote a technicist view of teaching and learning, rather than an empowering or emancipatory view. Examples of this ideological hegemony would include assumptions about social class, meritocracy, and political and economic legitimacy, among others. As Michael Apple has noted, such technicism in educational practice is both misleading and dangerous:

> The supposedly neutral language of an institution, even though it rests upon highly speculative data and may be applied without actually being appropriate, provides a framework that legitimates control of major aspects of an individual's or group's behavior. At the same time, by sounding scientific and "expert," it contributes to the quiesence of the public by focusing attention on its "sophistication" not on its political or ethical results. Thus, historically outmoded, and socially and politically conservative (and often educationally disastrous) practices are not only continued, but are made to sound as if they were actually more enlightened and ethically responsive ways of dealing with children. (1979, p. 144)

Turning to the case of language, ideology also plays a crucial legitimating role (see Coleman, 1996; Joseph & Taylor, 1990; Kress & Hodge, 1979; Milroy & Milroy, 1985). In her outstanding book *English with an Accent*, Lippi-Green addresses this phenomenon, with special emphasis on the "standard language ideology." Her argument is that

> Dominant institutions promote the notion of an overarching, homogenous standard language which is primarily white, upper middle class, and midwestern. Whether the issues at hand are larger social or political ones or more subtle, whether the approach is coercion or consent, there are two sides to this process: first, devaluation of all that is not (or does not seek to be) politically, culturally, or socially mainstream, and second, validation of the social (and linguistic) values of the dominant institutions. (1997, p. 65)

And, of course, at the heart of this process is the public school, where not only the standard language ideology is promoted but where a whole host of complex attitudes, ideas, and beliefs about language and language difference are conveyed and reinforced. In addition, of course, it is in the school context where such ideologies, attitudes, ideas and beliefs can be, and often are, contested and resisted. Indeed, it is through such contestation and resistance that the linguistic landscape of both the school and the society are sometimes modified and changed (see Fairclough, 1992; Osborn, 2000, 2002).

EPISTEMOLOGY AND THE CURRICULUM

The ideological content of both the formal and hidden curricula in public education in the United States has been well established and documented in general terms (see Altbach, Kelly, Petrie & Weis, 1991; Apple, 1990, 1995, 1996; Apple & Weiss, 1983). Extensive scholarly analysis has been done on such areas as social studies, the literary canon in English, sexism and racism in textbooks, and so on (see Luke, 1988; Woodward, Elliot & Nagel, 1988). As Apple and Christian-Smith have noted, "During the past two decades, a good deal of progress has been made on answering the question of whose knowledge becomes socially legitimate in schools" (1991, p. 1). As this suggests, one of the fundamental issues that must be addressed in any critical examination of the schooling process is that of epistemology (see Steedman, 1988; Steffe, 1995).

Epistemology, in a nutshell, refers to theories of knowledge and knowing, as well as to the origins, methods, and limits of knowledge. In the foreign language education context, epistemological issues play important roles in determining both how and what we teach (see Reagan, 1999). For instance, the audiolingual method (ALM) which characterized a good deal of foreign language education in the United States during much of the latter half of the twentieth century was based upon and grounded in behaviorist psychology and epistemology (see Chastain, 1976, pp. 109–129; Littlewood, 1984, pp. 17–21). More recent efforts to promote constructivist approaches to learning, which presuppose that knowledge is constructed by the individual learner, are grounded in a very different epistemological framework (see Reagan, 1999, 2002a; Williams & Burden, 1997). Constructivism, in essence, rejects positivistic and objectivist views of knowledge.[1] As Catherine Fosnot has noted,

> Constructivism is not a theory about teaching. It's a theory about knowledge and learning. Drawing on a synthesis of current work in cognitive psychology, philosophy, and anthropology, the theory defines knowledge as temporary, developmental, socially and culturally mediated, and thus, non-objective. Learning from this perspective is understood as a self-regulated process of resolving inner cognitive conflicts that often become apparent through concrete experience, collaborative discourse, and reflection. (1993, p. vii)

This does not mean that "all bets are off" with respect to knowledge, nor does it mean that "anything goes" in the search for knowledge.[2] In the context of foreign language education, what it does mean is that each individual's knowledge of a particular language is developmental—

regardless of whether we are concerned with the native language or a second/additional language. It also means that there is no absolute "It" out in the universe somewhere that constitutes "Spanish" or "German" or "Russian." There are, rather, millions of idiolects that together constitute each language. To be sure, there are standard or mainstream varieties of each language for which certain generalizations can be made, and it is with such generalizations that we are often concerned in the classroom context. However, at the same time we need to be aware of the fundamental arbitrariness of the norms of the mainstream or standard language. Chicano Spanish, for instance, uses *"Cuando vuélvamos . . ."* where mainstream Spanish would use *"Cuando volvamos . . ."*; the difference is not one of "correct" and "incorrect," but rather one of different grammatical rules in different varieties of Spanish. As Rosaura Sánchez has explained, "The difference . . . lies in a shift of stress in the nonstandard variety which automatically produces the dipthong. What we have done, in effect, is to regularize the stem of the verb in our variety: *vuelva, vuelvas, vuelva, vuélvamos, vuelvan*" (1981, p. 96).

Epistemology is important for a variety of reasons, not the least of which is that it raises issues about the legitimacy of knowledge, and the role of authority in determining this legitimacy (see, for example, Jansen, 1991). Linguistic purism is an excellent example of the conflation of generally accepted norms in language use and inappropriate conceptions of "correctness." In a widely used textbook for teaching Spanish to native speakers of the language in the U.S. context, for instance, Marie Esman Barker argues, "Barbarismo es el vicio defecto del lenguaje que consiste en pronunciar o escribir mal las palabras, o en emplear vocablos impropios. Aquí vamos a tratar de los "barbarismos" que caracterizan el habla del hispano en la región suroeste de nuestro país" (1972, p. 36). Although far from uncommon among language educators, such views are simply absurd from a linguistic perspective and are highly problematic epistemologically.

BIAS IN THE CURRICULUM

Educators have become very aware of and sensitive to explicit issues of bias in the curriculum in recent years, and teacher education students are commonly advised about identifying and rectifying such biases in the curriculum (see, e.g., Banks, 1994, pp. 117–121; Gollnick & Chinn, 1994, pp. 320–326). There is, at the very least, a rhetorical commitment to eliminating blatant bias in the curriculum in U.S. public education. Nonetheless, Anyon's observation about textbooks in general, and U.S. social studies textbooks in particular, remains largely valid. She argued that the textbook

> suggests a great deal about the society that produces and uses it. It reveals which groups have power and demonstrates that the views of these groups are expressed and legitimized in the school curriculum. It can also identify social groups that are not empowered by the economic and social patterns in our society and do not have their views, activities, and priorities represented in the school curriculum. . . . Omissions, stereotypes, and distortions that remain in "updated" social studies textbook accounts of Native Americans, Blacks, and women reflect the relative powerlessness of these groups. (1979, p. 382)

While progress has indeed been made in the elimination of blatant bias in the curriculum, the underlying assumptions, which play significant roles in the establishment and maintenance of ideological hegemony in U.S. society, remain very much intact and unchallenged. In the case of foreign language education, although obvious bias has been largely (though by no means completely) eliminated in textbooks and instructional materials in recent years, the underlying ideological and cultural biases for the most part remain unexamined and unaddressed. Although this is no doubt true of the wider curriculum as well, in the case of foreign language education the biases that can be identified are centrally concerned with the actual content and purpose of the formal curriculum and have the effect of essentially nullifying that curriculum's important elements (see Osborn, 2000). Even more significant are the generally unarticulated ideological assumptions about language, language learning, and language diversity that are present in the United States.

Both subtle and blatant bias impact foreign language instruction in the schools. A clear Eurocentric bias continues to be reflected in the languages most commonly offered in U.S. public schools, with the vast majority of students enrolled in French, Spanish, German, and Latin. Further, social class background often affects the student's decision to study a foreign language at all, and folk wisdom about the relative ease and difficulty of particular languages, as well as assumptions about the "appropriateness" of different languages for particular students, also affects which language the student is likely to choose (or be advised to take). For instance, Spanish is often seen as a relatively "easy" option by students, parents, counselors, and other teachers, while German and Latin are seen as more difficult and thus suited to more capable students. Thus, it could be argued that the language offerings of the school are grounded in historic sociopolitical power relationships and that the selection of the language to be studied by the student is further constrained by his/her social and educational background and expected life outcomes. Even beyond such biases, however, ideology plays an important role in the ways foreign language education programs are viewed in the United States.

THE FOREIGN LANGUAGE EDUCATION PARADOX

In the mid-1950s, Jacques Barzun, in a scathing indictment of foreign language education in the United States, suggested that

> boys and girls "take" French or Spanish or German . . . for three, four, or five years before entering college, only to discover there that they cannot read, speak, or understand it. The word for this type of instruction is not "theoretical" but "hypothetical." Its principal is "*If* it were possible to learn a foreign language in the way I have been taught, I should now know that language." (1954, p. 119)

Although foreign language teaching methods, textbooks, and curricula have undergone several major changes since Barzun wrote these words (see Birckbichler, 1990; Christie, 1989; Cook, 1996; Larsen-Freeman, 1986; Nunan, 1995; Richard-Amato, 1988; Richards & Rodgers, 2001), there can be little doubt that foreign language education remains, for the most part, relatively unsuccessful for the vast majority of students in U.S. schools. To a considerable extent, this is the result of factors well beyond the control of foreign language educators. For instance, Draper and Hicks (1996) have documented that only 33% of all students enrolled in grades 7–12 in the United States study a foreign language at all (though this nevertheless constitutes a significant improvement over recent years; indeed, these numbers represent an increase of more than one million students studying foreign languages since 1990). Of the total six million students in middle and secondary schools who do study a foreign language, very few ever achieve even a marginal degree of fluency in the target language. In short, the old joke that a person who speaks three languages is called a trilingual, one who speaks two languages is called a bilingual, and one who speaks only one language is called an American is far too close to the truth to be terribly humorous, at least for the foreign language educator.

How can this failure be explained? There are a number of factors that certainly contribute to the problems. Large numbers of structural and pedagogical constraints work against success in contemporary foreign language education programs in the United States (see Ortega, 1999; Reagan & Osborn, 1998). Among these constraints are the time devoted to foreign language teaching and learning, the lack of extracurricular institutional support for foreign language learning, institutional and individual biases with respect to which languages are offered and who takes which language, the public justifications for foreign language education, the articulated goals of foreign language education, and, finally, what might be termed the social expectation of failure with respect to the learning of foreign languages in the U.S. context.

Although various kinds of programs involving the teaching of foreign languages in the elementary school are gaining popularity in many parts of the United States (see Curtain & Pesola, 1994; Lipton, 1992), for the most part foreign language education still most often begins at either the middle or secondary school level for most students. This is, of course, far from ideal. While there are indeed some advantages to coming to the study of a second language later in life, as a general rule there is no doubt that the earlier one begins studying a second language, the better. In societies in which language learning is considered an essential component of a child's education, children routinely begin the study of foreign languages very early in their schooling (see Baldauf, 1993; Beardsmore, 1993a, 1993b; Ervin, 1991). Further, when foreign language learning begins is only one part of the broader problem. Perhaps even more important is the amount of time actually devoted to language teaching and learning. Typically, foreign language classes meet one period a day, allowing in most school districts for a maximum of fewer than 150 hours of language study per year—a maximum that does not, it should be noted, take into account such factors as teacher and student absences, fire drills, pep rallies, and so on, all of which reduce the amount of time actually devoted to language learning. To be sure, simply increasing the time spent studying a particular subject does not necessarily guarantee increased student learning, but by reducing instructional time beyond what is necessary does significantly increase the likelihood of student non-learning.

This hypothetical 150 hours of language study is very telling, since we do know roughly how much time is needed for the typical individual to acquire different levels of competence in different languages (see Liskin-Gasparro, 1982). Using the expected levels of speaking proficiency guidelines from the Foreign Service Institute, we find that in order to achieve a level 1 to 1+ on the 5-point Interagency Language Roundtable scale (which basically refers to "survival proficiency"), students with average aptitude for language learning require a minimum of 240 hours of instruction in French and Spanish, 480 hours for German, and even longer in the cases of the "less commonly taught languages" such as Arabic, Chinese, Japanese, and Russian (Hadley, 1993, p. 28; see also Brecht & Walton, 1994; Everson, 1993; Walker, 1989). In other words, given the time required for the acquisition of different languages, the time allocated to foreign language instruction in the schools in effect ensures that, over the course of two years of study, students will have had sufficient exposure to the target language to achieve at best minimal, survival levels of competence in the target language, and are in fact very unlikely to achieve even that.

The time-related constraints on foreign language education are illuminating because they so clearly conflict with what is known, both intuitively and empirically, about what is required for successful second language learning. The bottom line here would seem to be that since no one could seriously expect the current approach to foreign language education to succeed, the system is in fact expected, at least to some degree, to fail. On its own, this is an intriguing insight, but it is far from the whole picture.

These time constraints in foreign language education are further exacerbated by the lack of any significant external institutional support for foreign language learning. Voluntary foreign language clubs and the occasional school-sponsored field trip notwithstanding, students of foreign languages in U.S. schools have very few opportunities to utilize the target language in ways that are really meaningful. Content courses (such courses as social studies, literature, mathematics, and science) are almost never taught in foreign languages (except in bilingual education programs, which are generally not open to English-speaking students). Even the growing popularity of interdisciplinary approaches in the classroom has had little impact on the foreign language education in many school districts. In short, in the typical middle and secondary school, foreign language education is very much seen by students and non-foreign language educators alike as peripheral to the "real" school experience.

An additional problem in the context of foreign language teaching and learning in the U.S. setting is that of relevance or, perhaps more accurately, the perceived lack of relevance of foreign languages in the lives of students. To some extent, of course, the same is true for most subject matter. Relatively few students, I suspect, see the immediate contributions of algebra or U.S. history to their lives. Foreign languages are even further removed from students' daily lives. Unlike students elsewhere in the world studying English, for instance, who are (albeit to varying degrees) exposed to the language in advertisements, popular music, and contemporary culture, most students in the United States are unlikely to encounter significant opportunities to utilize the language they study unless they specifically and actively seek them out. Further, the curriculum of the typical foreign language class, although dramatically improved in recent years, remains largely artificial for most students. As Reagan and Osborn have noted,

> There has been a well-documented movement in the past twenty years or more away from "canned" expressions and sentences being used in the foreign language classroom toward more authentic communication and a utilization of realia. Textbooks have been engineered to focus on patterns of discourse that one might find in the target culture, which typically include behavior such as buying vegetables, discussing hobbies or school activities, and careers. Unfortunately, however, these discussions are typically no more meaningful to our students than the previous topics of discussion in foreign language classes. Most of our students will never buy vegetables in a Munich street market, ask for directions to the Eiffel Tower in Paris, or have a school schedule in Mexico City. This being the case,

it should not be particularly surprising to find that "foreign" languages remain foreign to most of our students. (1998, p. 54)

Finally, the last of the structural and pedagogical constraints against which foreign language education finds itself working is a widespread and general social expectation of failure. This social expectation of failure is in fact the thread that holds together the other structural, institutional, and pedagogical constraints discussed here. Foreign language education in the United States is clearly not successful for most students, nor could it be, given the way it has been, and continues to be, implemented in the schools. Further, it is clear that most students, parents, teachers, and policy makers do not seriously expect it to succeed. Rather, it serves an important tracking and sorting function in U.S. education—a function quite different from the arguments that foreign language educators sincerely offer for it. For the most part, the same is true in higher education as well. At the undergraduate level, completion of a certain number of foreign language classes often serves as a requirement for graduation, while graduate level programs commonly require the demonstration of reading proficiency in a foreign language but generally give no credit for course work to satisfy this requirement. In fact, in recent years many institutions have attempted to circumvent the foreign language requirement with the establishment of a cognate field, or even the declaration of computer language or statistics as satisfying the foreign language requirement. Even among the best-educated persons in our society, in short, competence in a second language is often seen as irrelevant, except in its limited role of serving to control and restrict access. The key to understanding the failure of foreign language education is in fact the assumption of monolingualism as the social norm, as discussed in chapter 2.

HEGEMONY IN FOREIGN LANGUAGE EDUCATION

If there are considerable ideological pressures on foreign language education from outside the profession, it must be recognized that language educators are themselves also contributors to some of the ideological challenges that face the profession. It is interesting to note that language educators in the U.S. context have traditionally been divided into three very distinct groups: "foreign language educators," "bilingual educators," and "English as a Second Language educators." This division is not merely semantic. Educators in each of these "second language education" professions see themselves as fundamentally different from the other groups. As Ortega has noted,

Together with [the] elitism perpetuated in much foreign language teaching, a second problem in the foreign language profession's orientation towards

> languages is a striking lack of sociopolitical awareness and a dismissal of the political nature of second language teaching within the foreign language profession. For instance, McKay and Wong surveyed journal articles from 1974 to 1987 which appeared in one TESOL and two foreign language major journals . . . and found that sociopolitical awareness and professional topics were the least reflected in all three professional journals. Foreign language scholarly writing appears to be unconcerned with issues of changing language attitudes, government language policy, the relationship between the profession and the community, and political action on language-related evens and issues to be taken by language professional organizations . . . many foreign language professionals declared having limited interaction with the English as a Second Language and bilingual education professions in terms of networking, teaching, and research. They tended to consider foreign language as apolitical and impartial regarding issues of language education, bilingual education, and language policy . . . and they often believed foreign language programs to be neutral and to exist as academic subjects independently of potential official English policies and of the funding processes affecting English as a Second Language or bilingual education. (1999, p. 248)

In short, the ideological context of foreign language education in the United States is not entirely external to the profession; as a well-known cartoon character once asserted, "We have met the enemy, and he is us."

NATIONAL STANDARDS AND FOREIGN LANGUAGE EDUCATION

The current debates about national standards in education can provide additional insight into common views and expectations of foreign language education. It is clear that an important aspect of the ideological content and functions of the curriculum is visible in the national standards movement (see Meier, 2000) as well as in the related debates about standardized testing (see McNeil, 2000). The debate about the content of the national standards in social studies, for instance, has been largely informed by and grounded in competing ideological perspectives (see Nash, Crabtree & Dunn, 1997). Similar controversy has surrounded discussions about national standards and standardized testing in English, science, and mathematics. In the case of foreign language education, the development of national standards have been far less controversial (see National Standards in Foreign Language Education Project, 1996). Indeed, the ACTFL standards have been widely accepted in the profession, and there are ongoing efforts to implement the standards in a meaningful way at the classroom level. To the best of my knowledge, there has been no significant public debate or controversy about the foreign language standards. This could be, at least in part, because the standards themselves are the product of foreign language educators who took their task seriously and produced standards that presupposed a commitment to meaningful language learning—that is, it may be that the people involved in the National Standards in Foreign Language Education Project simply did an outstanding job, and everyone recognizes this. While I do believe that the National Standards in Foreign Language Education Project was exceptionally well done, and while I hope that the lack of controversy about the standards is due to a general agreement about this, it seems to me more likely that the absence of discussion and debate is more reflective of a general apathy toward foreign language learning than it is with a broad acceptance of the national standards by the public. Groups and individuals care about what is taught in social studies and whether students can write clearly. They are, I think, far less concerned with whether students can communicate in a second language (unless, of course, the second language is English).

CONCLUSION

The title of this chapter was inspired by George Orwell's novel *1984*. Just as the world of *1984* was one of contradictions—the three slogans of the Party were, for example, "War is Peace," "Freedom is Slavery," and "Ignorance is Strength"—so too is the world of foreign language education in the U.S. setting characterized by contradictions. The challenge in making sense of this world, as has been suggested in this chapter, is to understand the ideological functions that undergird and support the methods, structures, and concepts of foreign language education. It is by paying attention to the generally unarticulated ideological functions served by foreign language education in our society that we can gain insight and understanding into the real challenges that face us as critical educators, and which, in turn, can assist us in developing curricular and methodological approaches that can in fact empower our students.

QUESTIONS FOR REFLECTION AND DISCUSSION

1. Rosina Lippi-Green is cited in this chapter with respect to her discussion of the concept of the "standard language ideology." What common ideological assumptions about "standard" and "nonstandard" languages can you identify? What are the implications of these assumptions for the foreign language classroom?
2. If epistemology is really important for educators to consider, as is suggested in this chapter, then why do teachers spend so little time discussing it? What does the lack of attention given to epistemology in public education discourse tell us about (a) the epistemological beliefs of educators, and (b) the role of epistemology in the teaching and learning process?
3. In recent years, some writers have begun to draw attention to what they call "linguicism"—the language and linguistic analog of racism, sexism, ageism,

and so on. How would you explain this concept? Why might it be an important one for foreign language educators to understand?

4. What are the implications for classroom practice (including both teaching methodology and student assessment) of the constructivist idea that all knowledge is developmental?
5. Jacques Barzun is quoted in this chapter arguing that "boys and girls 'take' French or Spanish or German . . . for three, four, or five years before entering college, only to discover there that they cannot read, speak, or understand it." Do you believe that this is still true of foreign language education in the United States? If so, how would you explain your own successful language learning?

FURTHER READING

There are a number of excellent works dealing with the themes explored in this chapter. See, for instance, Rosina Lippi-Green's *English with an Accent: Language, Ideology, and Discrimination in the United States* (1977), Susan Dicker's *Languages in America: A Pluralist View* (1996), and John Joseph and Talbot Taylor's *Ideologies of Language* (1990). For works dealing with constructivist epistemology, see Marion Williams and Robert Burden's *Psychology for Language Teachers: A Social Constructivist Approach* (1997), and Jacqueline Grennon Brooks and Martin Brooks's *The Case for Constructivist Classrooms* (1993).

NOTES

1. In recent years, there has been an immense amount of philosophical work done on epistemology, much of it outstanding (see Fenstermacher, 1997; Harris, 1992). Foundational works in the philosophy of science include Popper (1959), Kuhn (1970, 1977) and Lakatos & Musgrave (1970). For a good general introduction and summary of the field, see O'Hear (1989) and Klemke, Hollinger, & Rudge (1998). A powerful critique of much of the "postmodernist" philosophy of science can be found in Sokal & Bricmont (1998).

2. The philosopher of science Paul Feyerabend, who claimed to be an epistemological anarchist, did in fact in some places claim that "anything goes" but in other works seemed to back away from this view. His works are, in any event, wonderful reading, even if one disagrees with them (see Deurr, 1980, 1981; Feyerabend, 1981a, 1981b, 1987, 1991, 1993, 1995, 1999).

Chapter 4

Why Study Uzbek? Considering the Less Commonly Taught Languages[1]

Draper and Hicks (1996) report that fewer than half of all secondary students in American public schools study a foreign language. Of the six million students in middle and secondary schools who do study a foreign language, approximately 65% study Spanish, 22% study French, 6% study German, and 3.5% study Latin. The remaining 3.5% of students study a wide variety of other languages, including American Sign Language, Arabic, Chinese (both Cantonese and Mandarin), Greek, Haitian Creole, Hawai'ian, Hebrew, Italian, Japanese, Korean, Norwegian, Polish, Portuguese, Russian, Vietnamese, and a variety of both African and Native American languages (see Draper & Hicks, 1996, p. 305). It is with the languages studied by this 3.5% of the student population, as well as those languages that are not studied at all by students in the U.S. context, that this chapter is concerned. Specifically, our concern here will be on the need for what might be called a "social grammar" of the less commonly taught languages in general, with respect to their presence (or lack of presence) in the public school curriculum. In particular, we will be concerned with trying to identify some of the factors that seem to underlie the implicit linguistic hierarchy that governs the study of the different less commonly taught languages. As Walker has observed,

> Ninety-seven percent of the students of modern foreign languages in the public schools of this country are studying Spanish, French, and German . . . In American colleges and universities, Spanish, French and German enroll approximately eighty-five percent of the students of foreign languages. . . . A rough calculation presents a startling aspect of educational practice in the United States: *At least ninety-one percent of the academic study of foreign languages is directed toward languages used by twelve to thirteen percent of humanity.* (1989, p. 111, emphasis mine)

It is this phenomenon which is our concern here. It is also important to note that the focus of this chapter is on foreign language education in the United States and specifically excludes the use of less commonly taught languages in bilingual education programs. The use of less commonly taught languages in bilingual education in the United States, in essence, is transitional in nature, and the primary articulated objective (especially in programs using less commonly taught languages) is the transition of students into English-medium environments.[2] Thus, the fact that the less commonly taught languages may be used in such programs does not in any way detract from the central argument presented here.

There are a number of compelling reasons for us to be interested in the teaching and learning of less commonly taught languages. First and foremost, at least in terms of making a public case for the study of these languages, there is what can be called the geopolitical aspect of language teaching and learning. In essence, it is in the best interest of the society to produce sufficient numbers of linguistically competent individuals to function in the various national and regional languages that are used in areas of national political, economic, and strategic concern. For example, when the U.S. government identified 169 critical languages which "would promote important scientific research or security interests of a national or economic kind" (Crystal, 1997a, p. 344) in 1985, it was this geopolitical aspect of language teaching and learning that was at issue. In the aftermath of 11 September, the need for speakers of such languages as Arabic, Farsi, Pashto, Uzbek, and so on, became even more urgent—and the lack of speakers of such languages in the United States even more apparent.

Our need to understand others in the world provides another justification for studying the less commonly taught languages, since the languages themselves play an essential role in our ability to understand the speech communities that use them. As Robert Bunge has observed, "Language is not just another thing we do as humans; it is *the* thing we do. It is a total environment; we live in the language as a fish lives in water. It is the audible and visible manifestation of the soul of a people" (1992, p. 376, emphasis in original). It would, in short, be difficult to overstate the centrality of language to worldview and both group and individual identity. As Appel and Muysken suggested in their book, *Language Contact and Bilingualism:*

> Language is not only an instrument for the communication of messages. This becomes especially clear in multilingual communities where various groups have their own language: e.g. the Flemish in Belgium and the Gujeratis in India. With its language a group distinguishes itself. The cultural norms and values of a group are transmitted by its language. Group feelings are emphasized by using the group's own language, and members of the outgroup are excluded from its internal transactions. (1987, p. 11)

In addition, there are also pedagogical lessons to be learned from the experiences of teachers and students of the less commonly taught languages. As Roger Allen has explained with respect to teachers of Arabic, the contributions that teachers of non-Western languages

> may have for language teaching have until recently been ignored by the profession at large. It does not seem an exaggeration to claim that one of the results of the proficiency movement has been to bring the issues raised by the non-Western, less commonly taught, "critical," "exotic" languages very much to the attention of the language-teaching profession as a whole. (1992, pp. 236–237)

Although Allen is perhaps somewhat overly optimistic in terms of the extent to which the less commonly taught languages have been taken seriously by most language educators in the United States, his fundamental point is nevertheless an important and valuable one. There can be little doubt that teachers of less commonly taught languages bring with them very different sets of experiences with respect to foreign language pedagogy, and the discussion about and reflection on their experiences is almost certain to benefit both other less commonly taught language teachers as well as teachers of the more commonly taught languages (see Ihde, 1997). Beyond these lessons for foreign language education pedagogy, the teaching and learning of less commonly taught languages also impact on education in a number of other areas, among which are multicultural education programs, global education programs, critical language and language awareness programs, and finally, the teaching of the politics and political contexts of foreign language teaching and learning.

TRADITIONAL CATEGORIZATIONS OF THE LESS COMMONLY TAUGHT LANGUAGES

In a seminal article on the less commonly taught languages, Walker (1989) argued that, at least in the U.S. context, there is a fundamental distinction made between the traditionally taught languages (i.e., French, Spanish and German) and all others (the less commonly taught languages). Although it is not uncommon for the less commonly taught languages to be grouped together in this manner as something of a miscellaneous category (see, e.g., Brecht & Walton, 1994; Crookes, Sakka, Shiroma & Lei Ye, 1991; Everson, 1993; Ryding, 1989; Walker, 1991), this is inevitably misleading on a number of grounds, not the least of which is the problem of grouping together radically different kinds of languages. Indeed, Walker has suggested that "thinking of less commonly taught languages as a category of language is like thinking of 'nonelephants' as a category of animals" (1989, p. 111).

In attempting to address this problem, Walton suggests that the less commonly taught languages can be best understood as being divided in practice into three subgroups: (1) less commonly taught European languages such as Russian, Italian, Portuguese, and Swedish; (2) higher-enrollment non-Indo-European languages, such as Arabic, Chinese, and Japanese; and (3) lower-enrollment non-Indo-European languages such as Burmese, Indonesian, and Swahili (1992, p. 1). Jordan and Walton (1987) have even gone so far as to label the second and third groups the "truly foreign languages," emphasizing their presumed difficulty for speakers of English as well as their degree of difference from English. Jacobs (1996), in what could be considered a sort of linguistic one-upmanship, has offered an argument for the inclusion of American Sign Language in one of these categories as well. The key criterion that seems to be applied in making these distinctions is essentially the distance from English, in terms of such factors as phonology, grammar, lexicon, orthography, and spelling (see Hawkins, 1981, pp. 79–82; James, 1979).

Utilizing a five-point rating scale, the interlingual distance between any two languages can be determined and assigned a quantitative rating. Thus, in an analysis of the interlingual distances of English to French, German, Italian, Russian and Spanish, James (1979) determined the following scores:

French	12
German	10
Italian	6
Russian	16
Spanish	7

Thus, Italian and Spanish would be relatively easier languages for an English speaker to learn than would be French or German, with Russian constituting the most difficult language for English speakers to learn of those in James's sample. It is interesting to note that these results are actually fairly consistent with the Educational Testing Service's estimates of the classroom time required to meet various levels of linguistic proficiency in different languages (see Hadley, 1993; Liskin-Gasparro, 1982). Basically, the Educational Testing Service estimates divide target languages into four groups, ranging from those that are most quickly acquired by English speakers to those that require the most time. It is interesting to note that of the three commonly taught languages (French, German, and Spanish), two are in Group I (French and Spanish), and one is in Group II (German).

Although the division of less commonly taught languages by degree of difficulty for English speakers does have a certain amount of face validity, it does not really move us forward in terms of understanding why certain less commonly taught languages are more popular than others. If interlingual distance was really all that was at stake, then we would expect languages in Educational Testing Service Group I to be considerably more common than those in Group IV—and yet, that does not appear to be the case. Three of the four listed languages in Group IV (Arabic, Chinese, and Japanese) are among the more popular less commonly taught languages, while Group I includes a large number of languages that are virtually never taught in U.S. public schools (for example, Afrikaans, Danish, Dutch, Norwegian, Romanian, and Swedish), despite their presumed relative ease of acquisition. The problem, of course, is that decisions and choices about language are rarely made simply on grounds of ease of learning, or what might be called "hierarchies of difficulty" (see DiPietro, 1971, pp. 161–164); rather, such choices are deeply grounded and embedded in social, cultural, economic, political, demographic, and ideological beliefs and attitudes. It is in order to achieve a better understanding of these extralinguistic factors guiding language choice that a social grammar of the less commonly taught languages is needed.

TOWARD A SOCIAL GRAMMAR OF THE LESS COMMONLY TAUGHT LANGUAGES

If ease of acquisition does not provide an adequate or satisfactory explanation for why some less commonly taught languages are found in public school curricula in the United States and others are not, then what could explain this difference? The answer, as suggested above, requires a social grammar of the less commonly taught languages: a framework within which such factors as social, cultural, economic, political, demographic and ideological beliefs and attitudes can be taken into account. Although Hymes's (1996) analysis of the core assumptions about language in the United States, discussed in chapter 2, may help us to contextualize a social grammar of the less commonly taught languages, on its own this model is obviously far from sufficient for this purpose, as indeed are the related, and conceptually powerful, notions of linguistic imperialism and linguicism (see, e.g., Phillipson, 1988, 1992, pp. 50–57; Skutnabb-Kangas, 1988; Tollefson, 1995). Rather, what is needed is a framework for classifying the less commonly taught languages, coupled with a discussion of the explanatory factors for why particular less commonly taught languages fall where they do within this framework. It is to a discussion of such a framework that we now turn.

It is clear that there is a hierarchy of less commonly taught languages, but it is also clear, as we have seen, that this hierarchy is not one grounded in linguistic factors. In order to be useful, the hierarchy of less commonly taught languages is better envisaged as one reflecting the likelihood of a particular language being offered as a foreign language option in a public school. Thus, looking at foreign language education in the United States as a whole, we can talk about a hierarchy of five levels:

Level 1	Commonly taught languages
Level 2	Most commonly taught "less commonly taught languages"
Level 3	Rarely taught "less commonly taught languages"
Level 4	Never/virtually never taught "less commonly taught languages"
Level 5	The "non-languages"

Level 1 refers not to the less commonly taught languages at all but rather to the languages most commonly associated with foreign language education in the United States: French, German, Spanish, and probably Latin. Although there are significant differences with respect to student enrollment among these languages, all four are widely offered throughout the United States; certified teachers are generally readily available in all four languages (though, to be sure, there are periodic shortages); a variety of textbooks and supplementary pedagogical materials are available for all four languages; curricular guides are widely available and thorough; and all four languages are seen as fully legitimate objects of study. To a very significant extent, when one talks about foreign language education in the United States, it is with these languages that one is concerned.

Level 2 encompasses the less commonly taught languages that fairly routinely appear in public school curricula in most if not all parts of the United States—albeit considerably less frequently than even Latin—and serve far fewer students. Included among the Level 2 languages would be Russian, Chinese, Japanese and Arabic. It is interesting to note that these languages, the most commonly taught of the less commonly taught languages, all involve substantial orthographic challenges for English-speaking students, and all involve considerable interlingual distance from English (though learning Russian is obviously, on both counts, clearly easier for English speakers than learning the other Level 2 languages). Although shortages certainly exist, teacher certification in Level 2 languages is commonly possible and teachers for these languages can be found; textbooks and supportive materials are available (if limited); and curricular guides have been prepared in many states and local school districts.

Level 3 refers to the less commonly taught languages that do, on occasion, make their way into the public school curricula, but do so fairly rarely (even when compared with the Level 2 languages) and often in geographically restricted contexts. Included here would be such heritage languages as Polish, Italian, Portuguese, Modern Greek, Hawai'ian, Norwegian, and so on. The key here is that, for the most part, these languages are offered where they are in fact reflective of some element of the ethnic composition and makeup of the local population. In other words, to some extent Level 3 languages are actually examples of ethnic language or heritage language maintenance or revival efforts as much as truly foreign language efforts. Teaching certification is uncommon for Level 3 languages, and very often non-foreign language educators who speak the target language (often as native speakers) are employed to teach these languages. Textbooks and supplementary teaching materials are available but quite limited, and few formal curricular guidelines exist for most Level 3 languages.

Level 4 is by far the largest and most inclusive category and would include the overwhelming majority of the world's languages. Examples of Level 4 languages would include virtually all African languages, most Asian and Oceanic languages, indigenous Native American languages, and many smaller European languages, among others. This is, to some extent, a category of exclusion, in that it includes all languages that do not fit anywhere else. What holds this very large and diverse group of languages together (rather as a category of "nonelephants," as Walker [1989] would have it) is that they are virtually never offered as foreign language options in American public schools. As a general rule, teaching certification is not even possible in these languages; textbooks and pedagogical materials are difficult to come by and often of poor quality where they exist at all; curricula for public school classes do not exist; and, perhaps most important, there tends to be virtually no interest among either students or in the community at large for offering these languages. To a considerable extent, Level 4 languages are perceived, in the American context, as simply irrelevant.

The last category, Level 5, differs from the others in that it includes what can be termed "non-legitimate" languages—that is, languages and language varieties that the society appears to view as fundamentally different from "real" or "legitimate" languages. Such a distinction is, of course, linguistically nonsensical—the idea that there can be "legitimate" and "non-legitimate" languages makes no sense at all on any reasonable set of linguistic criteria. The distinction, though, is not linguistic but social and ideological, and it is all too commonly made in American society to dismiss certain languages as legitimate objects of foreign language study. Two of the better examples of this phenomenon are the cases of African American Vernacular English and American Sign Language, which we will explore in the next chapter. An especially interesting element of these Level 5 languages is the degree of controversy that often surrounds them. American Sign Language, for instance, is in fact offered in American public schools, and yet the resistance to it is surprisingly strong and often highly emotive in nature (see Vandenberg, 1998; Reagan, 1998a).

With respect to providing an explanatory model for why specific languages are located in a particular level, I would suggest that there are six fundamental factors which, taken together, determine a language's status. Specifically, these six factors are:

- the size of the language's speaker community;
- the geographic spread of the language (including its use as a second language, or lingua franca);
- whether the language constitutes a heritage language in the local American setting;
- whether the language is a language of wider communication;
- whether the language has an established and recognized literary/written tradition; and
- whether the language is a "living" or "dead" language.

It is important to note here that it is the interaction of these six factors that could be expected to determine the status of any particular language; no single factor could ensure either the presence or absence of a language in the public school curriculum. An additional factor that does not appear to be especially relevant in the contemporary U.S. context, but which has been important historically in the United States and continues to be so in many societies, is that of ideology (whether religious or political in nature). It is this factor that provides powerful explanatory and heuristic insight, for instance, into the anti-German language hysteria in the United States during the First World War, the role of the development of critical language training in the United States during the Cold War, and, more recently, some of the concerns among secularists in Turkey regarding the increased offering of courses in Ottoman Turkish, which is in some instances believed to be potentially symbolically linked to the rise of religious fundamentalism.

IMPLICATIONS FOR EDUCATIONAL POLICY AND PRACTICE

The articulation of a social grammar of the less commonly taught languages has significant and timely educational implications in the U.S. context in terms of foreign language pedagogy, multicultural and global education efforts, and the politics of education (especially with respect to critical and emancipatory education). In terms of foreign language pedagogy in the United States, an examination of the extralinguistic factors that determine the relative status of particular languages is an important aspect of language studies with which foreign language educators, and indeed all educators, need to be familiar (see Reagan, 1997a). Language is a profoundly social activity, inevitably embedded in a cultural, political, economic, and ideological context, and yet all too often language educators assume a narrow, essentially positivistic view of both language and language teaching. The consideration of the status of the less commonly taught languages can help to ameliorate this situation, just as serious discussion about foreign language teaching methods and strategies can generate important ideas and contribute to a cross-fertilization among foreign and second language teachers. In the past, this cross-fertilization has tended to move from the traditionally taught languages to the less commonly taught languages; a clear example of movement in this direction is Catherine Ball's interesting effort to incorporate text-based reading strategies in her teaching of Old English (see Ball, 1995). Along the same lines have been changes in the pedagogy of Latin in recent years (see LaFleur, 1992). The challenge here has been that the most common approach to the teaching of ancient and classical languages has tended to be and, with the possible exceptions of Latin and perhaps Classical Greek in some limited instances, continues to be essentially that of grammar-translation (see Smith, 1977). Similarly, the development of more student-friendly textbooks in some less commonly taught languages is another obvious example of such benefits. The possibilities for cross-fertilization, however, are in fact very much two-way. Indeed, as Allen has argued,

> As guidelines for such languages as Hebrew, Thai, Hausa, and Hindi take their place alongside Russian, Chinese, Japanese, and Arabic, we all begin to realise that teachers of languages from the various regions of the world have an enormous amount to contribute to, and learn from, each other about every aspect of their joint enterprise. (1992, p. 237)

A related area in which there is considerable potential for worthwhile interaction is between foreign language educators, teachers of English as a Second Language, and teachers working in bilingual education programs—where, incidentally, some less commonly taught languages are far more likely to appear than in the traditional foreign language curriculum. Although issues related to bilingual education programs in the United States are more generally addressed in Chapter 8, it is nevertheless important to stress here that there is a significant difference in educational aims and objectives between bilingual education programs and foreign language programs. This difference is perhaps best seen in terms of the kind of language proficiency that is our goal. In the literature on contemporary U.S. bilingual education, a common distinction is made between what are called basic interpersonal communicative skills and cognitive academic language proficiency (see Baker, 1993, p. 11; Spener, 1991, p. 440). The former refers to the language skills needed for casual conversational use of the L2, while the latter refers to the degree and kind of proficiency needed for intellectual and academic purposes. Bilingual educators argue that students achieve basic interpersonal communicative skills far sooner than cognitive academic language proficiency, and that this distinction makes necessary extended transitional programs for non-English-speaking students in the U.S. context. Although the distinction between basic interpersonal communicative skills and cognitive academic language proficiency is in fact questionable (see Martin-Jones & Romaine, 1986; Spolsky, 1989), it is an interesting one for discussion purposes here, since the kinds of language proficiency included in basic interpersonal communicative skills probably more than exceed typical expectations for student functioning in the target language in foreign language education programs.

Multicultural and global education programs, which have become increasingly popular in the United States in recent years, are another area where concerns with and interest in the less commonly taught languages are relevant. The fundamental challenge in such programs, from a linguistic perspective, is the minimal concern with language and language diversity that is generally found in multicultural and global curricula. There is, to be sure, a significant difference between the two types of programs in this regard: multicultural education programs do include some concern about language minority students (see Gollnick & Chinn, 1994, pp. 219–250; Ovando, 1993), though not, for the most part, about other language issues, while global education programs tend at best to give passing mention to language issues. Indeed, in the U.S. context, global education is most commonly completely separate from foreign language education and tends to be entirely monolingual in nature. As Reagan and Díaz have suggested,

> it simply does not make sense to think or talk about global education as a monolingual activity. Further . . . the idea that a global education curriculum could be developed, or that a global education unit could be taught, in a monolingual fashion (as, indeed, the literature seems not merely to accept but to assume) ought to be viewed by reasonable people in roughly the same way that claims about the world being flat are viewed—in short, as utter nonsense. To propose that we can prepare students to deal with issues of internationalization and globalization exclusively through the medium of English, with little or no exposure to other languages, is rather like imagining that we can prepare students to be scientifically literate by ensuring that they read their horoscopes each day and are taught to be sure to keep their healing crystals on hand in case of illness. In short, the very message of global education would seem to require that one challenge the dominance of monolingualism in our society. (1996, pp. 7–8)

Foreign language programs in elementary school contexts are an increasingly popular option in many parts of the United States (see Curtain & Pesola, 1994; Lipton, 1992). Although FLES (Foreign Language in the Elementary School) programs almost always provide students with an introduction to one of the commonly taught languages (most often French or Spanish), the same is not true for FLEX (Foreign Language Exploration/Experience) programs, where the focus is more on language awareness and exposure and less on acquiring a specific language. It is in FLEX programs that issues related to less commonly taught languages are most likely, and most easily, to be addressed in the elementary school context (see Lubiner, 1996; Reagan & Case, 1996).

Last, we come to the contribution that can be made by consideration of the social grammar of the less commonly taught languages to the politics of schooling and to the empowerment and emancipation of both students and teachers. Dell Hymes has argued, "It is probably through education—taken in its broadest sense, as schooling and instruction of all kinds—that the peculiar, latent, tacit American view of language most powerfully exercises cultural hegemony" (1996, p. 83). It is also, therefore, in educational institutions that we may have the best opportunity to challenge and repudiate this cultural hegemony—to engage, that is, in what Osborn has called "curricular nullification" (Osborn, 1998). This can be done through the inclusion of critical language exploration and awareness programs (see Andrews, 1998; Carter, 1990; van Lier, 1995), in foreign language classes themselves, and in other school contexts in which issues of language, power, and domination can be raised (see Fairclough, 1989, 1992; Reagan & Osborn, 1998), not to mention contexts in which issues of language rights can be discussed (see Phillipson, 2000; Skutnabb-Kangas, 2000a; Skutnabb-Kangas & Phillipson, 1995). As Michael Byram and his colleagues have pointed out in their discussion of language and culture teaching as political education,

> By making comparisons, learners are deliberately led into relativisation of their own perspective through prioritisation of the perspective of others. Comparison is not only a technique for highlighting similarities and differences as a means of making them more perceptible. It also serves as a step towards the acceptance of other perspectives, and the valuing of them as equally acceptable within their own terms. (1994, p. 177; see also Byram, 1989)

In short, the consideration of the social grammar of the less commonly taught languages provides us with a powerful opportunity to address a broad range of language-related issues in the school context, helping students to become more aware of the nature and role of language in society, of language bias and discrimination, and of the ways language is used and misused with respect to other social, political, and economic issues.

SPECIAL CHALLENGES IN TEACHING HERITAGE LANGUAGE SPEAKERS

Heritage language speakers always present special challenges in the foreign language classroom (see Valdés, Lozano & García-Moya, 1981), but in the case of many of the less commonly taught languages, such students present both unique opportunities and challenges. One example in which such opportunities and challenges can be seen especially clearly is in heritage speakers of Russian. Bermel and Kagan have noted,

> As our schools and universities see an ever-increasing number of students whose families emigrated from the former Soviet Union, we are faced with the dilemma of Russian-speaking students entering and interacting with language programs designed for the native speaker of English. These students intersect with our universities' Russian programs in a number of ways: they use it to leap various bureaucratic hurdles, including foreign language proficiency requirements; they come to us for objective certification of Russian-language documents; they participate in extracurricular activities that emphasize Russian culture; and, most important in an era of stagnant enrollments, in ever growing numbers they take courses in Russian language, linguistics, and literature. (2000, p. 405)

The heritage language speakers of Russian have positive implications for interest and enrollment in Russian courses and programs, both at the secondary and university levels. Such students also provide additional native speaker role models for nonnative speakers studying Russian, and given the limited opportunities for such interactions, this too is a positive outcome of the increasing numbers of heritage language speakers in Russian classes. Such students also, though, as a result of their émigré status, often display nonmainstream Russian language use. As Polinsky (1996) has observed, within the émigré community there is an increased permissiveness with respect to what constitutes "acceptable" Russian, and there are any number of examples of Émigré Russian that, while tolerated or even accepted fully in the émigré community, would be clearly unacceptable in a Russian context. Examples of such usage in both spoken and written abound. For instance, in a study of heritage speakers' written Russian, Bermel and Kagan (2000) have noted the following:

Spelling and Punctuation Errors

There is a general loss of appropriate punctuation, especially commas. Hyphens, spaces, and the hard and soft signs (ь and ъ) are often absent or misplaced, as in "что бы" and "что-бы" for чтобы ("in order to"), "потомучто" for "потому что" ("because"), and so on.

Grammatical Errors

Simplification of Russian forms, as well as interference from English forms, is fairly common among many heritage speakers of Russian. For instance, forms such as "около триста," "около трехста," and "около тристо" are found in place of the correct "около трёхсот" ("around three hundred")—examples where both parts ought to be, but only one (or none) is. An especially frequent error is the use of "кто" where Russian would require "который" (that is, where Émigré Russian has been influenced by the use of the English "who").

Confusion is also sometimes found in the use of prepositions, especially "в" ("in") and "на" ("on") (see also Kouzmin, 1982). In some instances, heritage speakers produce literal word-for-word equivalents of English rather than idiomatic Russian, as in the sentence, "*You and I have* different opinions." Mainstream Russian uses the phrase "у нас с тобой" for this construction, but among heritage speakers such constructions as "ты и я имеем" and "у тебя и у меня" are found.

Lexical Errors

Heritage speakers of Russian also demonstrate the inappropriate use of certain lexical items in Russian, sometimes as a result of uncertainty about the distinction between a general and a specific Russian term, and sometimes as a result of influence from English. Examples of the first problem include the substitution of a general word like "книга" ("book") for a more specific, and appropriate, word like "роман" ("novel"), or the use of "говорить" ("speak") for "спросить" ("argue"). Direct borrowings from English are also found.

Such changes in language use in the case of Russian have been made even more complex by the rapid rate of change in contemporary, post-Soviet Russian, which has also seen the influx of huge numbers of English borrowings. For instance, in recent years terms such as "тонер" ("toner"), "пейджер" ("pager"), "биг мак" ("Big Mac"), and "маркетинг" ("marketing") have all entered Russian (see Ryazanova-Clarke & Wade, 1999).

There are, of course, important pedagogical implications for all of these changes that are taking place, both in the mainstream language and in the émigré community. As Andrews has noted, "[A] measure of familiarity with various aspects of immigrant languages will allow instructors to address their [heritage language students'] needs with greater competence" (2000, p. 42). This means, in some instances, that curriculum, materials, and assessment must all be reexamined with respect to the special educational challenges and needs of the heritage language speaker.

REFLECTIONS ON LANGUAGE DIVERSITY AND LANGUAGE DEATH

Discussions of language diversity and the teaching and learning of less commonly taught languages lead to another, related, issue that has gained increasing attention in the past few years—language endangerment and, ultimately, the risk of language death (see Crystal, 2000; Dixon, 1997; Grenoble & Whaley, 1998; Nettle & Romaine, 2000). Just as language diversity has proven to be remarkably complex and difficult to determine (our best estimates are that there are approximately 6,000 languages in the world today, but even this is more a guess than a true estimate) (see Nettle, 1999), so too has language endangerment been difficult to quantify. Krauss, in a well-received statistic study of moribund languages around the world, has commented, "I consider it a plausible calculation that—at the rate things are going—the coming century will see either the death or the doom of 90% of mankind's languages" (1992, p. 7). Although they also cite the 90% figure, a more cautious note is sounded by Daniel Nettle and Suzanne Romaine in their book *Vanishing Voices: The Extinction of the World's Languages:* "How much of the world's linguistic diversity is endangered? The honest answer at this stage is that we don't know precisely, but when forced to guess, the proportion different linguists come up with is alarmingly high." (2000, p. 39).

The exact number of languages that are threatened with extinction, of course, is not important. What is significant is the scope of the problem, and that is all too clear already. Just as the biodiversity of our world is at risk, so too is its linguistic diversity. The analogy between biodiversity and linguistic diversity, although a powerful one that recurs often in the literature, is less than perfect. Most people understand, at least on some level, why the loss of biodiversity is undesirable. Far fewer individuals and groups are concerned about the loss of linguistic diversity, and some no doubt see such a development as a positive thing. And yet, language extinction in fact poses an incredible threat not only to our understanding of human language and cognition, but also to our knowledge of the natural world (see Crystal, 2000; Nettle & Romaine, 2000). It also presents very real challenges with respect to human rights (see Reagan & Osborn, 2002; Skutnabb-Kangas, 2000a; Skutnabb-Kangas & Phillipson, 1995; Phillipson, 2000).

To be sure, the challenge of language endangerment and language death is hardly one that can be solved by the foreign language educator. However, this does not remove all responsibility from our shoulders. Teaching about human language, language diversity, and the risks of language endangerment is as important component of a critical foreign language curriculum, whether in a less commonly taught language or in those more commonly taught.

CONCLUSION

This chapter has explored a number of issues related to languages about which most language educators have, at best, a very limited knowledge. Specifically, I have tried to develop a model for identifying and understanding the factors that appear to underlie the implicit linguistic hierarchy that governing the study of the different less commonly taught languages in the United States. In addition, we have briefly examined the phenomena of language endangerment and language death—phenomena that are of grave concern for most of the human languages spoken on the planet today. While no attempt has been made to answer the question posed in Joshua Fishman's (2001) book, *Can Threatened Languages Be*

Saved?[3] a case has been made for the relevance of such concerns for the foreign language educator—and, indeed, for his or her students. After all, as William Cuppy observed in his 1941 book *How to Become Extinct*, "Most of us feel that we could never become extinct. The Dodo felt that way too" (p. 165).

QUESTIONS FOR REFLECTION AND DISCUSSION

1. In chapter 3, the concept of ideology was discussed in considerable detail. What are the implications of this concept for an understanding of the teaching and learning of the less commonly taught languages in the U.S. context?
2. Walker's comparison of the category of "less commonly taught languages" to one of "nonelephants" in the animal kingdom is entertaining, but is it really a valid comparison? To what extent, and for what reasons, does it make sense to classify the less commonly taught languages as a single category?
3. Esperanto is not mentioned in this chapter, but it is in fact a "less commonly taught language." How does the case of Esperanto fit (or not fit) with the social grammar of the less commonly taught languages presented?
4. There is an important distinction between language evolution and language death. Consider the case of Latin,[4] which over time evolved into the modern Romance languages. Is Latin now a "dead language"? If so, when did it actually cease to be a living language? If not, how can we account for the fact that it no longer has native speakers?
5. This chapter is titled, "Why Study Uzbek?" Although it does not address this question directly, it does provide a contextualization for how one might answer that question. What kinds of reasons or justifications might one provide in responding to such a question?

FURTHER READING

By its very nature, the subject of the less commonly taught languages is one about which relatively little has been written in general; on the other hand, there are extensive bodies of literature about specific less commonly taught languages. Two excellent books that provide broad coverage of a number of less commonly taught languages, both edited by Timothy Shopen, are *Languages and Their Speakers* (1979) and *Languages and Their Status* (1979). For African languages, Bernd Heine and Derek Nurse's edited volume *African Languages: An Introduction* (2000) is both unique and outstanding. For Chinese, both Mobo Gao's *Mandarin Chinese: An Introduction* (2000) and Ping Chen's *Modern Chinese: History and Sociolinguistics* (1999) are useful. With respect to the issues of language endangerment and language death, see David Crystal's *Language Death* (2000) and Daniel Nettle and Suzanne Romaine's *Vanishing Voices: The Extinction of the World's Languages* (2000). The classic case study of language death is Nancy Dorian's *Language Death: The Life Cycle of a Scottish Gaelic Dialect* (1981).

NOTES

1. Parts of this chapter appeared in an earlier version in Reagan (2002c); see also Reagan & Vorster (2000).

2. See chapter 8 for a detailed discussion of this topic.

3. See also his earlier work on this topic, especially Fishman (1991).

4. Two works that would be helpful in responding to this question are Joseph Farrell's *Latin Language and Culture: From Ancient to Modern Times* (2001) and Françoise Waquet's *Latin, or, The Empire of a Sign* (2001).

Chapter 5

My Language Is Better Than Yours: Language Bias and Language Variation in the Classroom

In a recent book attacking multicultural education titled *Losing Our Language*, Sandra Stotsky (1999) includes a chapter titled, "Spanglish, Swahili, and Dialect: Innovative Ways to Deprive Children of Literate English." The central theme of Stotsky's book is that "In their zeal to boost ethnic self-esteem, provide role models for girls, promote the virtues of a multilingual population, and expand children's knowledge about other peoples and cultures, many educational publishers seem to have produced instructional tools more likely to produce multiple illiteracy than growth in reading" (p. 179).[1] Included among her concerns are the inclusion of words from languages other than English in basal readers, which she believes (without any compelling evidence whatsoever, I would add)[2] will "confuse both the children in the class who do not speak the language the words come from as well as those who do." What is intriguing in Stotsky's attack on linguistically inclusive teaching materials are the cultural and linguistic biases that underlie her views. She explicitly notes, for instance, that "one could easily justify the teaching of some commonly used Latin or French words or phrases," even as she rejects the use of Spanish terms. Indeed, although her examples are Spanish, in the title of the chapter she pejoratively refers to "Spanglish," just as she dismissively mentions Swahili and "dialect" (which is, in the context of her chapter, essentially a coded way of referring to African American Vernacular English).

The idea, which both implicitly and explicitly undergirds Stotsky's perspective, that some language varieties are better than others is a powerful and common one. It is also a profoundly wrong idea and one that has serious implications for classroom practice. What is surprising about this idea is the extent to which it has been virtually universally rejected by linguists, even as it remains commonplace among many educators. Nor, to be fair, is Stotsky alone. A book by Eleanor Wilson Orr titled *Twice As Less: Black English and the Performance of Black Students in Mathematics and Science* (1987), argues, "For students whose first language is BEV [Black English Vernacular] . . . language can be a barrier to success in mathematics and science" (Orr, 1987, p. 9). Orr's argument, in essence, was that certain linguistic features of African American Vernacular English (such as prepositions in the expression of selected quantitative relationships, as/than modes of expressing comparisons, and so on) could result in student misunderstandings of certain key mathematical relationships. Such arguments are demonstrably wrong (see, for instance, Baugh, 1988),[3] but this has not impeded their popularity with many mainstream teachers or with large segments of the general public.

The focus of this chapter, then, will be on addressing some of the issues that are involved in discussions of nonmainstream language varieties, as well as language varieties that are sometimes rejected as "legitimate" in educational discourse. We begin with a discussion of the terms "language" and "dialect," then explore the concept of "linguistic legitimacy," and finally, conclude by examining two particular cases in which language bias has played and continues to play an important role in U.S. education: African American Vernacular English and American Sign Language.

WHOSE DIALECT IS A LANGUAGE?

In everyday speech, we often use the terms "language" and "dialect" as if there were a meaningful distinction between the two. From a linguistic perspective things are actually far more complicated than this and, at the same time, far simpler. The problem, in a nutshell, is that the labels "language" and "dialect" are not, in fact, really linguistic terms at all. Rather, they express social and political conceptions and realities. As the linguist Max Weinreich is reputed to have said, "The difference between a language and a dialect is who's got the army and navy." In other words, the distinction between a language and a dialect is merely where a society wishes to draw it, based on social, political, economic, and even military factors. Even the criterion of mutual intelligibility does not work particularly well in facilitating this distinction: Norwegian, Swedish, and Danish, for instance, share a high degree of mutual intelligibility, but they are generally viewed, both by their speakers and by others, as distinct languages. At the same time, there are varieties of German that are mutually unintelligible to a significant degree (as there are varieties of English that are mutually unintelligible) (see Chambers & Trudgill, 1980, p. 5; also of interest here are Allen & Linn, 1986; Hudson, 1996; Romaine, 2000, pp. 1–31), and yet, there would seem to be consensus that both German and

English are unified, single languages, albeit perhaps characterized by significant internal variation.

Perhaps one of the best examples of this phenomenon in recent years has been the change that has taken place with respect to the language varieties that, at least during the latter half of the twentieth century, were known collectively as Serbo-Croatian (see Hawkesworth, 1998; Norris, 1993; Partridge, 1972). The deliberate construction of a single Serbo-Croatian language was an important element of social engineering during the Communist regime and was part of the broader effort to create a sense of Yugoslav national identity. Although Serbian and Croatian language varieties are indeed quite close, they are distinguished not only by their orthography (Serbian is written in the Cyrillic alphabet, while Croatian uses the Latin alphabet) but also by lexical differences. Even during the period in which the languages were officially unified, there were tensions (primarily on the part of Croatian intellectuals) related to the apparent dominance of Serbian forms. As John Lampe has noted,

> [C]ould a common Serbo-Croatian orthography and dictionary fairly be called Croato-Serbian as well? Croatian reservations turned into public protests when the first two volumes of the dictionary were published [in 1967]. Serbian variants of these two, overlapping, grammatically identical languages were consistently chosen over the Croatian variants. (2000, p. 305)

In the years following the breakup of the former Yugoslavia, efforts to emphasize the distinctive nature of each variety of the language intensified (see Glenny, 1996; Lampe, 2000), and there are now separate dictionaries, grammars, and so on, for Croatian, Serbian, and Bosnian (see, for example, Kroll & Zahirovič, 1998; Šušnjar, 2000; Uzicanin, 1996; Vitas, 1998), not to mention the emergence of the related Macedonian language in the Republic of Macedonia (see Kramer, 1999a, 1999b). Typical of the rhetoric found in such works is the following description of the "Bosnian language":

> The Bosnian language is spoken by 4.5 million people: Muslims, Serbs, and Croats living together for centuries in Bosnia and Herzegovina. . . . The Bosnian language is a symbiosis of the Serb and Croat languages, which are Slavic tongues, with strong Turkish and German influences. Bosnian is written in two alphabets: Cyrillic and Roman. (Uzicanin, 1996, p. 7)

As a consequence of these developments, we are now presented with a number of separate (albeit for the most part mutually intelligible) languages spoken by ethnically distinct groups, among which are Croatian, Serbian, and Bosnian. Regardless of the extent to which these languages are in fact mutually intelligible, their speakers have, by and large, decided that they are separate languages, and each speaker population has sufficient political legitimacy at the present time to enforce such a determination.

Even with respect to languages where one might expect greater clarity in this regard, we are often faced with complex and less than satisfying answers. For example, in response to the question, "How many Romance languages are there?" Rebecca Posner has commented, "An answer to this question that has been slightingly labeled *sancta simplicitas* is that there is only one: the languages are all alike enough to be deemed dialects of the same language. Another equally disingenuous answer might be 'thousands'—of distinctive local varieties—or 'millions'—of individual idiolects" (1996, p. 189). In short, the terms "language" and "dialect" are generally used in an ad hoc manner that has little to do with linguistics or with linguistic criteria. The question, "Is such-and-such a language or a dialect?" is simply not answerable from any body of the linguistic data. The answer, instead, must rely on non- and extralinguistic factors and must be made not by linguists but by the speakers of the language variety at issue and the wider community. From the perspective solely of linguistics, as Ronelle Alexander has noted, "Each dialect, in fact, is actually a separate language, with its own internally consistent system" (2000, p. 316).

THE CONCEPT OF "LINGUISTIC LEGITIMACY"

Language is at the heart of virtually every aspect of education, and indeed, of social life in general. Language serves as the primary medium through which much learning takes place, and the acquisition of socially and academically appropriate language forms (both oral and written) is generally seen as one of the principal goals for the educational experience (see Cleary & Linn, 1993). In addition, it is quite common for individual academic problems to be blamed on, or at least explained by, language differences. Underlying the educational discourse dealing with issues of language are a number of common assumptions about the nature of language, language structure, language difference, and so on, that tend to be shared by educators, parents, the general public, and indeed, by students themselves. Perhaps the most powerful of these assumptions concerns what counts as a "real" language, and, even more important, what does not count as a "real" language (see Reagan, 1997b, 1998a). At issue here is what can be called linguistic legitimacy: which language varieties are deemed by the society to be legitimate, and which are not.

This concept of linguistic legitimacy is both timely and important for educators—especially educators involved in the teaching of languages—to understand, since it touches on issues of social class, ethnicity, and culture, in addition to being embedded in relations of dominance and power.

Linguistic legitimacy as a construct is also important with respect to the implications it has for the development and implementation of educational policy, as made clear by the controversy about the 1996 Oakland, California, school district's decision formally to recognize Ebonics (that is, African American Vernacular English) as the dominant language of many of that district's students (see, for example, Bennet, 1996; Holmes, 1996; McWhorter, 1998; Olszewski, 1996; Schorr, 1997; Staples, 1997). Typical of much of the polemical rhetoric that surrounded that decision was the columnist Roger Hernandez's assertion, "The notion that black English is a language and that black kids are actually bilingual is ludicrous and patronizing. Ebonics is ungrammatical English. What students who speak Ebonics need to learn is that they are speaking substandard English and that substandard English brands them as uneducated" (1996, p. A–21). Essentially the same argument, although usually a bit more carefully and moderately articulated, is commonly found in educational settings and among educators. Perspectives such as that of Hernandez are common in our society, and may even, for many people, seem to be common sense. They are, however, flawed, and indeed are based on serious misunderstandings of language and linguistics, as we shall see in the two case studies that follow.

African American Vernacular English

There are very few debates about language capable of producing the kind of heat and passion engendered by discussions of African American Vernacular English, especially with respect to educational issues. In 1979, the *Martin Luther King Junior Elementary School Children vs. Ann Arbor School District* decision led to a widespread public debate about the nature and status of African American Vernacular English, not unlike that which recently took place with respect to the decision of the Board of Education in Oakland, California, to recognize African American Vernacular English as the primary language of a significant proportion of students in the school district (see Baugh, 1999, 2000; McWhorter, 1998; Mufwene, Rickford, Bailey & Baugh, 1998; Perry & Delpit, 1998; Rickford & Rickford, 2000; Smitherman, 1977, 2000). In both instances, strong emotions on both sides of the debate all too often drowned out more moderate voices, and in both cases the public debate obscured the linguistic and educational issues that needed to be addressed.

Many well-meaning individuals, educators and non-educators alike, have raised grave reservations and concerns about both *King* and the Oakland policy with respect to African American Vernacular English. The concerns that have been articulated most commonly include doubts about the nature and origins of African American Vernacular English, its recognition in educational settings, and, perhaps most important, its effects on student learning and student achievement. Also raised have been fears about the implications of identifying speakers of African American Vernacular English as non-English speakers, as well as concerns about the social and economic language needs of speakers of African American Vernacular English. A fairly typical critical response to the Oakland decision is that of Bill Maxwell, an African American columnist, who wrote: "Oakland, like many other districts nationwide, is failing in part because grown-ups there lack the courage to call Ebonics what it is: a bastardization that has few redeeming elements. . . . Ebonics is acceptable in rap, poetry and fiction. But it has precious few redeeming qualities in the real world and, therefore, must be avoided in public" (1997, p. B–2). While this response, like that offered by Roger Hernandez, is relatively polemical in nature, the underlying concerns it reflects are very real and legitimate and are certainly shared by many people, regardless of race. These are concerns that do need to be addressed and that can be addressed in a very compelling manner.

While a complete treatment of the social, linguistic, and educational aspects of African American Vernacular English is obviously not possible here, it may be useful to present a basic overview of what is actually known about the nature and origins of African American Vernacular English, as well as a brief discussion of possible educationally sound responses to the presence of large numbers of speakers of African American Vernacular English in the schools. It is to this that we now turn.

A good place to begin this discussion is with the labels used to refer to African American Vernacular English. Among the expressions and terms that have been, and continue to be, used in the literature to refer to African American Vernacular English are "nonstandard Negro English," "Black English Vernacular," simply "Black English," and, mostly in the popular literature, "Ebonics." Each of these labels has its own problems and limitations, as does "African American Vernacular English." All of these labels share the common problem that they imply that we are talking about a single language variety, that this variety is simply a variant of English, and that it is spoken by Blacks. Each of these assumptions is actually misleading at best. First, there is no single language variety that constitutes African American Vernacular English. In fact, there is a series of related language varieties (distinguished by both geographic variables and those of age, gender, social class, etc.) (see McWhorter, 1998; Mufwene, Rickford, Bailey & Baugh, 1998; Wolfram & Fasold, 1974, pp. 73–98). Second, the relationship of African American Vernacular English to mainstream American English is itself an area subject to considerable debate, as, indeed, is the extent to which African American Vernacular English can be said to constitute a language distinct from English. In fact, one of the problems with all of these labels is that they seem to create a false dichotomy between "White English" and "Black English" that not only is not reflective of linguistic reality (see Labov, 1972a, p. xiii) but is in fact fundamentally racist in nature (see Lanehart, 1998, 1999). Finally, although the vast majority of speakers of African American Vernacular English are in fact African American, certainly not all African Americans use African American Vernacular English, nor are all native users of African American Vernacular English in fact Black (see Baugh, 1999, 2000; McWhorter, 1998; Mufwene, Rickford, Bailey & Baugh, 1998; Perry & Delpit, 1998; Rickford & Rickford, 2000; Smitherman, 1977, 2000).

This having been said, the collection of language varieties that generally fall under the label African American Vernacular English do coexist with other varieties of American English and are both notably similar to one another and different in significant ways from other varieties of American English (see Labov, 1972a, pp. 36–37; McWhorter, 1998). Given the lack of consensus about the best label for this collection of language varieties, as well as the problems with each of the alternatives, then, I have chosen to employ the term most commonly used by linguists—African American Vernacular English (see Lanehart, 1998). What is most important to note in this regard is that the debates about what to call African American Vernacular English are themselves reflective of the very nonlinguistic and extralinguistic issues that color all aspects of the debates about African American Vernacular English. As Tom Trabasso and Deborah Harrison note with respect to the definition of "What is Black English":

> It is a political question since language has served as an instrument of political and cultural control whenever two cultures meet. It is a social question since certain forms of speech are admired, prestigeful, codified and promulgated while others are accorded low esteem, stigmatized, ridiculed and avoided. It is an economic question since many feel that "speaking proper" or some variety of Standard English is required for success in middle-class America. (1976, p. 2)

A much-discussed aspect of African American Vernacular English has to do with how this collection of language varieties developed—that is, with what the origins of the features discussed above might be. Most linguists today would accept what is called the "decreolist view," which maintains that the differences between mainstream American English and the varieties of African American Vernacular English can be best explained with respect to the creole origins of African American Vernacular English (Mufwene, Rickford, Bailey & Baugh, 1998; Trudgill, 1995, p. 50). As Elizabeth Traugott has commented,

> Viewed from the perspective of English-related pidgins and creoles, there seems to be no question that aspects of VBE [Vernacular Black English] can best be explained in the light of centuries of linguistic change, and development from a pidgin to a creole, through various stages of decreolization, to a point where VBE,

> though largely assimilated into the various English vernaculars, still has features which clearly distinguish it from them. To claim that VBE derives from a creole, therefore, is to focus on its social and linguistic history, and on the relative autonomy of the Black community in America. (1976, p. 93)

It should be noted here, though, that recent research has suggested that in many urban areas of the United States, the process of decreolization has not only stopped, it may actually have been reversed. In other words, as the urban Black population has been increasingly marginalized socially and economically, the language varieties that they speak may have begun to diverge from the surrounding mainstream varieties of American English (see Bailey & Maynor, 1987, 1989; Butters, 1989; Lanehart 1998, 1999). Among the linguistic features that may be developing in some contemporary African American Vernacular English varieties, for instance, is the use of the future resultative "be done" that has been documented by the sociolinguist John Baugh, as in the sentence, "*I'll be done killed that motherfucker if he tries to lay a hand on my kid again*" (quoted in Trudgill, 1995, p. 61).

The contemporary social and educational debates about African American Vernacular English rest on two fundamental and distinct arguments (see Schneider, 1989, pp. 2–3). The first of these two arguments focuses on the nature of African American Vernacular English in general terms, especially with respect to prescriptivist judgments about what constitutes "proper English" (see Wardhaugh, 1999), and how such judgments are related to the use of African American Vernacular English. The second argument concerns the relationship between African American Vernacular English and other varieties of American English, and is often presented in the terms of whether African American Vernacular English is really a distinctive language in its own right or whether it is simply a variety of American English. Each of these arguments is important from both a linguistic and an educational standpoint, and each merits our attention here.

That the nature of African American Vernacular English as a language should be at issue in contemporary discussions—although perhaps somewhat understandable socially, politically, and educationally—is nevertheless puzzling from a linguistic perspective. As Edgar Schneider has noted, "For more than twenty years, the dialect spoken by black Americans has been among the most salient topics of linguistic research in the United States" (1989, p. 1), and there is a huge body of very competent linguistic research dealing with various aspects of African American Vernacular English (see Baugh, 1999, 2000; Labov, 1972b, 1978; McWhorter, 1998; Mufwene, Rickford, Bailey & Baugh, 1998; Perry & Delpit, 1998; Rickford & Rickford, 2000; Smitherman, 1977, 2000). In fact, in sociolinguistics the study of African American Vernacular English has provided a central framework for much contemporary research. In other words, from the perspective of linguistics, the status of African American Vernacular English is well established: African American Vernacular English is a series of related language varieties, spoken primarily by African Americans, which are rule-governed and which differ in significant ways from other varieties of American English (see, for example Baugh, 1999, 2000; McWhorter, 1998; Mufwene, Rickford, Bailey & Baugh, 1998; Perry & Delpit, 1998; Rickford & Rickford, 2000; Smitherman, 1977, 2000).

One often-cited example of how African American Vernacular English differs from mainstream American English is the use of the "invariant 'be,'" which is used by African American Vernacular English-speakers to identify the habitual aspect of a finite verb (see Labov, 1993). Thus, the meaning of the African American Vernacular English sentence, "She be around" is best conveyed by the mainstream American English "She is usually around," while the African American Vernacular English "She around" would be best conveyed in mainstream American English as, "She's around right now." The implications of this distinction in the classroom context are made clear in the following conversation between a teacher and an African American Vernacular English-speaking student reported by Shirley Brice Heath:

> A teacher asked one day: "Where is Susan? Isn't she here today?" Lem answered "She ain't ride de bus." The teacher responded: "She *doesn't* ride the bus, Lem." Lem answered: "She *do* be ridin' de bus." The teacher frowned at Lem and turned away. (1983, p. 277)

This is a powerful example of communication breakdown in the classroom context and is arguably due not to any deficiency on the part of the student but, rather, to the linguistic limitations of the teacher. Lem responded accurately and appropriately to the teacher's question: he indicated that Susan had not ridden the bus on the day in question. The teacher, focusing on what she took to be an error in mainstream English, attempted to correct Lem by rephrasing his answer. Lem not only understood the teacher's correction, but he also recognized that she had not understood his point and replied by using a form of the habitual aspect to emphasize that indeed Susan did normally ride the bus but hadn't done so on this particular day. Even then, the teacher failed to understand Lem's point. The interesting feature of this miscommunicative event, I think, is that Lem is demonstrating considerably more metalinguistic knowledge and sophistication than is his teacher. As Warren and McCloskey have cogently noted,

> It appears that most Black English-speaking children understand more Standard English pronunciation and grammar than they use. . . . What aspects of Standard English they do not understand may be relatively superficial, at least from a linguistic standpoint (although perhaps not from a social one). The greater problem

may be that their Standard English-speaking peers and teachers do not understand Black English. (1993, p. 222)

And what of the classroom context of African American Vernacular English? The debate about African American Vernacular English is fundamentally an educational one, concerned with the most appropriate manner of meeting the needs of a particular group of students. I believe that the most important lesson to be learned with respect to the needs of African American Vernacular English-speakers is that language difference does not in any way constitute language deficit.[4] Although this has become something of a politically correct cliché in recent times, it is nonetheless worth emphasizing because while teachers and others may rhetorically accept the distinction between differences and deficits, all too often the distinction is not reflected in practice. Children in the public schools who are speakers of African American Vernacular English continue to be disproportionately misdiagnosed and mislabeled with respect to both cognitive and speech/language problems, and this alone would constitute a compelling justification for additional teacher preparation with respect to language differences—specifically those differences commonly found in the language of African American Vernacular English-speakers (see Perry & Delpit, 1998; Reagan, 1997a; Wolfram, 1979).

Embedded in much contemporary educational discourse about African American Vernacular English are, in fact, strongly held views of linguistic inferiority, as was suggested earlier with respect to Orr's *Twice As Less*. The position argued in *Twice As Less* is one that is, regardless of Orr's claims to the contrary, firmly grounded in a view known as "linguistic relativity." This view, which has its origins in the late eighteenth- and early nineteenth-century work of the German scholar Wilhelm von Humboldt, was given its clearest and most popular articulation in the work of Edward Sapir and Benjamin Whorf—after whom it is commonly named, as the Sapir-Whorf Hypothesis. In essence, the Sapir-Whorf Hypothesis is concerned with describing the relationship between the language we speak and our thoughts and thought processes. As Whorf himself argued, "[W]e dissect nature along lines laid down by our native languages . . . by the linguistic systems in our minds" (quoted in Crystal, 1991, p. 306). Perhaps the most common illustration of the Sapir-Whorf Hypothesis has been the example of the purported number of words in Eskimo languages for "snow." While there are credible examples that one could offer in support of the Sapir-Whorf Hypothesis, this particular example—widespread and common though it certainly is—turns out to be nothing more than a fiction (see Pullum, 1991, pp. 159–171).

A more recent articulation of the fundamental premises of the Sapir-Whorf Hypothesis has been provided by Penny Lee, who suggests, "Although all observers may be confronted by the same physical evidence in the form of experiential data and although they may be capable of 'externally similar acts of observation', a person's 'picture of the universe' or 'view of the world' differs as a function of the particular language or languages that the person knows" (1996, p. 87). In its most extreme forms, which all too often include works dealing with the education of children from nonmainstream linguistic backgrounds, this view of the relationship between thought and language is in fact deterministic in nature. Although there may well be elements of truth in a weak version of the Sapir-Whorf Hypothesis (see Elgin, 2000, pp. 49–71; Lee, 1996), there is widespread agreement among linguists, psychologists, and educational researchers that a strong version of the Sapir-Whorf Hypothesis is simply not credible or defensible.

An especially interesting facet of the public discourse about the Oakland policy, and one that has not received the attention it merits in much of the mainstream press, was the body of supposedly humorous jokes and take-offs that became relatively widespread in the aftermath of the decision. The many jokes that were circulated, both orally and especially on the Internet, about the Oakland policy were in fact based on flawed understandings of the nature of human language in general and African American Vernacular English in particular and inevitably resulted in the trivialization of important educational questions. In addition, this body of "humor" was not only misguided and offensive, it was in many instances demonstratively racist (for extended and powerful discussions of this point, see Baugh, 2000, pp. 87–99; Rickford & Rickford, 2000; Scott, 1998).

Basically, then, what the case of African American Vernacular English would seem to emphasize is that there is a fundamental distinction between what might be called "language-as-system" (that is, language as a linguistic phenomenon) and "language-as-social marker" (the sociological role of language). Further, in every society there is a hierarchy of linguistic variations, generally reflective of social class. It is this distinction that helps us understand why, in contemporary American society, African American Vernacular English and mainstream English can have the same linguistic status while having markedly different sociolinguistic status.

American Sign Language

In *Losing Our Language*, Stotsky (1999) not only challenges the inclusion of foreign languages and "Black dialect" (i.e., African American Vernacular English) in the texts but also other language varieties she believes to be nonmainstream. One example she cites involves a story about a ten-year-old deaf boy growing up in the late nineteenth century. Her critique of this story (which she awards "the prize for the most anticivic selection of the disabled" in the basal readers she examined) is based largely on her rejection of the cultural status of the Deaf community in general and on the view of the deaf as an historically oppressed community in particular (see pp. 128–132). Stotsky does not mention American Sign Language at all in her comments; indeed, she appears to believe that the American Sign Language passages in the text are simply examples of "deaf dialect." In spite of this oversight, however, her treatment of the Deaf as a cultural and linguistic community is in fact illustrative of a variety of misunderstandings about deafness, the deaf, and their language that remain fairly common in our society. These misunderstandings are significant and reflect the same overall deficit view of language difference already discussed in this chapter—as we shall see.

Since the 1970s, there has been a growing recognition that many individuals identify themselves as members of a common Deaf cultural community (in American Sign Language, this concept is expressed in the sign DEAF-WORLD [5]). Such a cultural conceptualization of deafness presents a significant challenge to the more popular view among hearing people of deafness as a disability. The difference is not merely a semantic one; it is fundamental to one's conception of what deafness is, what it means to be deaf/Deaf,[6] and how both individuals and society as a whole ought to address deafness. As Lane, Hoffmeister and Bahan have noted in their powerful book *A Journey into the* DEAF-WORLD,

> [W]hen hearing people think about Deaf people, they project their concerns and subtractive perspective onto Deaf people. The result is an inevitable collision with the values of the DEAF-WORLD, whose goal is to promote the unique heritage of Deaf language and culture. The disparity in decision-making power between the hearing world and the DEAF-WORLD renders this collision frightening for Deaf people. (1996, p. 371)

The dominant view of deafness in our society, which has been labeled the "pathological" view, defines deafness as essentially a medical condition, characterized by an auditory deficit. Such a perspective leads naturally to efforts to try to remediate the deficit. The pathological view of deafness is premised on the idea that deaf people are not only different from hearing people, but that they are, at least in a physiological sense, inferior to hearing people, in that hearing people can hear while deaf people cannot. If one accepts this common view of deafness, and the myriad assumptions that undergird it, the only reasonable approach to dealing with deafness is indeed to attempt to remediate the problem (see Aimard & Morgon, 1985). In other words, the pathological construction of deafness inevitably leads to efforts to try to help the deaf individual to become as much like a hearing person as possible—which is, of course, precisely what is done when one focuses on the teaching of speech and lip-reading in education, utilizes hearing aids to maximize whatever residual hearing a deaf individual may possess, and seeks to develop medical solutions to hearing impairment. This construction of deafness also leads to a sometimes implicit, sometimes explicit, rejection of the value of signing and other elements of the DEAF-WORLD. The historical debate among educators of the deaf with respect to whether or not signing of any sort should be used in deaf education is fascinating, in part because both sides in the debate presuppose a pathological construction of deafness (see Reagan, 1989). Recent discussions in both secondary and higher education in the United States about whether American Sign Language should "count" as a foreign language are also characteristic of the power of the pathological construction of deafness in public discourse (see Reagan, 2000b; Wilcox, 1988; Wilcox & Wilcox, 1997). This is not to suggest, though, that the pathological construction of deafness is monolithic. Within the framework of the pathological construction of deafness, there is in fact a wide range of responses to deafness, deaf people, and sign languages (see Reagan, 1995a). Relatively moderate approaches to deafness include the provision of appropriate assistive technology, speech therapy, and efforts to mainstream hearing impaired students in "inclusive" educational environments. Such efforts are, without doubt, well intentioned, and in some instances relatively successful in helping the hearing impaired individual to cope with and function in the hearing world (see, e.g., Banks, 1994).

The alternative construction of deafness is the sociocultural perspective, which is grounded in the experiences and history of the *DEAF-WORLD* and which stresses the sociocultural and linguistic aspects of Deafness (see, for example, Andersson, 1990, 1994; Kyle, 1990; Paul & Jackson, 1993; Quintela, Ramírez, Robertson & Pérez, 1997; Reagan, 1990a, 1990b, 1992b, 1995a; Sacks, 1989; Schein, 1989; Stokoe, 1980; Vernon & Andrews, 1990; Wilcox, 1989). As Carol Padden and Tom Humphries wrote at the start of their book *Deaf in America: Voices from a Culture,*

> The traditional way of writing about Deaf people is to focus on the fact of their condition—that they do not hear—and to interpret all other aspects of their lives as consequences of this fact. . . . In contrast to the long history of writings that treat them as medical cases, or as people with "disabilities," who "compensate" for the deafness by using sign language, we want to portray the lives they live, their art and performances, their everyday talk, their shared myths, and the lessons they teach one another. We have always felt that the attention given to the physical condition of not hearing has obscured far more interesting facets of Deaf people's lives. (1988, p. 1)

Describing this same phenomenon in an essay published in *The Atlantic,* Edward Dolnick wrote:

> Lately . . . the deaf community has begun to speak for itself. To the surprise and bewilderment of outsiders, its message is utterly contrary to the wisdom of cen-

turies: Deaf people, far from groaning under a heavy yoke, are not handicapped at all. Deafness is not a disability. Instead, many deaf people now proclaim, they are a subculture like any other. They are simply a linguistic minority (speaking American Sign Language) and are no more in need of a cure than are Haitians or Hispanics. (1993, p. 37)

In short, the sociocultural construction of deafness focuses primarily on Deaf people as a cultural and linguistic minority community (and, indeed, on that community as an oppressed one). The Deaf cultural community is, from this perspective, characterized by basically the same kinds of elements that would characterize any cultural community, among which are:

- a common, shared language
- a literary and artistic tradition
- a shared awareness of Deaf cultural identity
- endogamous marital patterns
- distinctive behavioral norms and patterns
- cultural artifacts
- a shared historical knowledge and awareness
- a network of voluntary, in-group social organizations (see Reagan, 1995a).

The single most significant element of Deaf cultural identity in the United States is, without a doubt, communicative competence in American Sign Language (see Lane, Hoffmeister & Bahan, 1996; Schein & Stewart, 1995; Valli & Lucas, 2001). American Sign Language serves multiple roles within the Deaf community, functioning not only as the community's vernacular language but also as an indicator of cultural group membership.[7] It is important to note here that this applies only to American Sign Language; other types of signing commonly used in North America (including both the contact sign language normally employed by hearing signers and the artificially constructed manual sign codes for English) fulfill very different functions and are viewed very differently by the Deaf community (see Lucas, 1989; Lucas, Bayley & Valli, 2001; Reagan, 1995c, 2000b). For instance, contact sign language is viewed as an appropriate means of communication with hearing individuals, while manual sign codes are widely rejected by the Deaf community as awkward efforts to impose the structures of a spoken language on sign.

Natural sign languages, such as American Sign Language, on the other hand, are those sign languages used in Deaf communities around the world in communicative interactions between and among Deaf people themselves. Such natural sign languages—which include not only American Sign Language but also Australian Sign Language, British Sign Language, Danish Sign Language, French Sign Language, Russian Sign Language, South African Sign Language, among others—are immensely complex linguistically.[8] It is these natural sign languages that constitute "sign language" in its strongest sense (see Reagan, 1990b, 1992a). These languages have emerged and evolved naturally and, as Sherman Wilcox has noted, "are fully developed human languages independent of the languages spoken in the linguistic communities in the same region" (1990, p. 141). Furthermore, different natural sign languages are related to one another in different ways, just as are spoken languages. We can talk about sign language families, which would consist of historically related natural sign languages (such as American Sign Language and French Sign Language), and contrast these to historically unrelated natural sign languages (for interest, American Sign Language and British Sign Language). It is interesting to note here, as these examples demonstrate, that the relationships between natural sign languages can, and do, differ dramatically from those of spoken languages. Thus, although they may share a written language (English), Deaf people in the United States and Britain use unrelated natural sign languages.

Since the 1960 publication of William Stokoe's landmark study *Sign Language Structures* (see Stokoe, 1960 [1993]), there has been a veritable explosion of linguistic, psycholinguistic, and sociolinguistic research dealing with American Sign Language, as well as with other natural sign languages (see Battison, 1978, 1980; Emmorey & Reilly, 1995; Fischer & Siple, 1990; Friedman, 1977; Klima & Bellugi, 1979; Kyle & Woll, 1983, 1985; Liddell, 1980; Lillo-Martin, 1991; Lucas, 1989, 1990, 2001; Schlesinger & Namir, 1978; Siple, 1978; Siple & Fischer, 1991; Valli & Lucas, 2001). The result is that we know far more about the nature and workings of natural sign languages than we did forty years ago, and the now well-established research base has been summarized by Robert Hoffmeister as follows:

> ASL [American Sign Language] is a language that has been misunderstood, misused, and misrepresented over the past 100 years. It is structured very differently from English. The structure of ASL is based on visual/manual properties, in contrast to the auditory/spoken properties of English. ASL is able to convey the same meanings, information, and complexities as English. The mode of expression is different, but only at the delivery level. The underlying principles of ASL . . . are based on the same basic principles found in all languages. ASL is able to identify and codify agents, actions, objects, locations, subjects, verbs, aspects, tense, and modality, just as English does. ASL is therefore capable of stating all the information expressed in English and of doing this within the same conceptual frame. ASL is able to communicate the meaning of a concept, through a single sign or through a combination of signs, that may be conveyed by a word or phrase (combination of words) in English. (1990, p. 81)

To sum up, then, the evidence is clear that American Sign Language is a legitimate language comparable in all significant ways to spoken languages. Although it utilizes a different modality from that employed by spoken languages, its operation is in no way inferior to spoken languages, and, of greatest concern for us here, it plays a key role in the sociocultural construction of Deaf identity. In fact, American Sign Language plays an important role in the construction of what could be termed the DEAF-WORLD worldview—that is, the way in which Deaf people make sense of the world around them. It does this in two distinct ways: first, through its role as linguistic mediator, and second, as an identifying facet of cultural identity. For instance, American Sign Language mediates experience in a unique way, as do all languages. The structures and vocabulary of American Sign Language provide the framework within which experience is organized, perceived, and understood, and this framework is inevitably distinct from the frameworks employed by other languages. For example, in American Sign Language if one describes a person as *VERY HARD-OF-HEARING*, it means that the person has substantial residual hearing, while *A LITTLE HARD-OF-HEARING* would suggest far less residual hearing. In other words, the concepts themselves are based on different norms than would be the case in English (where the meanings of these two expressions would be reversed).

The use of American Sign Language as one's primary vernacular language is arguably the single most important element in the construction of Deaf cultural identity. Deaf cultural identity presupposes communicative competence in American Sign Language, and is impossible without it. As Jerome Schein has explained, "[B]eing deaf does not in itself make one a member of the deaf community. To understand this, one has to remember that the distinguishing feature of membership in the deaf community is how one communicates" (1984, p. 130). It is not merely "signing" that is necessary, though—it is, specifically, the use of American Sign Language. Many hearing people sign, but relatively few are competent in American Sign Language. American Sign Language has historically functioned as a "language of group solidarity" for Deaf people, serving both as a badge of in-group membership and as a barrier to those outside the cultural community. Recently, as more hearing people have begun to learn American Sign Language, new complications have arisen with respect to issues of "ownership" of American Sign Language (see Lane, Hoffmeister & Bahan, 1996, pp. 70–77; Levesque, 2001), as well as concerns among some Deaf people about the use of American Sign Language by hearing individuals. As one leader in the Deaf community has noted,

> I have asked a number of deaf individuals how they feel about hearing people signing like a native user of ASL. The responses are mixed. Some say that it is acceptable for hearing people to use ASL like a deaf person on one condition. The

condition is that this hearing person must make sure that the deaf person knows that s/he is not deaf. Some people resent the idea of seeing hearing people signing like a native ASL user. Those who are resentful may feel sociolinguistic territorial invasion by those hearing people. (Quoted in Schein & Stewart, 1995, p. 155)

The role of American Sign Language in the construction of Deaf identity, then, is quite complex—it is clearly a necessary condition for Deaf cultural identity, but (as is demonstrated in the cases of hearing individuals who use American Sign Language fluently) not a sufficient condition for group membership. Indeed, for non-group members, use of American Sign Language can present significant challenges to one's credibility and status as a sympathetic outsider, and it is far from uncommon to find Deaf people who seek to "protectively withhold from hearing people information about the DEAF-WORLD's language and culture" (Lane, Hoffmeister & Bahan, 1996, p. 71).

It is interesting that just as the research base on American Sign Language has come into its own and as interest in the language has grown, challenges to its legitimacy have increased, especially as efforts have been made to include it as a foreign language option in many secondary schools and colleges and universities (see Belka, 2000; Jacobs, 1996; Wallinger, 2000; Wilcox & Wilcox, 1997). Among the more common objections to including American Sign Language as a foreign language option for students have been those that are concerned with the nature of American Sign Language (that is, with its status linguistically and psycholinguistically), the degree to which American Sign Language can be considered to be foreign, the degree to which advocates of American Sign Language are using the concepts of language and culture metaphorically rather than literally, and last, whether a nonwritten language is an appropriate choice for students, given the commonly articulated purposes of foreign language instruction in educational settings.

Many objections to the teaching of American Sign Language as a foreign language, as well as to its use in the education of deaf children, are based on the idea that American Sign Language is in some manner linguistically and psycholinguistically inferior to spoken language. Characteristic of this view is Myklebust's assertion that "Sign language cannot be considered comparable to a verbal symbol system" (quoted in Lane, 1992, p. 45), and, more recently, van Uden's claim that "The informative power of the natural sign language of the deaf is extremely weak" (1986, p. 89). However common and popular such views may be, they are nonetheless clearly and demonstrably false in both spirit and detail, as we have already seen. As Noam Chomsky once commented in an interview, "If deaf people have developed sign language, then there are no intellectual defects at all. Many people who are not deaf think that deaf people have deficits because we just don't understand their language" (1988, p. 196).

Perhaps among the more intriguing objections to viewing American Sign Language as a foreign language in American educational settings raised in recent years is that American Sign Language is not sufficiently foreign. As Howard Mancing has asserted, "In no way do I impugn the integrity of American Sign Language as a legitimate academic subject or as a well-developed, intellectual, emotional, subtle, sophisticated language. . . . It is all of that, but since it is *American* Sign Language it is not foreign by definition" (quoted in "Sign language," 1992, my emphasis). The issue raised here is basically one of definition. The obvious, ordinary language sense of "foreign" in the phrase term "foreign language" is that the language is foreign to the learner. If American Sign Language does not count as a foreign language in the U.S. context, then neither should native American languages, such as Navajo, nor even, perhaps, Spanish, which is at least as indigenous to North America as English and is certainly widely spoken as a native language in the United States.

Traditional defenses for the study of foreign languages as a part of a liberal education often rely on the close connection between language and culture. It is argued that only through the study of a people's language can their culture be properly understood, and that such study can provide an essential international or global component in an individual's education. Critics of the acceptance of American Sign Language as a foreign language have suggested that it does not meet this aspect of foreign language education on two counts: first, because the terms language and culture, when applied to American Sign Language and the culture of the Deaf community, are used metaphorically rather than literally, and second, because it is an indigenous rather than international language. As Thomas Kerth explains, "I think these people who talk about deaf culture and foreignness are using it in a metaphorical way, not literally, and when you get into the realm of metaphor the meaning gets obscured. Most would read a foreign language as one not spoken by Americans" (quoted in "Sign language," 1992). With regard to this claim that discussions of the Deaf culture are metaphorical rather than literal, all one can say is that this is a serious distortion of what members of that culture have actually said, written, and meant. There are a number of works devoted to the history, sociology, and anthropology of the American Deaf community, written by both deaf and hearing scholars (see, for example, Cohen, 1994; Fischer & Lane, 1993; Lane, Hoffmeister & Bahan, 1996; Padden & Humphries, 1988; Reagan, 1990a, 1992b, 2000b; Schein, 1989; van Cleve, 1993; Wilcox, 1989). These writings do not suggest that the concept of cultural Deafness is to be understood metaphorically; indeed, the overwhelming sense of these works is that the term is used in an absolutely literal sense. In short, the preponderance of the evidence clearly supports the view that the Deaf community constitutes a cultural community in precisely the same sense as would any other cultural community.

Kerth's second claim is closely related to the idea that American Sign Language is not foreign. However, here the suggestion is that since American Sign Language is used almost exclusively in North America, it cannot provide students with an international or global perspective. This is true in the case of American Sign Language, of course, to the same extent that it is a valid criticism of the study of the indigenous languages and cultures of North America, as noted earlier. The study of the Hopi, for instance, is also not "international" in the narrow sense that is being applied to American Sign Language and the Deaf community. However, one could certainly argue that the point of such an international requirement in a student's education is to expose the student to cultures and languages different from his or her own, and that there is no logical reason for this exposure necessarily to entail study of a culture and language of a different country.

One of the more common arguments, at least at the university level, against accepting American Sign Language as a foreign language has been that it is not a written language, and hence does not have a literature to which students can be exposed. This objection actually has two separate components; first, the claim that American Sign Language is not a written language, and second, that it does not possess a literature. Although it is technically not quite true that American Sign Language is not a written language—there actually are several notational systems that can be used for reducing it to written form—it is true that it is not a commonly written language. Indeed, the written language of the American Deaf community is English. Having granted, then, this first objection, what of the second—the claim that there is therefore a lack of a literature in American Sign Language?

Since American Sign Language is not normally written down, it obviously does not have a written literature in the way that French, German, Russian, Chinese, and English, among others, do. Of course, the same might be said of the vast majority of the languages currently spoken around the world. What American Sign Language does possess is a literary tradition comparable to the oral traditions found in spoken languages (see Reagan, 1995a). Nancy Frishberg, for instance, has identified three major indigenous literary genres in American Sign Language: oratory, folklore and performance art. Frishberg compellingly argues that

> American Sign Language has been excluded from fulfilling foreign or second language requirements in some institutions because of claims that it has no . . . tradition of literature. . . . [However,] a literary aesthetic can be defined prior to a written literary tradition, as in the case of Greek and Balkan epic poetry. We know that other languages which are socially stigmatized nonetheless adapt literature through translation and develop their own literary institutions. Non-Western cultures without writing traditions convey their traditions of history and philosophy within community-defined forms of expression. And, finally, the

presence or absence of writing (systematized orthography) has little relationship to the existence of a traditional verbal art form. (1988, pp. 165–166)

Further, it can be argued that the advent of the movie camera, and, more recently, the VCR, has made possible the compilation and transmission of the literary traditions and even the canon of American Sign Language in a way simply not possible before this century. Nor is it the case that such a literature is merely possible in theory; the extensive body of American Sign Language literature exists as a fact (see, for example, Bahan, 1992; Jacobowitz, 1992; Low, 1992; Rutherford, 1993; Wilcox, 2000). In short, American Sign Language does have a well-developed literature, albeit one not easily reducible to a written form, that is now both accessible and worthy of serious study (see Peters, 2000).

IMPLICATIONS FOR FOREIGN LANGUAGE EDUCATION

For the foreign language educator, the implications of the concept of linguistic legitimacy are profound. Language educators are very much at the forefront of the education that students receive with respect to the nature of language and language variation. Foreign language educators need to be aware of the issues surrounding the concept of linguistic legitimacy, as do all teachers, but they also need to understand the specific implications of these issues for the foreign language classroom. Students in the foreign language classroom not only need to be exposed to the mainstream variety of the target language, they also need to learn about other variations of the target language. It is by no means inappropriate for us to focus primarily on Parisian French in the French classroom, but it is very much a mistake to exclude from our teaching the different varieties of French spoken around the world (see, for instance, Hale, 1999; Natsis, 1999; Valdman, 2000). Further, in at least some instances local varieties of the target language may actually be incorporated into the formal school curriculum. This would, for instance, make sense in Spanish classes located in areas where there are large numbers of native speakers of the language who speak a nonmainstream variety of Spanish. It makes little sense, I would suggest, to teach a variety of the target language that has few local uses, when another variety might prove quite useful. Again, this is not to say that students should not learn the mainstream variety of the target language (or, in a case like Spanish, one of the mainstream varieties). However, if our students' second language interactions are most likely to take place with Spanish speakers for whom *troca* rather than *camión* is the recognized term for "truck," then surely both Spanish forms should be learned. What I would advocate, in short, is fairly simple: foreign language education should be informed by an understanding and sensitivity to the sociolinguistic aspects of the target language (for the case of French, see

Ball, 1997; for the case of Spanish, see Klee, 1998 and Mar-Molinero, 1997, 2000; for the case of German, see Johnson, 1998 and Stevenson, 1997).

Beyond encouraging such sociolinguistic understanding, the foreign language classroom is also an ideal place to help students begin to develop what can be called critical language awareness. In other words, the study of language needs to include not only the communicative and cultural aspects of language but also the often implicit political and ideological issues related to language. Students need to understand the ways in which language is used to convey and protect social status, as well as how it can be used to oppress and denigrate both individuals and groups. The foreign language classroom can either reinforce negative language attitudes and prejudices, or it can be used to empower students to better understand the social roles of language in society (see Lippi-Green, 1997). The choice is very much ours to make in our classrooms and in our interactions with our students.

CONCLUSION

The challenges to the legitimacy of African American Vernacular English and American Sign Language would appear to be quite different, and this is hardly surprising, since they are in many significant ways very different linguistic systems with very different histories, user communities, and so on. And yet, there are some remarkably similar common themes. In both instances, concerns about the legitimacy of the language inevitably involves related concerns about culture and, specifically, about the perceived lack of a cultural community tied to the language. The language communities that choose to use each of the languages under consideration are, in essence, themselves delegitimated as well—the African American cultural community is simply not discussed at all in the context of African American Vernacular English, while in the case of American Sign Language, the Deaf community is seen by outsiders as unsophisticated and parochial. Daniel Ling, for instance, a well-known and respected scholar, has gone so far in attempting to delegitimize the feelings and concerns of the Deaf community as to argue, "Members of the adult deaf community are not, by virtue of their deafness, experts on the education of hearing-impaired children and to argue otherwise is comparable to claiming expertise in pulmonary medicine simply because one breathes" (quoted in Neisser, 1983, p. 113). Indeed, as this quote suggests, in both of the cases discussed here, the very existence of a concomitant cultural community is often denied by those challenging the legitimacy of the language. Further, questions are raised about the linguistic structures of both languages—African American Vernacular English is dismissed as simply "broken" English, while American Sign Language is rejected as a derivative of English or as syntax-free or syntactically limited. Finally, it is interesting to note that challenges to the linguistic legitimacy of African American Vernacular English and American Sign Language are very commonly offered by those who are not themselves competent in the respective language. This fact is, on its own, quite intriguing, since under normal circumstances we would not consider individuals who do not speak a language to be credible judges about the value and structural components of the language.

We see, then, that the challenges to the legitimacy of both of these language varieties have been based on a variety of assumptions that, upon careful examination, prove to be both empirically and conceptually problematic. In both cases, it can be argued that the resistance to the language under consideration is misguided, misleading, and inappropriate. However, the debate is not simply a matter of misunderstanding. Rather, it reflects more general issues of language and cultural rights in society, and the way in which such rights are often overlooked or ignored. What is actually at issue in this debate is the question of how the "Other" in society is perceived and treated and the extent to which the dominant group in society is willing seriously to countenance pluralism. By challenging the legitimacy of particular languages (whether African American Vernacular English, American Sign Language, or any other language variety), we in essence denigrate and even reject the speaker communities of these languages, their cultures, and their worlds. The rejection of the linguistic legitimacy of a language—any language used by any linguistic community—in short, amounts to little more than an example of the tyranny of the majority. Such a rejection merely reinforces the long tradition and history of linguistic imperialism in our society. The harm, though, is done not only to those whose languages we reject, but in fact to all of us, as we are made poorer by an unnecessary narrowing of our cultural and linguistic universe. As Archbishop Desmond Tutu once noted about oppression in apartheid-era South Africa, "[A]t present nobody is really free; nobody will be really free until Blacks are free. Freedom is indivisible" (1983, p. 45). The same is true, I would argue, with respect to language, language rights, and linguistic oppression. So long as we reject the legitimacy of others' languages, we inevitably set overly parochial limits on our own culture, language, and world.

It is important to note that calling for the recognition of the legitimacy of all human languages and language varieties, and rejecting the false categorization of some language varieties as non-legitimate, does not in and of itself constitute any particular prescription for educational practice. Accepting a child's language as legitimate does not necessarily require that the child be taught through the medium of that language variety, nor does such acceptance automatically preclude instruction in or the learning of another language. The specifics of how speakers of African American Vernacular English, for instance, are to be schooled are in no way limited by the recognition of their language as real and legitimate.

This having been said, there are nonetheless clear social and educational implications that do in fact follow from the rejection of the concept of linguistic legitimacy. Perhaps most important in this respect is that the discourse related to the education of children from different language backgrounds must reflect the recognition of their languages and linguistic experiences as real, valuable, and appropriate and should seek to build on the individual child's background, to as great an extent as possible, in seeking to meet his or her needs. Our discourse, as Foucault has compelling argued, does indeed affect our perceptions and understandings as well as embodying "meaning and social relationships [and] constitut[ing] both subjectivity and power relations" (Ball, 1990, p. 2). Thus, our discourse about language and language diversity, in both social and educational settings, must itself be carefully reconsidered and subjected to critical reflection (see Reagan, 2002b).

It is not, however, only with our discourse that we must be concerned. Also clearly at issue is teacher knowledge, especially as such knowledge relates to language broadly conceived. Although teachers today are without doubt asked to function in classrooms in which language diversity is a daily fact of life, their preparation to deal with language diversity is all too often minimal at best. If classroom teachers are to be expected to function as applied linguists in their classrooms (as does, in fact, appear to be the case), then it becomes both urgent and essential that they receive appropriate preparation and training to enable them to meet such challenges (see Reagan, 1997a). At stake, too, are the kinds of research problems that are explored and the need to find ways to ensure that indefensible linguistic prejudices are not closing off potentially valuable areas of research.

In short, what is required is a change of both attitudes and practices with respect to our thinking about and responding to linguistic diversity in society and in the classroom. These changes, based on a better understanding of the nature of language, do not, as noted earlier, lead to any specific prescriptions for practice. What they do accomplish is to ensure that the linguistic needs of all children will be considered alongside their social, cultural, and educational needs. Whether we call what they speak a language, a dialect, or a language variety is really irrelevant. What does matter is how we address their needs, and that is what we should be discussing and debating.

QUESTIONS FOR REFLECTION AND DISCUSSION

1. In discussing Sandra Stotsky's (1999) book *Losing Our Language,* the author of this book singles out the title of one chapter in particular and indicates that the use of the word "Spanglish" in the title is pejorative. Do you agree? What

language variety do you believe Stotsky is talking about, and why might this term be considered offensive?

2. What do you believe is meant when someone talks about "proper English"? What are the social implications of this term? What are its educational implications?
3. In your view, is African American Vernacular English a language in its own right, or is it a variety of English? Should teachers be aware of the nature and structure of African American Vernacular English? Why or why not?
4. In this chapter, a case is made for the credibility of the sociocultural perspective on deafness. Insofar as this perspective is valid and compelling, what are its implications for inclusive education?
5. Do you believe that American Sign Language should be offered in U.S. public schools as a foreign language? What about in colleges and universities? Why or why not?

FURTHER READING

Among the books that seek to address some of the issues in this chapter are David Corson's *Language Diversity and Education* (2001), Rosina Lippi-Green's *English with an Accent: Language, Ideology and Discrimination in the United States* (1977), and Ronald Wardhaugh's *Proper English: Myths and Misunderstandings about Language* (1999). For more detailed discussions of African American Vernacular English, see John Baugh's *Beyond Ebonics: Linguistic Pride and Racial Prejudice* (2000) and *Out of the Mouths of Slaves: African American Language and Educational Malpractice* (1999), John McWhorter's *The Word on the Street: Fact and Fable about American English* (1998), John Rickford and Russell Rickford's *Spoken Soul: The Story of Black English* (2000), and *African American English: Structure, History and Use* (1998), a compilation edited by Salikoko Mufwene, John Rickford, Guy Bailey, and John Baugh. For more detailed discussions of American Sign Language and Deaf culture, see Lois Bragg's edited *DEAF-WORLD: A Historical Reader and Primary Sourcebook* (2001), Harlan Lane's *The Mask of Benevolence: Disabling the Deaf Community* (1992), Harlan Lane, Robert Hoffmeister and Ben Bahan's *A Journey into the DEAF-WORLD* (1996), Clayton Valli and Ceil Lucas's *Linguistics of American Sign Language: An Introduction* (2001), and Jerome Schein and David Stewart's *Language in Motion: Exploring the Nature of Sign* (1995).

NOTES

1. "Whole language" is another of Stotsky's targets. She explicitly condemns advocates of whole language for rejecting scientific research (see p. 308), while ignoring the very credible critiques of the very body of research upon which she

relies to defend phonics-based approaches to the teaching of reading (see, for instance, Coles, 2000). To some extent, the rhetoric in the so-called "reading wars" is fascinating—at least in part because of one side's efforts to monopolize the concepts of "research" and "science," while dismissing relevant data from other researchers as "non-scientific."

2. Stotsky's position here seems to be a variation on the widely discredited idea that bilingualism and multilingualism in childhood is problematic. In fact, the empirical evidence would seem to suggest just the reverse.

3. The fundamental problem with Orr's book is not so much that her views reflect a fairly extreme version of linguistic relativity but, rather, that she is simply wrong about her facts. Not only is the linguistic base with regard to what we actually know about the structure of African American Vernacular English dated and inaccurate but, as John Baugh has cogently argued, "despite claims to the contrary, Orr's book merely serves to perpetuate racist myths about the relationship between language and thought" (1988, p. 403). In other words, we need to look beyond simply the presence of language differences to find the cause of academic failure.

4. This is precisely the point, incidentally, that I believe that both Stotsky and Orr have missed.

5. The use of all capital letters is deliberate here. This is the normal practice for indicating when signs rather than words are being employed. Thus, DEAF-WORLD represents a specific sign in American Sign Language. This convention is especially important in instances in which American Sign Language has a sign that cannot be adequately or easily translated into English.

6. I have attempted here to follow the common practice of distinguishing between audiological *deafness*, which is represented with a lowercase "d," and cultural *Deafness*, which is represented with an uppercase "D."

7. An indication of the important role of American Sign Language in the establishment and maintenance of cultural identity can be seen, for instance, in the use of "name signs" (see Hedberg, 1994; Meadow, 1977; Stokoe, Casterline & Croneberg, 1976, pp. 291–293; Supalla, 1992; Yau, 1982, 1990, pp. 271–272; Yau & He, 1990). Name signs constitute a special category of signs in American Sign Language (and in other natural sign languages) and "seem to develop wherever a group of Deaf people have extended contact with each other and use sign language as their vernacular language. They are created for individuals within each generation or social grouping of Deaf people. Most typically, name signs originate in deaf school settings where Deaf children form an autonomous social world beyond the gaze of teachers . . . the name signs that Deaf adults bestow on each other later in life are determined by Deaf social norms and visual language structures rather than those of the 'outside' hearing society" (McKee & McKee, 2000, pp. 4–5). Further, "the acquisition of a name sign may mark a person's entry to a signing community, and its use reinforces the bond of shared group history and 'alternative' language use (in relation to mainstream society)" (McKee & McKee, 2000, p. 3).

8. Although our focus here is primarily on the case of American Sign Language, equivalent cases can be made for other natural sign languages (for

examples of recent work on European sign languages, for instance, see Edmondson & Karlsson, 1990; Prillwitz & Vollhaber, 1990a, 1990b). Not only is there extensive and growing literature on the linguistics of such natural sign languages, there is also growing focus on the both the politics and sociolinguistics of natural sign languages (see Lucas, 1989, 1995, 1996, 2001; Lucas & Valli, 1992; Penn & Reagan, 1990; Reagan & Penn, 1997).

Chapter 6

Language and Multiculturalism: Coming to Grips with Diversity

One of the changes that has taken place in U.S. education over the past quarter century is the concern with matters of diversity—and, in particular, with the growing acceptance, at least rhetorically, of multicultural education as an important part of public education. Cultural diversity has, in truth, been a fact of life for the vast majority of teachers and students in the public schools throughout U.S. history (see Spring, 1994; Weiss, 1982). What has changed is not the presence of large numbers of culturally and linguistically different students; what is new is how these students are viewed, and what kinds of educational programs and responses are available to serve them. Underlying these changes is a growing recognition, as Sonia Nieto has perceptively argued, that

> Our schools reflect the sociocultural and sociopolitical context in which we live, and this context is unfair to many young people and their families. The ideologies underlying many school policies and practices are based on flawed ideas about intelligence and difference. If we want to change the situation, it means changing the curriculum and pedagogy in individual classrooms, as well as the school's practices and the ideologies undergirding them. That is, we need to create not only affirming classrooms, but also an affirming society in which racism, sexism, social class discrimination, and other biases are no longer acceptable. (2000, p. xx)

The creation of such affirming classrooms is a difficult undertaking, to be sure, and the creation of such an affirming society is an even more difficult and daunting task. It is, though, what multiculturalism education is really all about. In this chapter, we will explore the foundations of multicultural education, with particular focus on the implications of multiculturalism and multicultural education for the foreign language classroom.

CONCEPTIONS OF CULTURE

In order to make sense of multiculturalism, as a theoretical construct and with respect to educational practice, it is essential that we begin with a discussion of what exactly we mean by "culture." The term is a slippery one, and this has led to a certain amount of confusion in educational discourse. There are, broadly speaking, two very different (albeit overlapping) conceptions of "culture": the aesthetic and the anthropological. Each has value and is appropriate in some settings and contexts, but the two are by no means interchangeable.

The aesthetic conception of culture refers to what has sometimes been called "high culture." Although the label itself is a loaded one, it does accurately convey the sociocultural understanding of the term that is intended. In essence, when one talks about aesthetic culture, one is concerned with music, art, literature, and so on—and not merely with these in general but with the examples of each that are presumed, on some set of criteria, to be the "best" available to us. Thus, the music of Mozart, the plays of Shakespeare, the paintings of Monet, and so on, are considered to be examples of aesthetic culture. The aesthetic conception of culture is deliberately judgmental, in that it is concerned with distinguishing great accomplishments in human history from more mediocre ones. Although often Eurocentric in historical practice, as an ideal the aesthetic construct of culture is universal in nature, drawing examples of excellence from all ages and societies. One important function of education has traditionally been seen as the introduction of students to aesthetic culture, since access to aesthetic culture requires a degree of formal and explicit training. It is in the context of the aesthetic conception of culture that one can say that a particular individual is "cultured."[1] In the context of foreign language education, aesthetic culture generally involves preparing students to read great literature in the target language and to be familiar with the other aesthetic accomplishments of the target society or societies (e.g., France and *le monde francophone,* Spain and *el mundo hispanico,* etc.).

Although the aesthetic conception of culture clearly has important educational implications, for the most part when contemporary educators speak of culture, they are concerned with a very different construct—with what can be termed the anthropological conception of culture. As Young Pai and Susan Adler have explained, when used in the anthropological sense, "culture is most commonly viewed as that pattern of knowledge, skills, behaviors, attitudes and beliefs, as well as material artifacts, produced by human society and transmitted from one generation to another" (2001, p. 21). In other words, culture refers to the complex and interactive sets of beliefs and practices that undergird social and community life—beliefs and practices related to language, behavioral norms, learning styles, family and kinship patterns, gender roles, the view of the individual and his/her relationship to the larger community, the historical awareness of the cultural community, and religious and spiritual beliefs and practices (see Cordeiro, Reagan & Martinez, 1994, pp. 2–7).[2] This is especially important with respect to educational practice, since, as Etta Hollins has explained,

> Culture is such an integral part of human existence that it becomes an invisible script that directs our personal lives. This invisible script can encapsulate and blind us to the factors that make us simultaneously unique from and similar to those from other cultures. Encapsulation can lead us to view the world as an extension of self. We may view those who are culturally different as aberrant, quaint, or exotic. Teachers who hold such views are likely to base classroom practices on their own culture and encourage students to conform to their perceptions and values. These teachers may be more successful with students with whom they share a common cultural and experiential background than those whose culture and experiences are different. (1996, p. 10)

It is in this anthropological sense that educators tend to be most concerned with understanding culture and its implications (see, e.g., Bennett, 1995; Gollnick & Chinn, 1994; Nieto, 2000; Sleeter & Grant, 1999). Although anthropologists in recent years have written extensively about the limitations and problems associated with the concept of culture (see Gupta & Ferguson, 1997), it is still a useful one for educators. However, it is also important to avoid the objectification of culture; although it obviously entails a social and communal identification, cultural identity is ultimately constructed individually. Furthermore, culture is not a static entity. It is constantly in a state of change (see Weibust, 1989). For the construct of culture to be useful in the classroom and school contexts, these important characteristics must be kept in mind.

For the foreign language educator, both conceptions of culture play important roles in the curriculum with respect to teaching about the target language and culture; what is sometimes less well recognized is that there are important pedagogical implications of students' cultural backgrounds that must also be addressed in the foreign language classroom, sometimes in ways that are unique in the broader and more general public school experience (see Osborn & Reagan, 1998).

DIVERSITY AND PLURALISM

It is important to understand at the outset that there is a substantial difference between cultural diversity and cultural pluralism. As the philosopher of education Richard Pratte (1979) has explained, cultural diversity refers to an empirical condition and is basically descriptive in nature, while cultural pluralism is a normative claim that seeks to suggest a particular course of action. In other words, when we say that a given society is culturally diverse, all we are saying is that there are different cultural groups in that society. We are not indicating whether or not we see the presence of diversity as a good thing, a bad thing, a problem, or a virtue. Thus, it is clear that most countries in the contemporary world are culturally diverse in nature, and this is most certainly true in the case of the United States (see Shinagawa & Jang, 1998). On the other hand, when we talk about cultural pluralism, a particular set of values is being presupposed. In essence, cultural pluralism entails two necessary conditions: first, there must be diversity present, and second, this diversity must be valued, respected, and encouraged (see Appleton, 1983). The extent to which the United States is actually committed to cultural pluralism is demonstrably far less certain than is its cultural diversity.

DEFICIT AND DIFFERENCE

The recognition of the presence of cultural diversity in fact leaves open a wide array of possible responses, only one of which is cultural pluralism. Perhaps most significant for our purposes here is the understanding that most social and educational responses to diversity focus on diversity in one of two quite distinct ways. Historically, the tendency in U.S. society (and in most others as well) has been to view cultural diversity in terms of the dominant culture—that is, the beliefs, attitudes, behaviors, and practices associated with the dominant culture are presupposed to be the norms against which other beliefs, attitudes, behaviors, and practices are judged. Thus, other cultures and cultural practices are seen as being deficient insofar as they differ from the dominant norm. In educational contexts, this has meant that children from nondominant cultural backgrounds are seen as arriving at school with deficits that must be corrected or overcome. In other words, one of the important functions of schooling, from such a perspective, is to provide remediatory or compensatory educational programs to enable children from nondominant cultural backgrounds to not only acquire the knowledge and skills necessary for successful assimilation into the dominant culture but adopt to these as their own, in place of the cultural patterns of their home background. In essence, this is precisely what efforts to "Americanize" children in the late nineteenth and early to mid-twentieth centuries in U.S. public schools were all about (see Spring, 1994). Such perspectives remain common among both pre-service and in-service classroom teachers. As Sleeter and Grant have noted,

> In our education classes, we have heard students refer to poor children as "disadvantaged," "socially deprived," "low socioeconomic," "culturally different," "culturally deprived," and "culturally deficient." Although different labels highlight different images—*socioeconomically* disadvantaged versus *educationally* disadvantaged—they all trace problems back to the child's living environment. (1988, p. 38)

This inevitably involves a sort of "blame the victim" approach to nonmainstream populations and also assumes a hierarchy of values related to cultural differences. Of course, such a phenomenon is by no means new. Almost two and a half millennia ago, in *The Persian Wars,* the Greek historian Herodotus observed, "If one were to offer men to choose out of all the customs in the world such as seemed to them the best, they would examine the whole number, and end by preferring their own; so convinced are they that their own usages surpass those of all others." Nonetheless, such views have profoundly negative consequences for children whose home culture is different from that of the school.

The alternative perspective on cultural diversity is that differences among cultures are just that: differences. Differences are best understood not as deficits at all but as differences that can provide clues for better and more effective teaching. As Abrahams and Troike argued nearly three decades ago,

> If we expect to be able to teach students from such [culturally different] groups effectively, we must learn wherein their cultural differences lie and we must capitalize upon them as a resource, rather that doing what we have always done and disregarding the differences or placing the students in the category of "noncommunicative," thereby denigrating both the differences and the students. (1972, p. 5)

The basic idea that underlies the difference approach to cultural diversity is that the power differential that separates dominant from nondominant cultural norms must be addressed. As Geneva Gay has explained,

> Future efforts to achieve democracy in this culturally pluralistic society must embrace composite, heterogeneous, and diverse understandings and actions, operating in concert with each other. This does not mean harmonizing, anesthetizing, or obliterating differences. Instead, it means genuinely accepting diversity as the new normative standard for creating national unity and human solidarity. It is what Molefi Asante means by achieving "pluralism without hierarchy." (1995, pp. 171–172)

Consider, for a moment, the implications of this concept of "pluralism without hierarchy" in the linguistic sphere. Not only does this entail rejecting the notion of linguistic legitimacy, as discussed in chapter 5, it also involves significant changes in the foreign language classroom, especially with respect to the child who arrives speaking a nonmainstream variety of the target language. Even more important, such a concept requires a fundamental rethinking on many teachers' parts about the role, place, and meaning of the "standard language" (see Milroy & Milroy, 1985).[3]

HISTORICAL RESPONSES TO DIVERSITY

As has already been suggested, given the presence of cultural diversity in any particular society, there are a number of ways in which the society can choose to address it. This means that cultural pluralism is but one of several possible ways of responding to the presence of cultural diversity. Pratte (1979) argues that there are at least five significant approaches to cultural diversity in any given society: assimilation, amalgamation, insular cultural pluralism, modified cultural pluralism, and the "open society" approach. These approaches, which he calls "ideologies of cultural diversity," in fact represent virtually every stage in the continuum that has traditionally characterized the assimilation of immigrants in U.S. society.

Assimilation, in essence, demands of all groups in the society conformity to the lifestyle, values, and mores of the dominant majority. In the U.S. context, assimilation refers basically to Anglo-Conformity and entails the presupposition of the superiority of Anglo-American cultural and linguistic patterns. For educators, assimilation meant, in the words of the educational historian Elwood P. Cubberley, that

> Our task is to *break up* their [the immigrants'] groups and settlements, to assimilate or amalgamate these people as part of the American race, and to implant in their children, as far as can be done, the Anglo-Saxon conception of rightiousness [*sic*], law, order, and popular government, and to awaken in them reverence for our democratic institutions and for those things which we as a people hold to be of abiding worth. (1909, p. 16)

Americanization, as this view of assimilation was commonly known in the nineteenth and twentieth centuries, was fundamental in nature, involving far more than mere compliance with the norms of the dominant culture. As Louis Brandeis explained,

> What is Americanization? It manifests itself, in a superficial way, when the immigrant adopts the clothes, the manners, and the customs generally prevailing here. Far more important is the manifestation presented when he substitutes for his mother tongue the English language as the common medium of speech. But the adoption of our language, manners and customs is only a small part of the process. To become Americanized the change wrought must be fundamental. However great his outward conformity, the immigrant is not Americanized unless his interests and affections have become deeply rooted here. And we prop-

erly demand of the immigrant even more than this—he must be brought into complete harmony with our ideals and aspirations and cooperate with us for their attainment. Only when this has been done will he possess the national consciousness of an American. (1954, pp. 340–341)

Amalgamation, like assimilation, assumes the need for a homogeneous society, and thus the desirability of subgroups conforming to established sociocultural norms. Amalgamation, which has been something of an idée fixe through much of U.S. history, is most commonly known as the ideology of the "melting pot." It suggests that diverse groups can and will be fused into a new, unique form—the American. Israel Zangwell perhaps best captured this notion in his play *The Melting-Pot,* in which the hero describes the process as follows:

America is God's crucible, the great Melting-pot where all the races of Europe are melting and re-forming. Here you stand, good folk, think I, when I see them at Ellis Island, here you stand in your fifty groups with your fifty languages and histories, and your fifty blood hatreds and rivalries. But you won't be long like that, brothers, for these are the fires of God you've come to—these are the fires of God. A fig for your feuds and vendettas! German and Frenchmen, Irishmen and Englishmen, Jews and Russians—into the Crucible with you all! God is making the American—the real American has not yet arrived. He is only in the Crucible, I tell you—he will be the fusion of all the races, the coming superman. (Quoted in Pratte, 1979, pp. 249–250)

The key difference between assimilation and amalgamation has to do, then, not so much with the final goal but, rather, with the extent to which the existing dominant culture remains dominant, as opposed to the extent to which a new dominant culture emerges from the mix of the various groups that constitute the society. In the U.S. case, assimilation is probably the more accurate term for much of what has taken place historically, although in some areas (such as food, intermarriage, and so on) amalgamation has also clearly taken place. American English is in fact a very good example of how these two ideologies of cultural diversity have been manifested in the linguistic sphere: our language is clearly English, but it is an English that differs from the British standard, in part because of the influences of native American languages, immigrant languages, and so on (see Ferguson & Heath, 1981).

Insular and modified cultural pluralism also share a series of assumptions, specifically with respect to the unique and valuable identity of each cultural group and the desirability of its continued maintenance as a community in the U.S. context. The difference between the two kinds of cultural pluralism has to do with the extent to which the cultural group accommodates to the mainstream, dominant culture around it. Insular cultural pluralism occurs when a group chooses to maintain its ethnic and linguistic identity apart from that of the surrounding culture. Thus, the Amish are a classic example of insular pluralism in our society. Many immigrant groups have also, at least for one generation, attempted to maintain such boundaries, though with notably less success. Modified cultural pluralism, on the other hand, refers to what is sometimes called "hyphenated Americanism": that is, the idea that one can simultaneously maintain ethnic identity and American identity, as is the case with an individual who identifies as Irish-American, German-American, Italian-American, Greek-American, Polish-American, and so on. Such "hyphenated Americanism," although very popular, can in fact be seen as a stage in the gradual process of assimilation.[4]

Pratte's fifth "ideology of cultural diversity," which is also his personal preference, is what he calls the "open society." Basically, the "open society" is a utopian social goal in which there is "no relative advantage or disadvantage to be had by anyone in the polity as a result of affiliation with a group" (Pratte, 1979, p. 70; see also Green, 1966). In other words, the idea of the "open society" is one based on a rejection of the public relevance of ethnicity, race, religion, language, and so on, as a basis for group association within the polity. Although the idea of a society organized in such a way that ethnic and cultural differences are simply irrelevant is a tempting one in some ways, it is not terribly credible in practice. The problem is that the "open society" necessarily presupposes that there are common, noncultural values that are shared across cultural groups. This is not the case: the very "noncultural" values that are essential for Pratte's "open society" are in fact attributes of specific cultures (and of Anglo-American culture in particular). In other words, Pratte's analysis, as attractive as it is on first glance, misses the fundamental point that it is not a question of whether the schools are to teach or encourage specific cultural values and practices, but a question of whose cultural values and practices are to be taught. It is this very point that many radical critics of multicultural education have emphasized, since to assume that dominant cultural values and practices are in some way neutral is to disempower students from other backgrounds (see Sleeter, 1991; Sleeter & McLaren, 1995).

MINORITY STATUS AND CULTURAL DIVERSITY

The issue of empowerment brings us to an important topic with respect to cultural diversity in society, and that is the nature of different cultural groups. As Sonia Nieto has pointed out,

> It is clear that certain peoples represent unique cases of subjugation in U.S. history. This is true of American Indians, who were conquered and segregated on reservations; African Americans, who were enslaved and whose families were torn apart; Mexican-Americans, whose land was annexed and who were then

> colonized within their own country; and Puerto Ricans, who were colonized and still live under the domination of the United States. In addition and probably not incidentally, they are all people of color, and the issue of race remains paramount in explaining their experiences. (2000, p. 239)

John Ogbu is a distinguished anthropologist who has spent much of his career trying to understand the factors that differentiate various cultural groups in U.S. society. Specifically, Ogbu has argued that there are fundamental differences among voluntary immigrants, voluntary minorities, and involuntary minorities, and further, that these differences have important ongoing social and educational implications (see Gibson & Ogbu, 1991; Ogbu, 1978, 1987, 1992). Involuntary minorities, such as those identified in the above passage from Sonia Nieto, find themselves in "castelike" positions with respect to the dominant culture. As Berreman has explained, race in the U.S. context is comparable to caste in that both involve "invidious distinctions imposed unalterably at birth upon whole categories of people to justify the unequal social distribution of power, livelihood, security, privilege, esteem, freedom—in short, life chances" (1999, p. 54).

The response of involuntary minorities to the dominant culture in general, and to education in particular, in turn differs dramatically from that of other groups in the society. Ogbu suggests that "subordinate minorities usually react to their subordination and exploitation by forming ambivalent or oppositional identities as well as oppositional cultural frames of reference" (1988, p. 176), which means that members of the group will develop attitudes, beliefs, and behaviors that are not only distinct from, but that challenge, those of the dominant group. Furthermore, individuals from such backgrounds who do attempt to cross the boundaries and function within the dominant culture "may experience both internal opposition or identity crisis and external opposition or peer and community pressures" (Ogbu, 1988, p. 176). This is a powerful insight, since it suggests that "*not learning* what the schools teach can be interpreted as a form of political resistance" (Nieto, 2000, p. 243). This approach to understanding the rejection of schooling and concomitant academic failure, which is commonly called "resistance theory," has been carefully articulated by a number of educational scholars in recent years and presents us with a very powerful lens for understanding the complexities of schooling in our society (see, e.g., Giroux, 1983, 1991, 1997).

MULTICULTURALISM IN EDUCATION AND SOCIETY

What, then, is multicultural education really all about? The problem in answering this question is that providing a clear definition of multicultural education is rather like trying to herd cats: there are too many people doing too many things under the rubric of multiculturalism, and any definition that works for some contexts and settings is unlikely to work in others. Just as cats are notably unwilling simply to fall into place and do as they are told, so educators have been reticent to restrict possible meanings of multicultural education. As Suzuki has noted,

> Many widely differing conceptualizations of multicultural education have been formulated. As a consequence, the various programs in the field often appear to have conflicting purposes and priorities. Many educators have come to view multicultural education as ill defined, lacking in substance, and just another educational fad. (1984, p. 294)

Further, as Christine Sleeter has observed, "[T]his is particularly a problem for people who know little about [multicultural education], since many well-intentioned but superficial school practices parade as multicultural education, such as food fairs, costume shows, and window-dressing contributions by people of color" (1991, p. 9). This has led to a number of problems, not the least of which has been the decontextualization of multicultural education, as Nieto has commented:

> Multicultural education cannot be understood in a vacuum. Yet in many schools it is approached as if it were divorced from the policies and practices of schools and from society. The result is a "fairyland" multicultural education disassociated with the lives of teachers, students, and communities. . . . Helping students get along, teaching them to feel better about themselves, or "sensitizing" them to one another may be meaningful goals of multicultural education. But these goals can turn into superficial strategies that only scratch the surface of educational failure if they do not tackle the far more thorny questions of stratification and inequity. (2000, p. 9)

The key to making sense of multicultural education as a truly significant kind of pedagogy has been provided largely by multicultural educators working in the tradition of critical pedagogy (see Irwin, 1996; Sleeter, 1991; Sleeter & McLaren, 1995). Their focus is not on diversity for the sake of diversity, nor on issues of sensitization but on issues of empowerment. In other words, multicultural education makes sense only as a strategy for empowering teachers, students, and communities. As Sleeter and McLaren argue in the introduction of their edited book *Multicultural Education, Critical Pedagogy, and the Politics of Difference,*

> Critical pedagogy and multicultural education require action. Both pedagogies attempt to contest the established historical order through a series of counter-hegemonic articulations, counternarratives, and countermyths that exist within a matrix of pedagogical discontinuities or ruptures. In other words, both address the configuration of sociopolitical interests that schooling serves. Criticalists do not believe that it is possible to provide value-free pedagogical knowledge—

> knowledge that is not the expression of the teacher's political or value commitments. All pedagogical efforts are infiltrated with value judgments and cross-hatched by vectors of power serving particular interests in the name of certain regimes of truth. (1995, p. 18)

James Banks, a leading advocate of multicultural education, has critiqued the epistemological foundations of public schooling in U.S. society by noting that "groups without power and influence often challenge the dominant paradigms, knowledge systems, and perspectives that are institutionalized within society. Knowledge and paradigms consistent with the interests, goals, and assumptions of dominant groups are institutionalized within the schools and universities as well as within popular culture. A latent function of such knowledge is to legitimize the dominant political, economic, and cultural arrangements within society" (1991, pp. 126–127). The role of multicultural education, on Banks's account, is to provide the necessary tools and settings in which such domination can be challenged:

> To empower students to participate effectively in their civic community, we must change the ways in which they acquire, view, and evaluate knowledge. We must engage students in a process of attaining knowledge in which they are required to critically analyze conflicting paradigms and explanations and the values and assumptions of different knowledge systems, forms, and categories. Students must also be given opportunities to construct knowledge themselves so that they can develop a sophisticated appreciation of the nature and limitations of knowledge and understand the extent to which knowledge is a social construction that reflects the social, political, and cultural context in which it is formulated. (Banks, 1991, p. 126)

To the degree to which it is successful, then, multicultural education is in fact a radical challenge to many existing educational beliefs and practices. In the context of the foreign language classroom, multicultural education has important and timely implications not just for what we teach, but also for how and why we teach. These are questions much more easily left unanswered, but it is only by addressing them that we can ensure that the educational process truly works to empower and liberate our students.

TOWARD A CRITIQUE OF CULTURAL RELATIVISM

Multiculturalism in the educational context has much to commend it, but as is true of most good things in life, it is not wholly and totally without blemish. The primary problem with contemporary approaches to multiculturalism education is their uncritical reliance on the doctrine of cultural relativism. Cultural relativism, in a nutshell, "assumes that all cultural values are of equal worth" (Spring, 2000a, p. 214). To some extent, as an operational procedure for anthropologists, this is a valuable and worthwhile starting point. It has, however, become something of an act of faith for many educators—an act of faith that is, in fact, very problematic in nature.

The philosopher of education Robert Ennis has examined the concept of relativism in considerable depth and has suggested that there are actually three logically distinct kinds of relativism: empirical relativism, elementary relativism, and sophisticated relativism (see Ennis, 1969, pp. 412–418). Each of these conceptions of cultural relativism is found in the educational literature, but as we shall see, they are fundamentally different in nature.

Empirical cultural relativism is by far the easiest and most straightforward of the three. As Richard Brandt has articulated it, the basic idea in empirical cultural relativism is that "the ethical [and cultural] judgments supported by different . . . groups are often different and conflicting in a very fundamental way" (1961, p. 433). Such a position is, I think, demonstrably true: different groups do indeed have different core values, and these values are in some instances in conflict. Empirical cultural relativism is, ultimately, concerned with factual claims, which distinguishes it from both elementary and sophisticated cultural relativism, which are normative in nature.

Elementary cultural relativism was most clearly articulated by William Graham Sumner when he argued that "In the folkways, whatever is, is right" (1940 [1906], p. 28). In other words, the standards and practices of a particular culture can only be evaluated within the context of that culture; no external evaluation is possible. Although such a position may initially appear quite appealing, it is nevertheless deeply flawed. As Ennis explains, such a view is inevitably self-contradictory in that it requires us to impress its core value (noninterference) on a culture that is committed to interfering with the culture of another people (1969, p. 413). It is additionally problematic in that it would seem to presuppose that all moral reformers are necessarily wrong, since they are challenging cultural norms, and further, that what is right or wrong is chronological in nature (for instance, that slavery was "right" until the society determined otherwise).

Sophisticated cultural relativism, as Brandt noted, argues not that there are not external standards of right and wrong but, instead, that "when the judgments of different . . . groups disagree, there is not . . . any way of establishing some one of them as correct; on the contrary, . . . conflicting principles are equally valid or correct" (1961, p. 433). Such a position, it must be admitted, is logically possible. The problem is that it is not one that can be realistically held in the real world. As Ennis observes,

> I do not think that any person whom I have heard express this position actually believes it, as evidenced by his own strongly held views about various contem-

> porary issues that affect him. . . . That a person is willing to take a stand and give reasons implies that he thinks he has at least a degree of justification for the position and that the position is better than the alternatives. . . . In the event that we should uncover a person who sincerely was unwilling to take a stand (and give reasons) on any issue, then I do not think that there is anything to do but wait until he becomes a human being. (1969, p. 415)

Although Ennis clearly demonstrates that empirical cultural relativism differs from elementary and sophisticated cultural relativism in that the former is descriptive while the latter two are normative and, further, that only in its empirical sense is cultural relativism logically defensible, this has not prevented educationists from conflating and confusing the three kinds of relativism. The result has been a confusion in much of the literature addressing multicultural educational issues about what is epistemologically credible and reasonable and what is in fact simply well-intentioned nonsense.

Perhaps among the better examples of the problem presented by non-critical manifestations of cultural relativism in contemporary U.S. education has been the growing popularity of Afrocentrism in many educational circles. Seen by its proponents as a unique discipline in its own right, rather than as an interdisciplinary approach to the study of Africa, Afrocentrism is best associated with the works of Molefi Asante (see Asante, 1988, 1990; Asante & Asante, 1990). In his words, Afrocentrism is intended to be "a new historiography founded on African aspirations, visions and concepts" (1988, p. 105). The Afrocentric literature has been widely criticized on a number of grounds, including historical misrepresentation and distortion (see, for instance, Howe, 1998; Lefkowitz, 1996b) and its inclusion and toleration of pseudoscientific claims and doctrines (see Howe, 1998; Ortiz de Montellano, 1995). In a powerful critique of the Afrocentric movement, Clarence Walker argues that

> Afrocentrism is a mythology that is racist, reactionary, and essentially therapeutic. It suggests that nothing important has happened in black history since the time of the pharaohs and thus trivializes the history of black Americans. Afrocentrism places an emphasis on Egypt that is, to put it bluntly, absurd. Furthermore, Afrocentrism caricatures Africa by homogenizing the diverse experiences of Africans across both time and place. (2001, p. 3)

Despite such criticisms and even the refutation of some of its central claims, however, Afrocentrism remains a widely tolerated facet of contemporary multicultural education.[5] It is in such a phenomenon that one sees clearly the risks associated with cultural relativism. As John McWhorter has argued, raising in-group self-esteem by "filling in an idealized vision of the black past and present" in such activities takes the place of logical argument, factual evidence and intellectual curiosity and thus can ultimately harm those it was intended to help (2001, p. 54).

CONCLUSION

The discerning reader will note the relatively minor role discussions of language and language diversity have played in this chapter. One might think that a bit odd, since we have been discussing cultural diversity and since, after all, language is a key component of cultural diversity. However, one of the more fascinating aspects of the ongoing discussions and debates in contemporary U.S. society about multiculturalism and multicultural education has been the very limited recognition of the role played by language diversity. Indeed, it is interesting that language is almost always dealt with in the standard textbooks concerned with multicultural education in a separate chapter, reinforcing the common notion that language diversity is somehow beyond the confines of multicultural education. The especially intriguing aspect of this is the idea, apparently widely accepted, that it is possible to effectively separate issues of language diversity from issues of cultural diversity. Just as the idea that one can have monolingual global education is absurd, so too the idea that it is possible to promote monolingual multicultural education is simply ridiculous. In fact, language diversity is a necessary component of any meaningful approach to multiculturalism, and this is especially true if one is concerned with critical and empowering multiculturalism. Critical language awareness can and should play a central role in such efforts, both with respect to the student's native language and in terms of other languages being studied. Further, within the foreign language classroom, the same issues and concerns that arise in public education in general emerge in language-specific ways and must be addressed by foreign language educators in ways that promote active, constructive learning on the part of students. It is also worth noting at this point that the historical response to linguistic diversity in the United States is reflective of an important and timely paradox: we have historically devoted considerable resources to encouraging children to abandon their mother tongues in favor of English, while at the same time struggling to make it possible for native speakers of English to learn other languages. One can, needless to say, easily imagine a very different approach to both activities that might benefit both groups.

QUESTIONS FOR REFLECTION AND DISCUSSION

1. How do aesthetic conceptions of culture and anthropological conceptions of culture inform the foreign language curriculum? What kinds of cultural con-

tent is involved in the foreign language classroom? What are the purposes of such content?

2. In this chapter, the author distinguishes between cultural diversity and cultural pluralism. Do you think that there is a comparable distinction to be made between linguistic diversity and linguistic pluralism? How might this distinction play out in social and educational terms?
3. What are the implications for the individual's native language of each of the five "ideologies of cultural diversity" identified in the chapter (i.e., assimilation, amalgamation, insular cultural pluralism, modified cultural pluralism, and the "open society")?
4. How can the foreign language educator contribute to efforts to empower students? To what extent does the curriculum in the foreign language classroom facilitate or impede such empowerment?
5. What are the implications of "resistance theory" for foreign language education in the United States? Can you imagine other contexts in which "resistance theory" might provide insights into the successes or failures of foreign language instruction?

FURTHER READING

The literature concerned with multicultural education is extensive. Among the best general introductory works are Sonia Nieto's *Affirming Diversity: The Sociopolitical Context of Multicultural Education* (3rd ed.) (2000), Donna Gollnick and Philip Chinn's *Multicultural Education in a Pluralistic Society* (4th ed.) (1994), Christine Sleeter and Carl Grant's *Making Choices for Multicultural Education: Five Approaches to Race, Class, and Gender* (3rd ed.) (1999), Christine Bennett's *Comprehensive Multicultural Education: Theory and Practice* (3rd ed.) (1995), Joel Spring's *The Intersection of Cultures: Multicultural Education in the United States and the Global Economy* (2nd ed.) (2000a), and James Banks's *An Introduction to Multicultural Education* (1994). A thought-provoking critique is provided in Robert Fullinwider's edited collection, *Public Education in a Multicultural Society: Policy, Theory, Critique* (1996).

NOTES

1. Although in the context of multicultural education, advocates of such "cultural literacy" as this implies have been quite controversial, their position is nevertheless an important one both historically and educationally (see, for instance, Bloom, 1987; D'Souza, 1991; Hirsch, 1987).

2. The challenge of discussing culture in a meaningful way, without either objectifying the concept or defining it so broadly as to make it useless, has been the focus of a considerable body of anthropological work (see Gupta & Ferguson 1997; Marcus & Fischer 1999).

3. Concerns about the social and political role of the standard language does not, of course, mean that there are no right or wrong answers in the foreign language classroom. There is a significant difference between a learner error and an alternative linguistic form acceptable within a particular speech community.

4. This is especially clear in terms of language, where as individuals move from identifying themselves as members of a particular ethnolinguistic group to "hyphenated Americans," one of the changes that generally appears to take place is competence in the former "home" language. Thus, one can be Swedish-American without necessarily speaking Swedish, while a claim to be Swedish would generally be taken to include competence in the language.

5. The Afrocentric literature has not, for the most part, directly targeted linguistic issues in education, beyond general support for Ebonics, which some Afrocentric scholars use to refer to a much broader collection of language varieties than simply African American Vernacular English. As Carol Blackshire-Belay defines the term, for instance, Ebonics includes "*all* languages of African people on the continent and in the diaspora that have created new languages based on their environmental circumstances" (1996, p. 20, n. 2). Such a definition is incredibly problematic from a linguistic perspective and would, in fact, include some language varieties that I suspect that Blackshire-Belay might wish to exclude (e.g., certain varieties of Afrikaans). Another example of the confusion in the Afrocentric literature about fairly basic linguistic concepts can be found in Bekerie's (1997) study of Ethiopic, in which the distinction between a writing system and a language is conflated almost beyond recognition.

Chapter 7

Delighting in Dead Languages: Critical Pedagogy and the Classics

There is a fairly common view of the Classics as a rather dry field of study, inhabited by elderly (generally male) professors who, among other things,

> travel all over Europe to track down and compare manuscripts. They scrutinize past editions and produce new ones of their own. This may involve them in the ticklish business of identifying errors made by careless copyists, that have then been reproduced in later editions; and of suggesting how those errors might be corrected to give a more accurate version of the text. Sometimes, even by the change of just a letter or two, a modern editor will present any reader who comes to consult the work a very different idea of some fundamental aspect, or crucial detail, of the classical world. (Beard & Henderson, 1995, p. 58)

Although such a description does represent what some classical scholars do, it is quite understandable that this will hardly sound exciting or important to most people.[1] In fact, the idea of the solitary scholar poring over old manuscripts looking for errors is precisely why so many people see Classics as boring, irrelevant, and a waste of time. And yet, Classics do have the potential to be incredibly exciting and interesting and can offer valuable insights into many contemporary issues and debates, as we shall see.

Classics, essentially, deal with the worlds of ancient Greece and Rome and with the Greek and Latin languages, including the literatures written in these languages, in particular.[2] One might think that such a focus would, at the very least, not be one subject to particularly intense ideological debate. To draw such a conclusion, though, would be a huge mistake. The Classics have in fact become something of a political and ideological minefield in recent years and have been a focus in many parts of the so-called "culture wars" in higher education in the United States. This is not necessarily a bad thing; it means that there is extensive public debate and argument about the place, content and role of the Classics, which also means that there is a growing recognition that, perhaps, the Classics do matter.

THE CONSERVATIVE CHALLENGE

Discourse and debate about the role and place of the Classics in contemporary U.S. education and society have, since the late 1980s, become increasingly combative in both academic and political circles. The impetus for this new discourse originated largely in conservative political circles and has presented two distinct but related critiques. The first, initiated with the publication of Allan Bloom's *The Closing of the American Mind: How Higher Education Has Failed Democracy and Impoverished the Souls of Today's Students* (1987) and E. D. Hirsch's *Cultural Literacy: What Every American Needs to Know* (1987), and supplemented by other conservatives such as William Bennett (1993, 1995), focuses on the perceived decline of knowledge of the humanities in general and the Classics in particular. The basic idea of these works has been that significant aspects of the common core knowledge necessary for one to be an "educated person" in a western society are no longer being taught and learned or at best are being distorted and watered down. The second critique has been targeted specifically on the teaching of the Classics in the United States and is characterized by the work of such figures as Victor Hanson, John Heath, E. Christian Kopff, and others. These individuals are classicists themselves, engaged in challenging what they believe to be destructive developments in the contemporary study and teaching of the Classics—especially such theoretical approaches as feminism, multiculturalism, and postmodernism.[3] Their challenges have gained considerable attention not only among other classicists but in the general media as well, due at least in part to the apocalyptic-sounding titles many of their books have taken: Hanson and Heath's (2001) *Who Killed Homer? The Demise of Classical Education and the Recovery of Greek Wisdom,* Hanson, Heath and Thornton's (2001) *Bonfire of the Humanities: Rescuing the Classics in an Impoverished Age,* and Kopff's (2001) *The Devil Knows Latin: Why America Needs the Classical Tradition.*

Although the fact that it has generated extensive public discussion about the Classics has certainly been welcomed by classicists, this conservative challenge has also been met with considerable resistance within the academy. As Page duBois has commented,

> I'm alarmed because I see in the popular press [the Greeks of antiquity] travestied by those who want to justify their political platform for America by

> means of a slanted, polemical appeal to the Western past, by a reductive, one-dimensional, shallow interpretation of Greek and Roman civilization. . . . These contemporary writers use the Greeks to argue for their views. Their positions lend implicit support to politicians and religious leaders who advocate so-called family values, restriction of women to their homes and the requirement of obedience to their husbands, and the dissolution of separation between Christianity and the state, while arguing for homophobia, militarism, xenophobia, and the restriction of immigration. Still other scholars sound the death knell for the study of antiquity, blaming those they call "multiculturalists." . . . I fear not only that such arguments will succeed in communicating their monolithic and polemically reductive ideas of the ancient world to readers, but also that classics as a field will wither . . . because of its association with reactionary ideas. (2001, p. 4)

The most interesting facet of this debate, I think, has not been the debate itself, nor even the particular issues around which such controversy swirls. Instead, what is especially interesting is the shared belief that the Classics should be studied, can and do speak to us today, and, as noted earlier, really do matter. We turn now to an exploration of why such a consensus, even in the midst of considerable disagreement about specifics, exists.

WHY THE CLASSICS SHOULD BE TAUGHT

In her landmark study *The Greek Way,* Edith Hamilton argued that the Greeks "were the first Westerners; the spirit of the West, the modern spirit, is a Greek discovery and the place of the Greeks is in the modern world" (1958, p. 15), and in a similar vein, Shelley commented, "We are all Greeks" (quoted in Farrell, 2001, p. 32). Both of these claims, most classicists would agree, are somewhat exaggerated, but both also contain more than a kernel of truth. Much of western civilization does indeed have its origins in classical Greece, though of course much does not as well. Greece, though, does hold a special place in our history and heritage, and it is certainly appropriate to suggest that an understanding of ancient Hellas can provide illumination into many aspects and facets of our own historical development. Greek literature—Homer, Sophocles, Euripides, and so on—is foundational for the study of western literature in general, just as Greek philosophy still provides much of the fundamental framework for contemporary philosophical discussion and debate. If it is not quite true, as Ralph Waldo Emerson once claimed, that "out of Plato come all things that are still written and debated among men of thought" or as is sometimes attributed to Alfred North Whitehead, that "all philosophy is but a footnote to Plato," it is nevertheless hard to imagine philosophy without Plato.[4] Whether in literature, philosophy, mathematics, the sciences, architecture, political theory, history, linguistics, astronomy, the arts, or medicine, ancient Greek society played a pivotal role that continues to affect us all. As Mary Beard and John Henderson have pointed out,

> We are *all* already *Classicists,* however much (or little) we think we know about the Greeks and Romans. We can never come to *Classics* as complete strangers. There is no other foreign culture that is so much part of our history. . . . It is precisely the centrality of *Classics* to all forms of our cultural politics that binds Western civilization to its heritage. (1995, p. 31)

The significance of Greece, especially when coupled with that of Rome, has, then, important implications for our understanding of the origins and development of our own society, culture, and heritage. Beyond this purely historical function, though, the study of the Classics can also provide us with valuable critical insights into many of the problems and challenges faced by human beings of all ages in all societies. The Greek contributions to western civilization are remarkable and awe inspiring, but the Greeks were human beings, with all of the foibles and limitations of human beings. Their societies were not, by any means, utopias. As Page duBois has reminded us, "The classical Athenian male citizen kept slaves, subjected women, hated and frequently brutalized his enemies, and forced slaves to work and die in the city's mines. Ancient democracy was based on exclusion and frequently on imperial expansion, on the Athenian state's ambitions throughout the Mediterranean world" (2001, p. 19). Furthermore, the ancient Greeks were quite diverse in any number of ways, and their societies were far more complex, complicated, ambiguous, and varied than one is sometimes led to believe by overly idealized images of Athens in its Golden Age. Nor did classical Greece simply emerge from its own roots as a unique civilization; we know that it was the product of considerable cross-cultural contact, with both the civilizations of Egypt and Phoenecia (see, for instance, Burkert, 1992, as well as the more controversial work of Martin Bernal [1987, 1991, 2001]). Indeed, it is this very complexity of Greek society that makes the study of Classics so potentially powerful and informative.

The Classics, in short, can be studied not only for what they can teach us about the world of antiquity, and about the debts of our own society and culture to that world, but also for what they can teach us about human culture and society writ large. While it is true that "so much of Western culture turns on centuries of exploration of the legacy of the classical world that it lies *somewhere* at the roots of pretty well all we can say, see, or think" (Beard & Henderson, 1995, p. 122), it is also true many of the answers attempted by the ancient Greeks were less than satisfactory. They did, though, ask the right questions (or at least many of the right questions), and it is in this questioning that we can see the relevance of the study of the Classics most clearly.

WHAT SHOULD BE TAUGHT: THE CONTENT OF THE CLASSICS

The Classics, by its very nature forms an incredibly broad and interdisciplinary field of study. It involves history, art, literature, linguistics, archeology, and any number of other disciplines. At its core, both historically and today, is the study of the two major languages of the classical world: Greek and Latin. It is possible, of course, to study many aspects of the Classics without actually studying either Latin or Greek, and many people have done so. The same can be said of any cultural community: it is certainly possible to study about France and francophone culture without knowing or studying French. And yet, such study, valuable and worthwhile though it obviously can be, allows one at best an indirect access to the culture being studied. Proust and Molière can be read in English, to be sure, but there is inevitably a loss when one relies on translations rather than on texts in the original language. Language study can provide insights into culture that are simply not achievable in other ways.

If we accept the centrality of the study of Latin and Greek as a given for classical studies, then what way should the curriculum be organized, and what should its general content be? The best contemporary answer to this question has been provided by the National Standards in Foreign Language Education Project (1996). This project, which had as its goal the creation and articulation of national standards for foreign language education in the United States, provided a blueprint for conceptualizing foreign language learning standards. The fundamental organizing principle of the *Standards for Foreign Language Learning* are the "five C's": communication, cultures, connections, comparisons, and communities (see Lafayette, 1996; Phillips, 1999). Specifically, each of the "C's" refers to a broad, general objective, or goal, for students engaged in the study of any foreign language, modern or classical:

Communication: Students will be able to communicate in languages other than English.

Cultures: Students will gain knowledge and understanding of other cultures.

Connections: Students will connect with other disciplines and acquire new information.

Comparisons: Students will develop insight into the nature of language and culture.

Communities: Students will participate in multilingual communities at home and around the world. (National Standards in Foreign Language Education Project, 1996)

The standards, of course, because of their generic nature, must be made language specific. In the case of the classical languages, the *Standards for Foreign Language Learning* have been adapted in the *Standards for Classical*

Language Learning, a collaborative undertaking involving the American Classical League, the American Philological Association, and regional classical associations (see National Standards in Foreign Language Education Project, 1999, pp. 153–196). It is important to note at this point what the *Standards for Classical Language Learning* is intended to be, and what it is not intended to be. It is, in essence, "a statement of what students should know and be able to do" as a consequence of studying Latin or Greek, but it is not, and cannot take the place of, a particular course curriculum (National Standards in Foreign Language Education Project, 1999, p. 159). As the authors of the *Standards for Classical Language Learning* clearly explain,

> This document is not meant to be a classroom tool. It is not a curriculum for a Latin or Greek course; it is not a guide for daily lesson planning. *Standards for classical language learning* does not mandate methodology; it is not textbook bound. It does not tell how to teach. It provides a destination, not a road map. (National Standards in Foreign Language Education Project, 1999, p. 159)

Although not intended to be a road map, the *Standards for Classical Language Learning* nevertheless do provide incredibly valuable insights into what the purposes of classical language study should be in contemporary U.S. society. Each of the "five C's" is taken as a general goal, under each of which are subsumed two standards. Each standard is then provided sample progress indicators, at the beginning, intermediate and advanced levels. Given the significance of the *Standards for Classical Language Learning* for the teaching and learning of the Classics in contemporary U.S. education, it is appropriate for us to consider each of the goals, as well as the standards related to each goal, in some detail here.

Communication, the first of the "five C's," in the context of classical languages refers primarily to the skills of reading the target language. As is noted in the *Standards for Classical Language Learning,* "the written messages from the ancient world, from epic poetry to Pompeian graffiti, are the major source of knowledge and our major line of communication to the Greeks and Romans. *Reading, then, is the first standard and the key to communicating with the ancient world*" (1999, p. 161, emphasis in original). This does not mean that oral proficiency is completely absent as a possible goal in the Latin or Greek classroom; indeed, some quite good materials have been developed to facilitate oral language development in these languages (see, for instance, Traupman, 1997). It does, though, make clear one of the important ways in which the teaching of classical languages does differ from the teaching of modern languages. This emphasis is reflected in the two standards related to the goal of communication: (i) students read, understand, and interpret Latin or Greek, and (ii) students use orally, listen to, and write Latin or Greek as part of the language learning process. Such standards differ dramatically from those established for modern languages, where students are expected to engage in conversations, provide and obtain information, express feelings and emotions, exchange opinions, and so on, in the target language (see, for example, the *Standards for Learning Spanish* in National Standards in Foreign Language Education Project, 1999, pp. 431–474).

The second of the "five C's," cultures, in the context of the classical languages refers specifically to the cultures of the Greco-Roman world. As is true of communication, the goal of cultures in fact overlaps and intersects with all of the other general goals of the *Standards for Classical Language Learning.* As part of the process of gaining knowledge and understanding of the Greco-Roman world, students are expected to demonstrate an understanding of the perspectives of the Greeks and/or Romans as revealed both in their practices and in their products (both literary and otherwise).

Connections between the Classics and core subject areas (such as English, mathematics, science, social studies, foreign languages, etc.) should be readily and fairly easily made by students. Especially valuable in this respect are interdisciplinary experiences and activities, which can be made particularly worthwhile as students utilize their knowledge of Latin or Greek to access authentic works that relate to other subject areas. One area in which such connections are commonly made is that of specialized vocabularies, whether in politics and government, science and technology, or whatever, where significant numbers of English words are derived from Latin and/or Greek roots.

The fourth goal of the *Standards for Classical Language Learning* is comparisons, which refers to the student's ability to develop insights into his or her own language and culture. One of the traditional arguments for the study of the classical languages has been that such study helps students understand the structure and workings of their own language. While this view is problematic if taken too seriously (the grammar of English differs in significant and important ways from those of Latin or Greek), it is certainly true that many students first acquire an understanding of grammar from the study of Latin or Greek and, beyond this, may recognize and use elements of both Latin and Greek to increase their knowledge of their own language—especially in terms of the structure and vocabulary of their own language. As the authors of *Athenaze: An Introduction to Ancient Greek* explain in their introduction,

> One of the widely recognized goals of classical language study is attainment of a better understanding of English. With regard to the study of Greek, this means largely a knowledge of Greek roots, prefixes, and suffixes that appear in English words. The influence of Greek on English has been especially notable in scientific and medical terminology, but it is also evident in the language of politics, philosophy, literature, and the arts. (Balme & Lawall, 1990a, p. vii)

Similarly, students can make use of their knowledge of classical cultures and civilizations to better understand both the evolution and contemporary reality of their own culture.

Finally, the fifth goal of the *Standards for Classical Language Learning* is that of communities—specifically, the student's ability to participate in wider communities of language and culture. As the authors of the *Standards for Classical Language Learning* explain, this goal:

> Focuses on the application of the knowledge of Latin or Greek to wider linguistic and cultural communities extending from school to later life. Knowledge of Latin or Greek enables students to develop a full understanding and appreciation of classical influences in today's world as they encounter new language-learning situations and other cultures. Students understand the link between classical languages and certain professional fields through their specialized terminology. Understanding Greco-Roman culture provides students with a basis for interpreting events of the modern world. The tools of technology and telecommunication provide links to the resources of the worldwide classical community. (National Standards in Foreign Language Education Project, 1999, pp. 166–167).

Articulated in the manner laid out in the *Standards for Classical Language Learning*, the case for the Classics would appear to be quite strong, and the content to be taught both clear and relevant. We turn now to the rather vexing question of how such content should be taught.

HOW THE CLASSICS SHOULD BE TAUGHT

In their book *Who killed Homer? The Demise of Classical Education and the Recovery of Greek Wisdom*, Victor Hanson and John Heath spend an entire chapter arguing that one of the challenges in the teaching of Classics is that "teaching Greek is not easy"; indeed, they emphasize that "the problem is that Greek is fairly difficult" (2001, p. 161). Well, yes—Attic Greek is a fairly difficult language, and, as they note, it "comes at a price" to students. However, this is also, I would suggest, somewhat misleading. After all, learning any language in a formal classroom setting is a time-consuming process that takes a great deal of effort. There are no "easy" or "painless" ways to learn a foreign language, whether modern or classical, regardless of what one might read in airline magazines and the like. To be sure, some languages do take more time and trouble to learn than do others, but it is by no means self-evident that Attic Greek is uniquely difficult in terms of its complexity. Hanson and Heath are correct in noting that "the would-be Greek student must absorb the myriad rules of verb formation, the addition of vowel prefixes, reduplication of letters, vowel contractions, infixes, and suffixes" (2001, p. 163), but the student of Zulu is faced with some eighteen classes of nouns, subject and object concords, copulatives, and a remarkably complicated verbal system (see Poulos & Msimang, 1998). The student of Chinese is faced with a simpler grammar but a far more complex and difficult written language (see Gao, 2000; Yip Po-Chin & Rimmington, 1997). In short, while classical Greek may indeed be a daunting challenge for learners, it is far from alone.

Apart from noting that teaching the Classics (or any language) is not easy, we should also note that, as Donald Mastronarde has observed,

> There is no one best way to teach elementary Greek or to learn it. Any successful course will depend on a complex interaction among the classroom teacher, the textbook, and the students, with their varying learning-styles and differing degrees of dedication to a challenging project. (1993, p. vii).

Taking student and teacher differences into account, and fully recognizing that different approaches will work well in different contexts, some general points about the teaching of classical languages can nonetheless be made (see Nikel, 1974). Although the teaching of Latin and Greek in the United States remained, for the most part, grounded in the grammar-translation approach for some time, in recent years this has changed as teachers of classical languages have increasingly begun to employ more communicative approaches, especially at the start of language study, to language teaching and learning. As Paula Saffire and Catherine Freis note in their textbook *Ancient Greek Alive,* "Students find the conversational method the most natural and least intimidating way to begin ancient Greek, and they always remember what they learned through speaking. . . . Our students always regret when we drop conversation, and far into the second semester they tell us they wish we were still speaking Greek" (1999, p. xvii). To be sure, the learning of Latin and Greek in contemporary society is, as Hanson and Heath have argued, "an entirely artificial process," (2001, p. 167), and a full-blown communicative approach to teaching Latin or Greek is obviously inappropriate. This does not, however, mean that such an approach should be dismissed out of hand, nor does it imply, as Hanson and Heath suggest, that teachers "who try to turn a dead language conversational, whose clever artifice can for a while teach students to talk in Attic Greek of the fifth century B.C. about the weather or Christmas presents given and received, are, unfortunately, usually touched. If they continue in that sort of business, we usually find them almost demented" (2001, p. 169). In fact, at the very least, anecdotal evidence strongly suggests that such teaching can help to make the initial language learning experience for students of the classical languages both more effective and welcoming. As Balme and Lawall note in the teacher's handbook that accompanies *Athenaze: An Introduction to Ancient Greek,*

We also recommend that teachers encourage their students to study the vocabulary and to reply to the exercise questions *orally*. Not only is the sounding of a language the natural way of learning it, but the combination of the two senses of sight and hearing can greatly facilitate the learning process. (1990b, p. iii)

In short, whatever instructional approach or combination of approaches that results in students wishing to learn more about the Classics, and becoming excited about language learning in general and the Classics in particular, would seem to be preferable to any approach that does not accomplish this. I recognize, though, that such a view of the Classics may not be universally shared. As J. E. Sharwood Smith wrote in the later 1970s,

Perhaps the value of exercising the mind on elementary Latin has sometimes been dismissed too readily. I have heard a distinguished professor of Sociology, whose first training was in Classics, argue that . . . Latin exercises are the finest possible propaedeutic to Sociology, because they are eminently boring and because they teach an exact attention to language—high toleration of boredom and a trained attention to language being more valuable ingredients of a good sociologist than starry-eyed enthusiasm for changing the world. Distinguished professors of Sociology have such *mana* that one cannot afford not to listen to them, but, unless all professors of Sociology are prepared to make proficiency in Latin composition a condition of entry to their over-populated courses, the recommendation of Latin for its superior power to induce boredom would be, now of all times, a short cut to extinction. (1977, pp. 28–29)

So, while the potential power of Latin (and Greek as well, one assumes) to bore students may for some be an adequate justification for their place in the curriculum, for most of us alternative arguments focusing on the fascination and relevance of the Classics for modern life are likely to be more moving.

TEACHING THE CLASSICS AS CRITICAL PEDAGOGY

Critical pedagogy is difficult to define, in part because it does not, in the words of Peter McLaren, "constitute a homogenous set of ideas" (1989, p. 160). Rather, critical pedagogy is defined and manifested in a wide variety of ways by many different scholars and educators who share certain common assumptions and objectives but differ in many other important ways.[5] At its heart, critical pedagogy has as its core objective "to empower the powerless and transform existing social inequalities and injustices" (McLaren, 1989, p. 160). It is, as Joan Wink has suggested, "a process that enables teachers and learners to join together in asking fundamental questions about knowledge, justice, and equity in their own classroom, school, family, and community" (2000, p. 71). In this, critical pedagogy is actually remarkably similar to some of the traditional goals associated with the study of Classics. As M. I. Finley commented,

> The study of ancient history is in the last analysis not just the study of antiquity, and surely not of antiquities. It should serve to enrich the students' understanding of society, politics and culture in terms of, and in the interests of, their own experience and ultimately of the situations they will face in society. (Quoted in Smith,1977, p. 62)

To be sure, study of the Classics has rarely lived up to this expectation, and to some extent has certainly been used historically to perpetuate sexist, classist, and racist views. This misuse of the Classics and the classical tradition should not blind us to the very real value of that tradition. As Page duBois has written,

> One of the great rewards of reading history is the realization that things have not in fact always been the way they are now, that people in other times and places have organized human societies, of whatever size, differently. If we allow ourselves to be open to the myriad lost possibilities of human cultures, we amplify our present often limited sense of human potential. We can throw open the narrow window through which many people now see the ancient world, and look at much more that is recognizable in our repertory of human possibility and in our inheritance from the ancient dead. (2001, pp. 22–23)

And what are these possibilities? Contemporary Classics scholars have been engaged in a wide range of research activities that seek to address the very core issues of both classical and modern societies. Among the issues that have been, and continue to be, discussed and debated—and which can and should be incorporated into the study of the Classics—are such matters as:

- the role and place of women in classical societies (see Katz, 1999; Lardinois & McClure, 2001; Rousseau, 1995),
- feminism in classical studies as well as in Classics as a field of study (see McManus, 1997),
- imperialism and nationalism (Rose, 1999),
- old age (Falkner & de Luce, 1989),
- democracy and its limits (Hansen, 1997),
- democracy and hegemony (Wohl, 1996),
- definitions and implications of ethnicity and identity (Cartledge, 1995; Gill, 1996; Hall, 1989),
- language and identity (Rouchette, 1997; Swain, 1996), and
- conceptions of honor and shame (Cairns, 1993).

In short, virtually any contemporary controversy at the very least has antecedents in classical antiquity from which we can learn. Further, as we already noted, the Greeks sought answers to the most fundamental questions of human existence—questions about the good life, justice, knowledge, ethics, and so on. These are the questions at the heart of the "human conversation," and it is here that the goals of critical pedagogy and those of the Classics—and, indeed, of education in general—coalesce.

CONCLUSION

Mary Lefkowitz, a leading critic of Martin Bernal's work, recently observed, "Classicists in the late modern world . . . have more than enough grounds for paranoia. We are reminded daily that our subject is useless, irrelevant, and boring—all the things that, in our opinion, it is not" (1996a, p. 4). The study of Classics can and should be useful, relevant and exciting. Consider, for instance, Mary Beard and John Henderson's broad and evocative definition of the classics:

> *Classics* concerns whole cultures, and the whole range of our responses to those cultures. And so it concerns what is salacious, sordid, or funny, no less than what is informative or improving. Indeed . . . the same material from the ancient world may be both funny *and* improving, salacious *and* informative—the difference depending largely on the different questions we choose to ask of it, and on the different ways we frame our responses . . . . But that *whole range* of responses includes not just our responses to the ancient world itself, but also to the *study* of *Classics*, to the way it is taught, to the educational values it is seen to represent, and to its traditions of scholarship. . . . *Classics*, and particularly the teaching of the Latin and Greek languages, is deeply embedded in all kinds of modern images of education, schooling, and culture as a whole. (1995, p. 109)

Given such a perspective, as well as the potential for the study of the Classics to help to empower and liberate students, the real question, perhaps, should not be why some students should study Latin or Greek, but rather, why all students are not expected to do so.

QUESTIONS FOR REFLECTION AND DISCUSSION

1. In what ways are the teaching of Latin and Greek different from the teaching of modern foreign languages? In what ways are they similar? What lessons can be learned (a) by teachers of modern languages from the experiences of teachers of classical languages, and (b) by teachers of classical languages from teachers of modern languages?
2. In chapter 4, we discussed the concept of "language death." How does this concept apply to languages such as Latin and Attic Greek, which no longer have native speakers, but which are still widely taught, studied, and read?
3. The relationship between Latin and Greek in antiquity was an interesting and complex one. Farrell has noted that there is a "poverty topos" running through the history of Latin literature that presents Latin as derivative of and inferior

to Greek (2001, pp. 28–29). How does this compare to earlier views of English vis-à-vis Latin? What similar kinds of attitudes can you identify in the modern world?

4. In your view, how can the study of Latin or Greek "empower the powerless and transform existing social inequalities and injustices," as is suggested in this chapter? What are the implications of such goals for the curriculum? For teaching methods?
5. The study of classical languages almost always refers to the study of Latin and Greek. It could also include the study of many other ancient languages—Hebrew, Aramaic, Syriac, Assyrian, Babylonian, Hittite, Phoenician, and so on. What advantages might there be to offering students the option of studying one of these other ancient languages? What barriers or problems might exist?

FURTHER READING

The best general introduction to Classics as a field of study, in my view, is Mary Beard and John Henderson's *Classics: A Very Short Introduction* (1995). For an excellent study of the history of Latin, see Joseph Farrell's *Latin Language and Latin Culture* (2001); for Greek, see Geoffrey Horrocks's *Greek: A History of the Language and Its Speakers* (1997). Werner Jaeger's three-volume study *Paideia: The Ideals of Greek Culture* (1971a, 1971b, 1973) remains an invaluable reference and classic.

NOTES

1. Although such activity does, I admit, sound less than fascinating, it can in fact be quite important. For instance, as Beard and Henderson have explained, "How accurately . . . the Romans understood the geography of the province of Britain is an important question not only for our evaluation of ancient science and techniques of mapping, but also in discussions of Roman imperialism. How much, that is, do we imagine that the Romans really knew about their conquered territories? The answer to this partly depends on whether you believe that the Roman historian Tacitus compared the shape of the island to a 'diamond', *scutula*, in Latin (as all the manuscripts, and most old editions, have it), or to a 'shoulder-blade', *scapula* (as an editor of the text, writing in 1967, thought would be better" (1995, pp. 58–59).

2. The teaching of Classics generally focuses on classical Latin and Attic Greek, though New Testament Greek is also widely studied, albeit for primarily religious purposes. In addition, the study of post-classic Latin, although not generally a major concern of classical scholarship, is also potentially important. For typical examples of New Testament Greek texts, see Dobson (1993), Mounce (1993), Wallace (1996, 2000), Wenham (1965), and Young (2001). For discussions related to the study of non-classic Latin, see Farrell (2001) and Waquet (2001); the most common text for medieval Latin is Harrington (1997).

3. There is actually a third controversy that overlaps but is distinct from the other two, and that is the debate about the work of Martin Bernal (1987, 1991,

2001). Bernal's work has received both considerable praise and criticism within the Classics community. See, for instance, Berlinerblau (1999) and Lefkowitz and Rogers (1996).

4. Whitehead provided a very powerful, albeit conservative, rationale for the study of the Classics in his landmark work *The Aims of Education* (1949, pp. 69–83).

5. Key figures writing about critical pedagogy include Paulo Freire, Michael Apple, Henry Girouz, and Peter McLaren, among others. A good general introduction to critical pedagogy is Kanpol (1994).

Chapter 8

Fallacies, Factoids, and Frustrations: Bilingual Education in the United States

Bilingual education in the U.S. context has proven to be an incredibly controversial and contentious topic in recent years among both educators and the general public. As was the case with African American Vernacular English that we explored earlier, much of the debate about bilingual education is grounded less in empirical evidence than in personal beliefs and experiences, misunderstandings about the nature of language in general and bilingual education in particular, and in political and ideological biases. As María Estela Brisk has argued,

> Much of the debate on bilingual education is politically motivated, more suitable for talk shows than for improving schools. The United States can create quality bilingual education for the increasingly diverse student population, but only if we observe what really happens in our schools. If we continue to deal with bilingual education as a label, the sterile debate on how abruptly language minority students should be Americanized and Anglicized will continue to isolate many of our students. (1998, p. xv)

The realities of bilingual education in the United States are in fact quite complex, and simplistic presentations of the issues often do far more harm than good as we try to meet the needs of an important and growing part of our school-age population.

A good place to begin our discussion of bilingual education is with what might be termed "common assumptions." There are, I believe, some common, core assumptions shared by virtually all educators, policy makers, and indeed, by most individuals in the general public that relate to the issues that we will be addressing. Specifically, there appears to be a consensus in our society that:

- All children need to acquire competence in mainstream English.[1]
- All children need to master not only language skills but other subject matter as well.
- All children deserve to feel loved, cared for, and respected.
- All children need to be held to high but attainable standards of performance.
- All children should feel safe and secure in the school environment.
- All children need to be exposed to a curriculum and school experience that will empower them to change their own world.

What is interesting about these assumptions is that none really dictates particular classroom practices, nor do any prescribe specific educational policies. In part because of this, these core assumptions are not particularly controversial, I suspect, and most educators would see them simply as conditions for "good education." Nonetheless, I do recognize that some groups and individuals in our society will reject one or more of these assumptions, and in those cases, I believe there exists a fundamental value difference that must be addressed prior to dealing with any particular social or educational policy issue.

The fundamental question about students who arrive at school not speaking English, or not speaking English fluently, is what kinds of methodological and pedagogical approaches are most likely to result in positive social and educational outcomes. That is, what is at stake is ultimately a matter of pedagogical effectiveness—what works best for the children involved. To be sure, there are constraints on effectiveness as a criterion for educational practice. Not everything that works is acceptable; no matter how effective it might be to use electrical shocks to increase student motivation to learn, for instance, no reasonably sane educator or policy maker is likely to advocate it. Similarly, there are certain fundamental rights (including language rights) that must be observed in the educational process. All this having been said, within reasonable constraints we are concerned with what works best to achieve legitimate and desirable educational ends.

A note on terminology is appropriate here. A wide variety of labels have been used to describe the kinds of students with which this chapter is primarily concerned: non-English speakers, language minority/minority language students, limited English-proficient students (LEPs), potentially English-proficient students (PEPs),[2] and, more recently, English language learners (ELLs). In addition, such students are commonly labeled "bilingual" in school parlance, although this label generally ceases to be used once they are competent in English (that is, once they actually are bilingual). The challenge here is to find a label that avoids suggesting a deficiency on the part of the child, while at the same time indicating that language skills in English are not present or fully present. For our purposes here, I have chosen to use the term "minority language student," albeit with the caveat that in many school settings, the home language of the child is in fact the majority language in his or her school—albeit not the dominant language, at least in a sociopolitical sense.

THE NATURE AND PURPOSES OF BILINGUAL EDUCATION

Bilingual education in the U.S. context is concerned with providing minority language students with a schooling experience that prepares them for life in U.S. society. It is important to begin with this statement, since much of the propaganda and debate about contemporary bilingual education programs in the U.S. might lead one to think otherwise. Bilingual education programs are not programs that ignore the need for acquisition of English; indeed, the acquisition of English is one of the most important outcomes of effective bilingual education programs. In fact, bilingual education programs seek to accomplish three broad goals:

- Knowledge of the subject matter being taught in the classroom, including mathematics, science, social studies, art and music, language arts, and any other content in the curriculum.
- Literacy skills, initially in the child's first language that then transfer to the second language (English).
- Language skills in both English and the native language.

Each of these broad goals is a significant and core aspect of bilingual education, and the research base for each is actually quite strong, as we will see later in this chapter. Apart from the educational research for each of these goals, though, even common sense alone would support each goal. As for the first, we know that under the best of circumstances, second language learning takes time and effort. While the language minority child is acquiring English, she or he is, for the most part, not learning whatever else is being taught. In most cases, this means that for several years the child is disconnected from the standard curriculum. The purpose of providing content area instruction in the child's native language is, then, quite simple: to ensure that while English is being learned, the child is not losing or falling behind with respect to subject area content. Given the socioeconomic background of large numbers of language minority students, such instruction is essential if the schooling experience is to be a positive one. This argument is particularly strong when we are talking about initial literacy skills. Learning to read is the foundation of the elementary schooling experience, and, as Stephen Krashen has noted,

> If we learn to read by reading, it will be much easier to learn to read in a language we already understand. . . . Once you can read, you can read. The ability

to read transfers across languages. . . . This characterization helps us understand what the advantages are in providing first language support: Knowledge gained through the first language makes English input more comprehensible and literacy gained through the first language transfers to the second. (1996, p. 4)

Finally, bilingual education has as its ultimate goal a functioning bilingual individual. In other words, while some programs in the United States and elsewhere are subtractive in nature (that is, have as their objective the replacement of the native language with the socially dominant language), good programs are additive in nature, building on the child's existing language competence. In a sense, of course, what this means is that we view the minority language child as one who comes to school not with a deficit (that is, not being able to speak English), but rather, as one who comes with important language skills in a language other than English that can be used as a foundation for both English language learning and for the development of further language skills in the native language. There is an interesting, and telling, paradox involved in the debates about bilingual education. As María Estela Brisk has commented,

The paradox of bilingual education is that when it is employed in private schools for the children of elites throughout the world it is accepted as educationally valid. . . . However, when public schools implemented bilingual education for language minority students over the past 50 years, bilingual education became highly controversial. (1998, p. 1)

In other words, the debate about bilingual education in the U.S. context has a great deal more to do with politics, ideology, and issues of social class than it does with education per se.

WHAT THE RESEARCH *REALLY* SAYS

One of the common features of discussions and debates about bilingual education in the United States is the claim that such programs, although perhaps well intentioned, simply do not work—or, at the very least, that the research on the effectiveness of bilingual education is inconclusive. Typical of such claims is Rosalie Porter's assertion that

The bilingual education establishment is fighting to maintain its primacy and prerogatives unchallenged, even though bilingual programs have, in the majority of cases, proven unsuccessful. . . . If there were convincing evidence that children learn their school subjects better if they are taught in their native language, then we could continue to approve the temporary segregation [of students in bilingual education programs]; but that case has not been substantiated. (1990, pp. 6–7)

We are often presented with rather sweeping generalizations about bilingual education, not only in terms of the effectiveness of such programs, but also making a number of other claims about language minority students and their education. The issues involved are certainly controversial; as Stephen Krashen has commented,

> Bilingual education is under attack. Letters to the editor, editorials, and talk show hosts repeat the same arguments nearly daily. Bilingual education, they say, doesn't work. Students in bilingual programs do not learn English and those who have never had bilingual education appear to do very well without it. Also, they claim that most parents and teachers don't want it. In addition, there is also the feeling that English is in trouble and that programs such as bilingual education contribute to the erosion of English in the United States. (1996, p. 1)

Such generalizations about and critiques of bilingual education programs are undoubtedly common and popular, and clearly represent the views of a not insubstantial part of our population. To some extent, such views are understandable, especially when they coincide with other beliefs about language and language acquisition. As we discussed in the first chapter of this book, many of these beliefs are actually examples of language mythology—and, as we shall see, many of the common beliefs about the "facts" in the debate about bilingual education turn out to be far from accurate. How, then, if this is indeed the case, have such beliefs about bilingual education been able to gain such popularity and credence?

The answer to this question is grounded in the nature of bilingual education programs in the first instance and in the nature of educational research in the second. As Katherine Samway and Denise McKeon have observed, "[A]ttempts to compare bilingual education programs with other programs serving L2 students have produced seemingly conflicting answers" (1999, p. 70). This is the case to a large extent because of the incredible diversity of programs that are labeled "bilingual." More often than not, comparative studies of bilingual education programs are not really comparative at all; they involve very different models, approaches, and curricula—all of which are subsumed under the general (and misleading) label of "bilingual education." As Hakuta and Gould have argued,

> Much of the research evaluating programs for L2 students appears to suffer from three serious shortcomings: (1) It obscures the striking diversity of programs in design and quality (including the availability of resources, materials, and trained staff), (2) it obscures the way in which language is actually used for instructional purposes, and (3) it obscures the linguistic, social, and academic characteristics of students. (1987, pp. 38–45)

This does not mean, however, that no conclusions at all can be drawn from the research that has been conducted. Although much of the research is indeed flawed, much of it is also quite good. In fact, the research literature is quite clear with respect to the general indicators that characterize effective programs for meeting the needs of language minority students (see Samway & McKeon, 1999, pp, 75–79). The six indicators that are most strongly supported by the research evidence are:

Indicator 1: High expectations need to be held for all language minority students (see Collier, 1992; Lucas, Henze & Donato, 1990; Minicucci & Olsen, 1992; Pease-Alvarez, García & Espinosa, 1991; Tikunoff, Ward & van Broekhuisen, 1991).

Indicator 2: There is integration of language development with subject matter development (see Crandall, 1987; Lindholm, 1987; Snow, Met & Genessee, 1989; Tikunoff, Ward & van Broekhuisen, 1991).

Indicator 3: There is support for content development through the students' first language (see Collier, 1992; Ramirez, Yuen, Ramey, Pasta & Billings, 1991; Tikunoff, Ward & van Broekhuisen, 1991).

Indicator 4: Comprehensive staff development and training are provided for all faculty and staff (see Lucas, Henze & Donato, 1990; McKeon & Malarz, 1991; Tikunoff, Ward & van Broekhuisen, 1991).

Indicator 5: There is active and meaningful support for school leaders and administrators (see Lindholm, 1987; Lucas, Henze & Donato, 1990; McKeon & Malarz, 1991; Tikunoff, Ward & van Broekhuisen, 1991).

Indicator 6: The entire school environment is supportive of the learning of minority language students (see Gándara & Fish, 1994; Guthrie, 1985; Lindholm, 1987; Lucas, Henze & Donato, 1990; Tikunoff, Ward & van Broekhuisen, 1991).

Nor is this all that can be learned from the existing research base on bilingual education. Stephen Krashen has, in my view, compellingly argued that programs that successfully meet the needs of language minority students are characterized by four elements: (1) comprehensible input is English is provided (in ESL, sheltered subject-matter teaching), (2) subject matter knowledge is presented in classes taught in the students' first language, (3) literacy development takes place initially in the students' primary language, and (4) there is continued development of the students' primary language (1996, p. 65). The case for the use of the language minority student's native language as a bridge to English is, in short, strongly supported by the research base.

What is interesting about the debate about the research base on bilingual education has been its ideological and political nature rather than what the actual studies themselves would appear to suggest. Jim Cummins, for instance, has observed that

> The academic debate on bilingual education in the United States contrasts markedly with the treatment of the issue in the media. Media articles on bilingual

education have tended to be overwhelmingly negative in their assessment of the merits of bilingual programs. . . . By contrast, the academic debate lines up virtually all North American applied linguists who have carried out research on language learning as advocates of bilingual programs against only a handful of academic commentators who oppose bilingual education. These opponents tend to come from academic backgrounds other than applied linguists. (2000, p. 201)

It is, in short, in the political sphere, rather than in the academic sphere, that the real controversy about bilingual education swirls, and it is in that sphere that we must look if we really want to understand the debate about bilingual education in contemporary U.S. society (see González & Melis, 2001a, 2001b).

LANGUAGE RIGHTS IN EDUCATION

Thus far in this chapter, we have examined bilingual education in terms of pragmatic matters—that is, in terms of the extent to which the research would seem to indicate that it is an effective way of teaching language minority students English, while at the same time ensuring that they learn other content matter. Although the evidence does strongly support good bilingual education programs, at this point I would like to suggest that there are in fact broader and more important reasons for supporting such programs—reasons that are only tangentially concerned with pragmatic matters. Specifically, what I want to argue here is that on the international level there has been a growing interest in and concern with the linguistic human rights of the individual in recent years (see, for instance, Phillipson, 2000; Skutnabb-Kangas, 2000a, 2000b; Skutnabb-Kangas & Phillipson, 1995), and that this international attention to issues of language rights has direct and important implications for the education of language minority children in the United States. As Joel Spring has explained,

The [United Nations'] Convention Against Discrimination in Education and the concerns of indigenous peoples highlighted the importance of language rights. As exemplified by Singapore, Mauritius, the United States, and other postcolonial nations, language rights are a potential source of conflict in multicultural societies. It is generally recognized that there is an inseparable relation between language and culture. Particular words often embody cognitive and affective meanings that defy translation into other languages. In addition, literary and oral traditions depend on the preservation of language. In other words, the right to one's culture requires the right to one's language. (2000b, p. 30)

The discourse on human rights has evolved in significant ways in the past century. As the British philosopher Brenda Almond has noted,

The Second World War involved violations of human rights on an unprecedented scale but its ending saw the dawn of a new era for rights. Following their heyday

> in the seventeenth century . . . rights played a crucial role in the revolutions of the late eighteenth century. In the nineteenth and early twentieth centuries, however, appeal to rights was eclipsed by movements such as utilitarianism and Marxism which could not, or would not, accommodate them. . . . The contemporary period has seen a further shift in their fortunes and today they provide an accepted international currency for moral and political debate. In many parts of the world, irrespective of cultural or religious traditions, when issues or torture or terrorism, poverty or power are debated, the argument is very often conducted in terms of rights and their violation. (1993, p. 259)

Discussions and debates about rights impact legislation, social policy, and, ultimately, the quality of life of both groups and individuals. As Robert Phillipson, Mart Rannut and Tove Skutnabb-Kangas have argued,

> The history of human rights shows that the concept of human rights is not static. It is constantly evolving in response to changed perceptions of how humans have their fundamental freedoms restricted, and the challenge to the international community to counteract injustice. (1995, p. 16)

The past century, then, has witnessed not only challenges to and abrogations of human rights but also growing awareness and articulation of such rights. One area in which such awareness has been relatively late to develop, in spite of ongoing and often egregious violations of group and individual rights, is that of language. As recently as the mid-1980s, Gomes de Matos could write, "Although ours has been said to be 'the age of rights' . . . there has not yet been a thorough, well-documented, carefully thought out discussion of the crucial problem of the human being's linguistic rights" (1985, pp. 1–2). Given the centrality of language to self-identification and to our sense of who we are, and where we fit in the broader world, it is interesting that a concern with language rights has taken so long to emerge. And yet, such concern has emerged in recent decades, and the scholarly and political literature dealing with issues of language rights has increased dramatically both quantitatively and qualitatively (see, for instance, Annamalai, 1986; Herriman & Burnaby, 1996; Olivier, 1993; Skutnabb-Kangas, 2000a, 2000b; Skutnabb-Kangas & Phillipson, 1995). Although it is clear that we have a long way to go in terms of raising consciousness about language rights, and while such rights are far from universally recognized, let alone observed, the fact that the issue itself has been put on the table for discussion and debate itself constitutes a promising development.

The fundamental challenge presented by debates about language and language policy is essentially one of achieving balance between the competing goods of social unity and access on the one hand, and respect for and toleration of diversity on the other. Basically, the question that policy makers are trying to address in such debates is the extent to which pluralism, as a necessary condition for a democratic social order, applies to the issue of language. At the heart of this discussion, of course, is the issue of language rights. In other words, to what extent, and in what ways, are language rights human rights? Also relevant here is the related question of whether language rights apply only to the individual, or whether there are rights that are "group rights" (that is, rights that apply to a community rather than solely to the members of that community by virtue of some common, shared feature of the individuals in the community) (see Coulombe, 1993; Tollefson, 1991, pp. 167–200, 1995). This is actually a far more complex matter than it might at first seem, since language rights are "preeminently social, in that they are only comprehensible in relation to a group of other human beings with whom the language is shared and from which personal and cultural identity is achieved" (MacMillan, 1982, p. 420). In other words, debates about language rights are unique in that, as Kenneth McRae argued, "societies characterized by linguistic pluralism differ from those characterized by racial, religious, class or ideological divisions in one essential respect, which stems from the pervasive nature of language as a general vehicle of communication" (1978, p. 331). This having been said, the concept of group rights is itself somewhat problematic, potentially leading to an apartheid-style mandate of ethnic obligation, even as the alternative of linguistic imperialism looms large (see Pennycook, 1994, 1998; Phillipson, 1992).

In working toward a conception of "language rights," a good place to begin the discussion is with *The U.N. Declaration on the Rights of Persons Belonging to National or Ethnic, Religious and Linguistic Minorities* (18 December 1992), in which representatives of the international community attempted to articulate the nature of the human and civil rights that ought to be accorded members of minority groups (see Skutnabb-Kangas, 1994). This *Declaration* was a follow-up to the Universal Declaration of Human Rights, necessitated by the widespread violation of the second article of the Universal Declaration of Human Rights that prohibits discrimination against individuals based on language. Specifically, three articles of the *Declaration on the Rights of Persons Belonging to National or Ethnic, Religious and Linguistic Minorities* are relevant for our purposes here. First, Article 2.1 prohibits what might be termed active discrimination against members of minority groups:

> Persons belonging to national or ethnic, religious and linguistic minorities (hereinafter referred to as persons belonging to minorities) have the right to enjoy their own culture, to profess and practice their own religion, *and to use their own language, in private and in public, freely and without interference or any form of discrimination.* (Article 2.1, my emphasis)

This, in a sense, is the negative force of the *Declaration,* in that it focuses on simply prohibiting actions and policies that unfairly target minority groups. The *Declaration* goes far beyond this negative constraint, however, and in Articles 4.2 and 4.3 specifies what can be called positive language rights:

> States shall take measures to create favorable conditions to enable persons belonging to minorities to express their characteristics and to develop their culture, language, religion, traditions and customs, except where specific practices are in violation of national and contrary to international standards. (Article 4.2)

> States should take appropriate measures so that, whenever possible, persons belonging to minorities have adequate opportunities to learn their mother tongue or to have instruction in their mother tongue. (Article 4.3)

These explicit statements of both negative and positive aspects of language rights differ in significant ways, of course, from the constitutional provisions governing the issue of language rights in the United States, and, indeed, of those in many countries. They are even further, in many instances, from actual government policies and practices, especially (although by no means exclusively) with respect to the rights of indigenous peoples. In fact, a central feature of the draft Declaration of Indigenous Peoples Human Rights, which was developed by the Working Group on Indigenous Populations of the United Nations Sub-Commission on Prevention of Discrimination and Protection of Minorities in the 1990s (see Spring, 2000b, pp. 35–37), was focused on the issue of language rights in education:

> Indigenous children have the right to all levels and forms of education of the State. All indigenous peoples also have this right and the right to establish and control their educational systems and institutions providing education in their own languages, in a manner appropriate to their cultural methods of teaching and learning. (Article 15)

In the "Preface" to her powerful and compelling book *Linguistic Genocide in Education—or Worldwide Diversity and Human Rights?* Tove Skutnabb-Kangas emphasizes both the ties between linguistic diversity and language rights and the relatively weak treatment of language rights in contemporary global society:

> Linguistic human rights are a necessary (but not sufficient) prerequisite for the maintenance of linguistic diversity. Violations of linguistic human rights, especially in education, lead to a reduction of linguistic and cultural diversity on our planet . . . language in education systematically gets a poorer treatment than other basic human characteristics. Very few international or regional human rights instruments grant binding educational linguistic human rights, despite pious phrases. The present binding linguistic human rights in education clauses are

completely insufficient for protecting and maintaining linguistic diversity on our globe. (2000a, p. xii)

Not only are language rights in the educational context insufficiently protected; they are in fact routinely ignored and violated around the world (see Grenoble & Whaley, 1998; Nettle & Romaine, 2000). And what of the United States? The proponents of the "U.S. English" Movement and their allies are correct in noting that there is no official language in the United States and that our language policies have emerged in a somewhat chaotic and inconsistent fashion. More to the point, language policies and language practices at all levels of U.S. society have historically involved extensive violation of individual language rights, and in fact continue to do so. There is, to put it mildly, absolutely no reason whatever to believe that the sorts of changes advocated by the supporters of the "U.S. English" Movement are likely to change this situation. If anything, the rhetoric of such groups suggests just the opposite (see Baron, 1990; Crawford, 1992a, 1992b, 2000; Macedo, 2000). The right of the child to an education in his or her native language is violated on a daily basis throughout the United States, but even beyond this, the denigration and exclusion of languages in both school and society constitute an ongoing assault on meaningful language rights (see Reagan, 1997a, 1997b). The history of U.S. language policy has been accurately summarized as follows:

Except for very brief periods during which private language rights have been tolerated and certain limited public rights have been permitted, the history of language policy in the United States has generally been one of the imposition of English for an ever wider range of purposes and the restriction of the rights of other languages. (Hernández-Chávez, 1995, p. 141)

Indeed, if we look at the history not only of immigrant languages, but even more, the history of indigenous languages in North America, what we find is not merely a history of neglect, but in fact what is arguably a history of deliberate cultural and linguistic genocide (see Boseker, 1994; Hernández-Chávez, 1995)—a history shared, unfortunately, with the treatment of indigenous peoples and their languages both in Canada (Fettes, 1992, 1994, 1998) and in Latin America (see Hamel, 1995a, 1995b). Using a term like "linguistic genocide" may strike some readers as too polemical, but it is in fact a fairly accurate description of what has taken place.

Ultimately, questions of language rights are questions of language policy, and they reflect underlying assumptions about the nature of language as well as issues of power, equality, and access in society. As James Tollefson has noted,

The policy of requiring everyone to learn a single dominant language is widely seen as a common-sense solution to the communication problems of multilingual

> societies. The appeal of this assumption is such that monolingualism is seen as a solution to linguistic inequality. If linguistic minorities learn the dominant languages, so the argument goes, then they will not suffer economic and social inequality. The assumption is an example of an ideology which refers to normally unconscious assumptions that come to be seen as common sense . . . such assumptions justify exclusionary policies and sustain inequality. (1991, p. 10)

The desire for simple solutions to complex problems and challenges is perhaps understandable, but it is also dangerous. The tendency to address rights issues as pragmatic or empirical matters, as is often the case, is also both misleading and wrong. The question, in short, is not whether instruction in the mother tongue is pedagogically most effective (although the evidence would suggest that it is), any more than whether capital punishment reduces crime—in both cases, fundamental human rights must be understood to remove the question from the empirical realm and move it to the normative realm. Only by placing the questions in the right discourse context can we hope to come to reasonable and justifiable solutions—and, at least in the case of language rights, we have a long way to go before this becomes a reality.

CONCLUSION

Bilingual education presents language educators with a special challenge. Throughout this book, I argue that the study of language needs to include not only the communicative and cultural aspects of language but also the often implicit political and ideological issues related to language. Students need to understand the ways in which language is used to convey and protect social status as well as how it can be used to oppress and denigrate both individuals and groups. Central to the discussion and, indeed, to the understanding of such issues is an understanding of the nature, purposes, and foundations of language rights. Language rights, like language attitudes, are inevitably going to be either challenged or reinforced in all educational settings, but arguably nowhere more significantly than in the foreign language classroom. The foreign language educator, in short, has a powerful and important role to play in ensuring that students become aware of language rights as a component of human rights, both in their own lives and in the lives of others. This means that an awareness of and sensitivity to the issues surrounding bilingual education in general, and language minority students in particular, should in fact be of grave concern to the foreign language educator.

To argue that language educators should advocate for language minority students is not to suggest that all bilingual education approaches and programs should be supported. Good, effective bilingual education has a demonstrated positive impact on student learning; bad bilingual education is simply bad education and should be rejected as such. Perhaps the best advice one can give in this regard is that offered by Stephen Krashen:

> Opposition to bilingual education has never been more intense. I would like to suggest a simple means of overcoming this problem: Make bilingual education so successful that there is simply no doubt of its effectiveness. . . . While bilingual education is doing very well, it can do much better. In my opinion, bilingual programs will not realize their true potential unless they do a much better job of providing a print-rich environment in the primary language, and encouraging children to read. The case for reading in bilingual education rests firmly on theory and research. (1996, p. 65)

Insofar as bilingual and other language educators take Krashen's advice to heart, the education of all children in our society—language minority and language majority alike—will benefit.

QUESTIONS FOR REFLECTION AND DISCUSSION

1. This chapter begins by identifying six common, core assumptions about meeting the needs of language minority students that are, the author claims, "shared by virtually all educators, policy makers, and indeed, by most individuals in the general public." Review this list of assumptions and decide whether or not you agree with them. Are there any that you would word differently? Why?
2. A common practice in foreign language education is to immerse the student in the target language to as great a degree as is possible. How, and why, is this practice different from the approach taken in most contemporary bilingual education programs in the United States?
3. María Estela Brisk is quoted as arguing, "The paradox of bilingual education is that when it is employed in private schools for the children of elites throughout the world it is accepted as educationally valid. . . . However, when public schools implemented bilingual education for language minority students over the past 50 years, bilingual education became highly controversial." What are the social and educational lessons that can be learned from this paradox?
4. What are the implications of the concept of linguistic human rights for minority language students in the U.S. setting? To what extent are these rights currently honored and to what extent, and in what ways, are they violated?
5. What are the implications of the concept of linguistic human rights for students enrolled in foreign language courses in the U.S. setting? Are there different implications depending on the student's first language?

FURTHER READING

Bilingual education has been an area in which there have been a significant number of outstanding introductory works published in recent years. Among those that I believe are most helpful in understanding the complexities of contemporary bilingual education are Colin Baker's *Foundations of Bilingual Education and Bilingualism* (3rd ed.) (2001), María Estela Brisk's *Bilingual Education: From Compensatory to Quality Schooling* (1998), Jim Cummins's *Language, Power and Pedagogy: Bilingual Children in the Crossfire* (2000), and Ofelia García and Colin Baker's edited *Policy and Practice in Bilingual Education: Extending the Foundations* (1995). For individuals interested in the growing literature on language rights, Robert Phillipson's edited *Festschrift* for his wife, Tove Skutnabb-Kangas, entitled *Rights to Language: Equity, Power, and Education* (2000) provides a broad, general introduction to many of the core issues.

NOTES

1. The late Laurie McDade once took me to task for suggesting that, in the context of contemporary U.S. society, linguistic differences can, in fact, constitute pragmatic social deficits. Her position was that radical pedagogy requires that linguistic differences be used as a way of emphasizing "the power of the hegemonic discourse of language competence to silence and displace a critical inquiry into the gap between the promise of attained competence and the access to multivocal students to accomplish more than just 'limited mobility' in their lives" (1987, pp. 77–78). I argued then, and would still maintain, that while this is all well and good, the lack of competence in the dominant language variety of the society nevertheless effectively eliminates almost any chance of individual advancement. Ultimately, the point at which Laurie and I disagree is the likelihood of radical social change in the near future. If one believes that our society, as currently constituted, is likely to experience significant changes with respect to power, hegemony, and class, then the argument for ensuring that students have access to the dominant language variety is, admittedly, far less compelling.

2. I find the use of the term "potentially English proficient," although well intentioned, nevertheless somewhat bizarre. Presumably every human being is "potentially English proficient"—just as each of us is also "potentially Spanish proficient," "potentially Russian proficient," and "potentially Zulu proficient." To use this term, it seems to me, is to miss the point. Yes, every child could learn English. The question is whether they are in a social and educational context in which that is a goal.

Chapter 9

Language for Oppression, Language for Liberation: Language Policy as Applied Sociolinguistics

In many parts of the contemporary world, specific language policies serve important functions in supporting the social, cultural, political, and educational agendas and policies of different governments and regimes. As Tollefson has noted,

> Language policy is a form of disciplinary power. Its success depends in part upon the ability of the state to structure into the institutions of society the differentiation of individuals into "insiders" and "outsiders." . . . To a large degree, this occurs through the close association between language and nationalism. By making language a mechanism for the expression of nationalism, the state can manipulate feelings of security and belonging . . . the state uses language policy to discipline and control its workers by establishing language-based limitations on education, employment, and political participation. (1991, pp. 207–208)

Language policies can have such powerful effects and such broad reach because, as Robert Cooper has noted, "Language is the fundamental institution of society, not only because it is the first human institution experienced by the individual, but also because all other institutions are built upon its regulatory patterns" (1989, p. 182). There is an extensive body of literature devoted to language policies in various nations, as well as in international bodies, including recent work that focuses especially on the role of language policy in educational settings (see Tollefson, 2002). Such scholarship is immensely valuable and has much to teach us as language educators. In addition, the study of language policy, which has been largely concentrated on other societies, has significant implications for our own society as well. Indeed, the debates about African American Vernacular English, bilingual education programs, and even the status of foreign language education programs are all examples of language policies in the U.S. context—and all, as we have seen, are certainly in need of more careful and thoughtful analysis than they most often receive.[1]

In this chapter, our focus will be on the nature of language planning as an applied sociolinguistic activity. We begin with a broad overview of the nature and purposes of language policy activities, then turn to the functions of language policy, its formation and implementation, and its evaluation. We follow this with a discussion of the use and misuse of language policy to achieve social, political, and educational ends. The chapter concludes with a case study that will, I hope, make clear the power and significance of language policy in education: that of pre- and post-apartheid South Africa.

LANGUAGE POLICY IN SCHOOL AND SOCIETY

Language planning and language policy formulation and implementation have been, and continue to be, important elements of national social and educational policy in many societies, and this has been especially true in the developing world as efforts are made to address the legacy of colonialism and, in many cases, the ongoing presence of considerable cultural and linguistic diversity (see, for example, Mazrui & Mazrui, 1998; Phillipson, 1998; Reagan, 1996; Schiffman, 1996; Weinstein, 1990). Questions of national and official language selection; orthographic selection and spelling standardization, language use in government, judicial, and educational settings; and language status and power are rarely made easily, and seldom avoid a considerable degree of controversy and conflict. As Phililp Altbach has noted, "Language is a key to the intellectual situation in many Third World nations. Language also plays a role in the distribution of knowledge, since the medium through which material is communicated determines accessibility. Many Third World nations are multilingual states in which questions of language policy are often politically volatile" (1984, p. 234). Such controversy is especially common where language policies are concerned with the provision of education, and this is understandable, since, as Kennedy commented, "The close relationship between use of a language and political power, socioeconomic development, national and local identity and cultural values has led to the increasing realization of the importance of language policies and planning in the life of a nation. Nowhere is this planning more crucial than in education, universally recognized as a powerful instrument of change" (1983, p. iii).

The role of language policies as a component of more general social and educational planning and policy analysis is, in short, an important facet of understanding development in many societies. Language policy as an element of national development strategy can best be understood as the deliberate attempt to change or in some way alter existing language usage and thus to resolve various types of language problems and controversies (see Christian, 1988; Cobarrubias & Fishman, 1983; Cooper, 1989; Kennedy, 1983; Lambert, 1990; Tollefson, 1991). As Eastman has explained, "Language planning is the activity of manipulating language as a social resource in order to reach objectives set out by planning agencies which, in general, are an area's governmental, educational, economic, and linguistic authorities" (1983, p. 29).

An important point that needs to be emphasized here is that language policy is profoundly political in nature (see McKay, 1993; Pennycook, 1994, 1998; Phillipson, 1992; van Dijk, 1995). Language policies involve public decisions about language, its use, status, and development—decisions that have overwhelming significance socially, economically, educationally, and politically for both society and the individual. Language policy cannot be separated from such concerns, nor, indeed, would it be appropriate to try to do so. Language policies are, in short, inevitably ideological and political in nature, and this fact must be taken into account in trying to understand them (see Tollefson, 1991, pp. 22–42).

FUNCTIONS OF LANGUAGE POLICY

Language policies can focus on issues of language status (status planning), on issues of internal development (corpus planning), or on combinations of these two types of language-planning activities (see Cobarrubias, 1983b; Williams, 1992, pp. 123–147). Status planning refers to efforts by a government or institution to determine what language or languages are to be used in particular spheres of use. The identification of a country's official language, for instance, constitutes status planning, as would a decision about what language should be used in schools. Corpus planning is often a result of status planning; it refers to efforts to standardize, elaborate, and perhaps purify a language selected for use in a particular sphere of language use (see Cluver, 1993b, p. 59).

Language policy activities, both status planning and corpus planning, can serve a number of different, although sometimes overlapping, functions: language purification, language revitalization, language reform, language standardization and modernization (see Nahir, 1977; Eastman, 1983, p. 28). Furthermore, each of these functions of language policy is reflected and manifested in virtually every sphere of human life: in the political sphere (the language of political debate and discourse, etc.), the judicial sphere (the language of law, as well as the language used by the police and courts), the religious sphere (the language used for worship, as well as the language in which key religious texts are written), the cultural sphere, the commercial and economic sphere (the language of business and industry), the educational sphere (the language of instruction, additional languages studied by pupils, etc.), and the interpersonal and familial sphere (the language used in the home, with relatives, and so on).

Ultimately, language policies are concerned with "deliberate efforts to influence the behavior of others with respect to the acquisition, structure, or functional allocation of their language codes" (Cooper, 1989, p. 45), and thus, with efforts to change society. In this, of course, language policies are similar to all social and educational policies. They are, basically, attempts to engineer human society.

THE FORMULATION AND IMPLEMENTATION OF LANGUAGE POLICIES

Language policy formulation and implementation can, at least for heuristic purposes, be conceptualized as consisting of four interrelated, and to some extent overlapping, components: (1) the initial fact-finding phase; (2) the establishment and articulation of goals, desired outcomes, and the strategies to be employed in achieving these goals and outcomes; (3) the implementation process; and (4) the evaluation of all aspects of the language planning process (see Reagan, 1983). During the first stage of this process, information about the setting in which the language policy is to be implemented is gathered. Clearly, the more information that is available to those involved in making policy, the better. It is, of course, also important that the information available be accurate—not a small point, regardless of whether one is an outsider or an insider in the setting in which the policy is to be implemented. In any event, two sorts of information must be gathered if the language policy is expected to have a significant and positive impact. The first of these is a clear understanding of the sociolinguistic setting in which the language policy is to be implemented. Especially important in this context are the common patterns of linguistic behavior and usage. The second sort of necessary information is that which will provide a reasonably accurate understanding of other relevant social, economic, and political processes and developments. It is only with a combination of these two kinds of information that a realistic perspective on need determination and assessment of needs and wants can be gained and utilized by those involved in the policy-making process.

The second step in the process of developing language policies involves identifying and articulating the goals, strategies, and outcomes to be achieved by the policies. This process will take place on several levels. The goals will serve to define and delineate the expected (and desired) outcomes of the language policy to be effected, while the strategies for achieving these outcomes, which are normally seen as primarily a technical matter, will provide the basis and direction for the implementation of the language policy. It is important to note here that in some instances it is quite common for there to be a distinction between the real purposes and goals of a particular policy, and the articulated or stated goals of the policy, and that this distinction is one we need to be aware of in understanding and evaluating language policies.

The implementation of the language policy, which is the third step in the language planning process, is in many ways the central focus of much of the language policy literature. This phase entails the mobilization of resources, general finance and personnel management, motivation, and supervision of those concerned both with the management of the language policy program and with its target populations, and preparation, sequencing, and coordination of related aspects of the language policy (such as the development of textbooks, etc.) (Rubin & Jernudd, 1971).

The last step in the process of language planning, and often the most neglected, is that of evaluation. Evaluation of the language policy should take place in two senses—both as an integral, ongoing component of all phases of the language planning process, and as a final, cumulative examination of the successes and failures of the language policy (mainly, although not exclusively, in terms of the correlation of goals and outcomes). Insofar as the predicted outcomes are still considered valid ones, the actual outcomes ought to be, as a consequence of evaluation, brought continually closer to the articulated goals of the language policy.

The model of the process of language planning that I have presented here is essentially a normative one, which is to say that this is how we might advocate that policies related to language should be made. However, such a model all too often does not actually describe or reflect reality. In fact, language policies and related policy decisions are frequently made solely or primarily on the basis of short-term political expediency, misguided assumptions and beliefs, and a range of extralinguistic factors. It is also true, however, that language policies can quite often be unsuccessful (sometimes spectacularly so), often precisely because of the way in which they were designed and implemented, as we shall see later in this chapter.

THE EVALUATION OF LANGUAGE POLICIES

The evaluation of social and educational policies has become something of a growth industry over the past half century, as both the number and relative importance of policies has grown in U.S. society. It is, of course, not only appropriate but reasonable for us to seek to determine if the policies that we fund are effective at accomplishing their ends and purposes. However, much of the evaluation activity related to both social and educational policies has tended to be technicist in nature, presupposing the legitimacy and desirablity of the policies being evaluated. In other words, evaluation most often is concerned simply with determining whether, and how well, stated objectives have been met or achieved, not with examining those objectives themselves. Although this is obviously an important matter, it begs the broader question of the ethical value of the policy examined. An extreme version of this process would be for us to examine the scheduling of trains in Nazi Germany to determine whether the transportation of people to the death camps was being optimally effected. The evaluation of the effectiveness of the policy must, in short, be understood to be separate from the ethical evaluation of that policy.

As a way of addressing this matter, the philosopher Donna Kerr (1976) has suggested four tests that any good public policy must pass. These four tests, and the fundamental questions that they seek to raise, are:

The desirability test: Is the goal of the policy one that the community as a whole believes to be desirable?

The justness test: Is the policy just and fair? That is, does it treat all people in an equitable and appropriate manner?

The effectiveness test: Is the policy effective? Does it achieve its objectives?

The tolerability test: Is the policy resource-sensitive? Is it viable in the context in which it is to be effected?

These four tests are quite useful in evaluating language policies and can serve as a working model for analyzing different language-planning processes, providing us with a series of questions that can be used in evaluating different language policy options and, indeed, can be used in evaluating other sorts of social and educational policies as well. Even more, they necessarily require us to focus our attention not only on matters of effectiveness but also on broader social, ethical, and philosophical matters related to the particular policy.

THE USE AND MISUSE OF LANGUAGE POLICY

Language policy as an applied sociolinguistic activity has the potential to function either as a tool for empowerment and liberation or as a means of oppression and domination. This is the case, in part, because language planning and language policy activities often involve both implicit and explicit goals and objectives. Further, and closely related to the presence of both implicit and explicit goals and objectives in language planning and language policy, is the fundamentally political and ideological nature of such activities (see Cobarrubias, 1983a; Joseph & Taylor, 1990; Phillipson, 1992). Indeed, not only can language policy be used for good or ill—there are abundant cases of both sorts of uses of language policy and language planning. We turn now to an especially powerful example of where language policy was used to accomplish what most of us would agree were morally despicable ends and is now being utilized to achieve far more defensible and progressive ends: the case of pre- and post-apartheid South Africa.

LANGUAGE POLICY FOR OPPRESSION AND EMPOWERMENT[2]

The late twentieth century was a time of incredible change. One of the more exciting and promising events of the period was the end of apartheid and the establishment of a truly democratic society in South Africa. The post-apartheid period in South Africa has been one in which political, social and economic change has taken place on an incredibly widespread scale as the society attempts to redress the harms and injustices perpetuated by the apartheid regime. Given the historic importance of language policy activities in South African society, it is hardly surprising that this is an area that has received significant attention from the new government (see de Klerk & Barkhuizen, 1998; Mtuze, 1993; Reagan, 2000a). This fact alone would make the South African case worth a careful and thorough reexamination, but in fact there are even broader reasons for focusing on issues of language policy in contemporary South Africa. As Jan Blommaert noted,

> The 1990s . . . have been marked by a renewed interest in language planning. The historical changes in South Africa triggered a new enthusiasm among language scholars, and almost automatically drove them into the direction of language planning issues because of the nature of the political-ideological debate surrounding the end of apartheid. Issues of national and subnational identity, of culture and language, featured prominently in almost any debate on the future of South Africa, and the new Republic set an important precedent by allowing eleven languages to be used as official languages instead of the usual one, two or four of most other African states. Here was a country which championed multilingualism as a symbol of political and cultural pluralism. (1996, p. 203)

The South African case raises a number of important issues of concern for those interested in language policy: issues of multilingualism, linguistic diversity, linguistic integration, linguistic equity, and language rights. Further, South Africa is fascinating for those interested in matters of language because it is characterized by elements of both the "developed" and the "developing" worlds, and thus, to some extent, provides us with a microcosm of the broader international issues related to language. By far the wealthiest and most developed of all the nations of Africa, South Africa has a well-developed infrastructure that in many ways parallels those of western Europe and North America, a large and well-educated professional work force, and significant natural resources, including a very modern and productive agricultural sector. At the same time, South Africa is a society with fairly extensive linguistic diversity, a low literacy rate, serious problems of social and economic inequity, limited resources that are insufficient for meeting the expectations of most people in the society, and a rapidly growing population for which its infrastructure is nowhere near adequate. From a linguistic perspective, South Africa is a reasonably diverse society in which English plays a key role both as a native language of some South Africans and as a common lingua franca for others, but is by no means demographically a majority language in the society.

In the years since the 1994 election, South Africa has begun seriously and thoughtfully to address many of the challenges related to language and language policy that will face virtually all societies in the years ahead. Its experiences in this regard are both telling and significant and have far broader implications for other societies. In this section of the chapter, recent developments in South Africa with respect to language policy will be explored, and possible lessons for efforts to promote linguistic diversity in multilingual settings will be identified.

South African society is characterized by extensive diversity. The society is multiracial, multicultural, multireligious, and multilingual. Indeed, the diversity present in contemporary South Africa is arguably nowhere manifested more clearly than in the case of language. In addition to Afrikaans and English, which during the apartheid era served as the country's co-official languages, nine indigenous African languages and five Indian languages are spoken. The situation is further complicated by the presence of a number of immigrant languages, languages used primarily or exclusively for religious purposes (Arabic, Hebrew, and Sanskrit), sign languages, and various kinds of nonstandard languages and language varieties. Despite this high degree of linguistic diversity, which is of course far from uncommon elsewhere in the developing world, South Africa also shares a number of linguistic characteristics with the world's so-called developed nations. The country's linguistic diversity includes a language of wider communication, English, which is widely spoken throughout the country and by at least some members of all of the different ethnolinguistic groups. There are a high level and degree of bilingualism and even multilingualism, reflecting the educational level of the population as well as the extensive intergroup contact that continues, in spite of the legacy of apartheid, to characterize South African society (see Kaschula & Anthonissen, 1995). And, although still far too low to be acceptable, and certainly skewed disproportionately toward certain groups at the expense of others, the literacy rate in South Africa is impressive when compared with that of virtually any other African society (see, for example, National Education Policy Investigation, 1993b, pp. 69–70; Pretorius & Lemmer, 1998; Prinsloo & Breier, 1996).

Language and the *taalstryd,* or "language struggle," has been a central point of disagreement and debate throughout the history of South Africa, especially, though by no means exclusively, in the educational sphere (see, for example, Hartshorne, 1987, 1992). Under the apartheid regime, the language medium question was most controversial in Black education, where the policy of initial mother-tongue instruction was widely denounced as an attempt to retribalize black South Africans (see Alexander, 1989). To some extent, though, it must be remembered that the mother-tongue policy was in fact a reflection of the historical *taalstryd* which took place in the white community of South Africa in the nineteenth and early twentieth centuries, since that struggle deeply influenced both white perceptions and government policy with regard to language policies in education. This earlier *taalstryd* had focused in part on the rights of Afrikaners to educate their children in their mother tongue, in the face of ongoing efforts at anglicization (see Reagan, 1986a, 1986b, 1986c; Steyn 1980, 1987). Although the tensions between English and Afrikaans were never eliminated, government policies of what might be termed "active official bilingualism," coupled with English and Afrikaans speakers attending their own-medium schools, worked to mitigate what tensions existed between the two subgroups of the white population.

Language remained a highly controversial issue in black education throughout the apartheid era, however (Alexander, 1990; Hartshorne, 1987; Marivate, 1993; Reagan, 1984, 1986a, 1986b; Reagan & Ntshoe, 1987). Somewhat ironically, it was the Nationalist government that supported mother-tongue schooling for blacks, while blacks themselves, for the most part, opposed such schooling. It is this irony that provides, at least in part, a key to understanding the apartheid-era (and, indeed, much of the post-apartheid) debate on language policy in South African education (Heugh, 1995; Reagan, 1986a, 1986d, 1998b). The apartheid regime consistently favored mother-tongue schooling for blacks (and, in fact, for almost all children in the country), but for quite different reasons than those used to defend mother-tongue instruction for white children (see Hartshorne, 1987, 1992; Reagan, 1998b). It is clear that mother-tongue programs for blacks were not only consistent with the ideology of apartheid, they functioned as one of the pillars of apartheid in perpetuating both racial and ethnolinguistic divisions in South African society (see Reagan, 1987b). Mother-tongue schooling for blacks was employed from the passage of the Bantu Education Act of 1953 to the end of the apartheid era to support the social and educational goals of Verwoerdian-style apartheid (Thompson, 1985). The apartheid regime used such programs to reinforce ethnic and tribal identity among black schoolchildren, seeking to "divide and conquer" by encouraging ethnolinguistic divisions within the black community (Hartshorne, 1987, 1992; Heugh, 1985. For a discussion of this phenomenon in other colonial settings, see for example Mansour, 1993, pp. 58–61). As Barnard perceptively noted,

> *Moedertaalonderwys* . . . is not the Afrikaans term for mother-tongue instruction. It is a political concept which has its roots in the dogma of Christian National Education. According to this dogma, each "race" or "*volk*" has its own identity which sets it apart from all others. . . . Surely one has to wonder and become suspicious when there is this insistence on the part of the authorities to force upon all children, against the wishes of their parents, a particular language. . . . What is being attempted is certainly not mother-tongue education in the interests of the children but the enforcement of "*moedertaalonderwys*" as an instrument of social control and subjugation, as a means to an end. (Quoted in Heugh, 1987, pp. 143–144)

Given this historical background, it is easy to understand the resistance to mother-tongue education, as well as to mandatory instruction in Afrikaans (see Reagan, 1985, 1987a), found in many parts of the black community during the apartheid era. Indeed, schooling designed to emphasize ethnic and cultural differences all too often falls prey to this sort of "pluralist dilemma." As the Australian scholar Brian Bullivant observed some years ago, programs designed and intended to encourage ethnic identification, including various kinds of multicultural education programs in many western societies, "are ideal methods of controlling knowledge/power, while appearing through symbolic political language to be acting solely from the best of motives in the interests of the ethnic groups themselves" (1981, p. 291). This was clearly the case in South Africa, though few blacks were taken in by the rhetoric of pluralism. Unfortunately, the legacy of apartheid includes suspicions about mother-tongue instruction in any form, which has led to ongoing tensions with respect to educational language policy in post-apartheid South Africa. As Nkonko Kamwangamalu has observed,

> [A]s a result of apartheid policies, for the black people in South Africa mother-tongue education has been synonymous with inferior education. Consequently, they have tended to resist such education and to opt, instead, for English-medium education. However, as the literature shows, English-medium education has tended to be elitist and has failed to promote literacy in South Africa, much as it has failed in the rest of the continent . . . mother-tongue education might become an alternative to English-medium education provided that it is "cleansed" of the stigma it has been carrying since the heyday of apartheid. (1997, p. 249)

In the aftermath of the 1994 election, the Government of National Unity, as well as the new constitution, recognized eleven official languages, rejecting the historical bilingual policy (which reflected only the linguistic diversity of white South Africa) with a multilingual policy more accurately reflecting the reality of South African society (see Department of National Education, 1997). Further, the *Reconstruction and Development Programme* of the African National Congress called for the development of "all South

African languages and particularly the historically neglected indigenous languages" (1994, p. 71). It is important to note here that this commitment to multilingualism did not entail maintaining all public and private sector services in all eleven official languages, which would have been almost certain to prove cost prohibitive. Such a scenario would have assumed that past models of bilingualism would be superimposed on current realities—that is, that the absolute equality of English and Afrikaans sought by the apartheid regime (primarily as a component of Afrikaner political ideology) would be the model for the language policy to be pursued by the democratic government of South Africa with respect to all eleven official languages. This, of course, need not be the case, and in fact has quite clearly not been the case in contemporary South Africa. Rather, the focus of the new constitution with respect to official languages and issues of language rights is intended to be as inclusive as possible, and supportive of multilingualism, but also pragmatically and economically feasible (see Constitutional Assembly, 1997; Department of National Education, 1997). The challenge that the new constitution attempts to meet is to ensure individual language rights (no small matter in a nation in which roughly half the population do not speak English) and to symbolically emphasize the multilingual and multicultural nature of the society, while at the same time allocating resources in a economically and politically responsible manner. Although one could see such efforts on the part of the government as disingenuous and even misleading, given the de facto dominant status of English in South Africa (see Verhoef, 1998a, 1998b), such a view is not really merited by the realities of the situation. Indeed, the government has made a significant commitment to the promotion of multilingualism in South Africa and is in fact engaged in a very much up-hill battle to do so in the context of the immense economic and social power of English (see Barkhuisen & Gough, 1996; Chick & Wade, 1997; Chisange & Kamwangamalu, 1997; Heugh, 1993), as we shall see.

With the end of the apartheid era and the election of a democratic government in South Africa, language policy in general, and in education in particular, has inevitably received considerable attention as the institutions of South African society are transformed (for detailed discussions of contemporary language policy in South Africa, see Alexander, 2001; Beukes, 1991a, 1991b, 1992, 1996; Beukes & Barnard, 1994; Chick, 1992; Cluver, 1992; Desai, 1991, 1994; Heugh, 1995; Kashoki, 1993; Pieterse, 1991; Prinsloo & Malan, 1988; Prinsloo, Peeters, Turi & van Rensburg, 1993; Reagan, 1990c, 1995b; Ridge, 1996; Schuring, 1991; Swanepoel & Pieterse, 1993). One powerful example of this concern with language policy, especially in the educational sphere, is *A Policy Framework for Education and Training,* which is a discussion document issued by the Education Department of the African National Congress and which sets out proposals related to issues of education and training (African National Congress,

1995). Included in this document are four lessons that are identified as being of the utmost importance in order that the "cycle of language oppression be broken" in South African society in general, and in education in particular:

- Language policy in education should be the subject of a nation-wide consultative process, to ensure that proposed changes in policy have the broad consent of the language communities which will be directly affected by them.
- No person or language community should be compelled to receive education through a language of learning they do not want.
- No language community should have reason to fear that the education system will be used to suppress its mother tongue.
- Language restrictions should not be used to exclude citizens from educational opportunities. (African National Congress, 1995, p. 62)

In order to ensure that these lessons are reflected in any language policy to be developed in South Africa, the African National Congress discussion document goes on to identify general principles upon which educational language policy should be based. These principles include the right of the individual to choose which language or languages to study and to use as a language of learning (medium of instruction); the right of the individual to develop the linguistic skills, in the language or languages of his or her choice, which are necessary for full participation in national, provincial, and local life; and the necessity to promote and develop South African languages that were previously disadvantaged and neglected (African National Congress, 1995, p. 63). It seems clear, then, that both the lessons to be learned from past experience and the general principles upon which educational language policies are to be based are reflective, in large part, of concerns about past practices in South Africa and are intended to be consistent with the goal of a democratic and nonracial language policy, as well as with the constitutional recognition of the equality of the eleven official languages of South Africa.

An excellent example of the sort of approach to language policy formulation envisioned by the African National Congress is the National Education Policy Investigation's work on language (National Education Policy Investigation, 1992a, 1992b, 1993a, 1993b). The National Education Policy Investigation was a project undertaken by the National Education Coordinating Committee between 1990 and 1992 that explored policy options in the educational sphere "within a value framework derived from the ideals of the broad democratic movement" (National Education Policy Investigation, 1992b, p. vi). The National Education Policy Investigation sought to set the stage for ongoing protracted and extensive debates about educational policy issues. Indeed, at one point in the mid-1990s, more than sixty separate committees around the country were involved in discussions of national language policy. The focus of the National Education Policy Investigation can clearly be seen in the final concluding paragraph of the language report, which argues that

> Any [language policy] option that is chosen can have an empowering or a disempowering effect on learners, depending on its suitability for the particular school's context, on how it is implemented, and on how it relates to the national language policy of the country. There is no one policy that is ideal for all schools. Language policy for education needs, therefore, to be flexible without being so laissez faire as to allow the perpetuation of present discriminatory policies or ill-informed choices of alternatives to them. (1992b, p. 93)

Current efforts now under way in South Africa are moving in accord with this admonition, and it is clear that the government has had the expectation that, as a consequence, the educational language policies that are in the process of being developed are far more likely to receive broad popular support than have past policies (see Reagan, 1995b). Perhaps the most outstanding example of this has been the reception of the final report of the Language Plan Task Group (LANGTAG). This group was created in 1995 by Dr. B. S. Ngubane, the Minister of Arts, Culture, Science and Technology, with the explicit task of devising a national language plan for South Africa. The final LANGTAG report, issued in August 1996, clearly attempted to achieve the following objectives, which had been identified by Dr. Ngubane:

- All South Africans should have access to all spheres of South African society by developing and maintaining a level of spoken and written language which is appropriate for a range of contexts in the official language(s) of their choice.
- All South Africans should have access to the learning of languages other than their mother tongue.
- The African languages, which have been disadvantaged by the linguicist policies of the past, should be developed and maintained.
- Equitable and widespread language services should be established. (Language Plan Task Group, 1996, p. 7)

In short, what is occurring with respect to language policy in the contemporary South African context, at least from the perspective of the government, is an ongoing effort to democratize the language planning process and to ensure the protection of language rights for all South Africans. More specifically, the government is engaged in a multifaceted effort in the sphere of language policy and language planning, including not only status and corpus planning but also language attitude planning and the articulation and implementation of protections for individual language rights.

Status planning has already taken place in terms of the selection of the country's eleven official languages, as well as in the ongoing development of language medium policies in the educational sphere (Beukes, 1992). Further, one of the more interesting and unusual aspects of the status planning process in the South African case has been the inclusion of the status of South African Sign Language in the discussions and debates about language policy (see Penn 1992, 1993; Penn & Reagan 1990, 1995, 1999; Reagan & Penn 1997). Unlike such discussions related to American Sign Language in the U.S. context, the South African debate did not revolve around questions of whether South African Sign Language is a real language but, rather, simply around what its constitutional status should be. Although ultimately not included as an official language in the new constitution, South African Sign Language does nevertheless enjoy constitutional recognition and support—and in fact the significance of its exclusion as an official language would seem to be primarily symbolic in nature, since the language and educational rights of the deaf individual are clearly protected by the constitution (Constitutional Assembly, 1997; see also Office of the Deputy President, 1997).

Corpus planning is an area in which South Africa has had extensive experience. The support and development of Afrikaans as an official language in South Africa were an incredibly powerful example of corpus planning (see Steyn, 1992, 1998), but even in terms of African languages, there have been long-term efforts at corpus planning. As Heinz Kloss noted in the late 1970s,

> Committees have been working for some twenty years on languages like Southern Sotho, Pedi, Zulu, and Tsonga, to create scientific vocabularies in those languages with a view to the production of school books in them at the upper secondary level. . . . In South Africa, more qualified scholars, White and Black, are working on this "linguistic engineering" than in all the rest of Africa. Even Swahili is well behind the South African languages in educational development, in spite of its easy lead in political status. (1978, p. 21)

While true, Kloss's comments ignored an important aspect of the corpus planning efforts during the apartheid period. A more critical, and accurate, view of these efforts was provided by the African National Congress, which observed,

> The languages of the people are not permitted to be developed by them in their own way. Ignorant and officious White professors sit on education committees as arbiters of African languages and books without consultation with the people concerned. The grotesque spectacle is seen of the White government of South Africa posing as a "protector" of so-called Bantu culture and traditions of which they know nothing. (Quoted in Heugh, 1987, p. 269)

Perhaps the central difference between contemporary corpus planning efforts and those of the past is to be found not so much in particular decisions or policies as in the advent of democratic language planning activities grounded in the communities in which the affected languages are actually used (see, for example, Department of Arts, Culture, Science and Technology, 1997; Mtintsilana & Morris, 1988).

Beyond status and corpus planning, however, a significant focus of contemporary language planning activities in South Africa is on what might be termed language attitude planning (Finchilescu & Nyawose, 1998; Louw-Potgieter & Louw, 1991; Verhoef, 1998b). Language attitude planning in the South African context actually has both an articulated and an unarticulated purpose. The articulated purpose is to raise consciousness about the multilingual nature of South African society, to increase toleration and acceptance of language differences, and to encourage the growth of individualism, bilingualism, and multilingualism in the country's languages (see Beukes, 1996; Heugh, Siegrühn & Plüddemann, 1995; King & van den Berg, 1992; Mawasha, 1996; Verhoef, 1998a). The unarticulated but nevertheless powerful purpose of language attitude planning in contemporary South Africa is to attempt to address the concerns about the future of specific languages in the country—most notably Afrikaans (see Brink, 1984; Cluver, 1993a; Combrink, 1991; Kriel, 1998; Maartens, 1994; van Rensburg, 1993, 1997; Webb, 1992) but also European languages (see Department of Education and Culture, 1992; B. Smit, 1993, 1996; U. Smit, 1994; Strike, 1996) and many of the African languages (Baai, 1992; Msimang, 1992; Mutasa, 1996; see also Robinson, 1996). Indeed, changing common negative attitudes about the African languages in South Africa is one of the greater challenges faced by language planners in the new regime, as indeed has been the case in many other post-independence countries (see Rahman, 1996, 1998; Ramanathan, 1999; Sarinjeive, 1997, 1999; Schiffman, 1996; Schmied, 1991; Schuring, 1991). Hardly surprisingly, it has been in the educational sphere where such efforts face the greatest resistance, due both to the historical significance of mother-tongue schooling and the very real practical advantages of English (see Barkhuisen & Gough, 1996; Chick & Wade, 1997; Chisange & Kamwangamalu, 1997; Heugh, 1993; Ndebele, 1987; Peirce, 1989; Tollefson, 2000).

Finally, the establishment and promotion of language rights have been an ongoing concern of the post-apartheid South African government (see Co-ordinating Committee on the National Action Plan, 1998; Department of Arts, Culture, Science and Technology, 1999; Desai, 1994). This concern with language rights in South Africa has in many ways paralleled a growing international interest in language rights, and in the South African case, such matters have demonstrably been taken seriously both in terms of constitutional and legal policy and in terms of practice (see Mamdani,

2000; Musker, 1997). And yet, while all this may sound quite promising and is certainly a dramatic improvement on the apartheid past, it is by no means the whole story. What seems to be taking place in contemporary South African society is that the linguistic market has created a context in which competence in English is the primary criterion for economic success and social mobility, and this context has been clearly recognized and acted upon by the population (see Gaganakis, 1992). The result has been a decline in the teaching and learning of most other languages (see Reagan, 2000a; Strike, 1996) in the country[3] and an incredible growth in the teaching of English. To be sure, this growth has also inspired increased emphasis on critical language awareness in the teaching of English (see Fairclough, 1989, 1992, 1995; Janks, 1991, 1997; Janks & Ivanič, 1992), and the clear success of English in the marketplace has raised serious ideological concerns both in South African and elsewhere (Bamgbose, Banjo & Thomas, 1997; de Kadt, 1996; Holborow, 1999; Krishnaswamy & Burde, 1998; Lowenberg, 1995; Mansoor, 1993; Phillipson & Skutnabb-Kangas, 1996). Nevertheless, perhaps the clearest lesson that contemporary South Africa has to teach us has to do with the overwhelming dominance of English, a dominance supported both by economic factors and by tacit government acquiescence in the face of considerable linguistic diversity. It is interesting that this has been the case even given strongly articulated language policies that encourage and support multilingualism. Issues of linguistic toleration, language rights, and the relationship of language to ethnic identity notwithstanding, the economic return on competence in English is effectively overwhelming efforts to encourage competence in other languages (see also Mazrui & Mazrui, 1998; Pennycook, 1994, 2000; Phillipson, 1992; Phillipson & Skutnabb-Kangas, 1995). English-medium schooling is rapidly becoming the dominant model in much of South Africa; the study of other languages (European, Afrikaans, and even indigenous African languages) has substantially declined and is continuing to do so (see Reagan, 2000a); publications and other kinds of media are increasingly dominated by English; and even in Parliament and government circles, the language of daily operation tends to be English. Although neither Afrikaans nor most of the indigenous African languages are in any immediate danger, a language shift toward English is clearly taking place at an accelerated rate, and the number of spheres in which languages other than English can be used is rapidly declining. What is constitutionally a multilingual society is in fact a diglossic one in which English is the high variety and other languages are low varieties (see Kamwangamalu, 1998). In short, what the South African case now appears to demonstrate at this point in time is the incredible power of the English language, and, in fact, the threat that such power poses to virtually all other languages, especially in multilingual environments.[4]

CONCLUSION

Our discussion thus far might lead one to believe that issues of language policy take place only at the national and international levels. If this were in fact the case, there would still be compelling reasons for foreign language educators to be interested in and concerned with such undertakings. However, in reality language policies exist on all levels of society—and one of the places in which they are actually most powerful is in the context of the school (see, for instance, Lambert, 1994). All schools have language policies, though these policies may be implicit or explicit, and all teachers are involved in the implementation of these language policies. As David Corson has compellingly explained,

> School language policies are viewed by many in education as an integral and necessary part of the administration and curriculum practice of schools. A language policy . . . identifies areas of the school's scope of operations and program where language problems exist that need the commonly agreed approach offered by a policy. A language policy sets out what the school intends to do about these areas of concern and includes provisions for follow-up, monitoring, and revision of the policy itself. (1999, p. 1)

The decision about the language (or languages) to be used as the medium of instruction in the school is a language policy decision, as are decisions about what other languages are to be taught, how language will be taught, the relative significance of different languages in the school context, and so on. For the foreign language educator, this means that our very existence as a profession depends on language policies. The need for students to study a foreign language as a component of their general education is, then, part of the language policy discourse and practice in any school. Which foreign languages are to be taught is likewise a language policy decision.

Beyond such direct concerns, language policy should also be of concern to foreign language educators in terms of our efforts to promote the sort of critical language awareness in students that is being advocated in this book. Among the key concepts that critical language awareness approaches to language and language study seek to convey to students are the following:

- People have the power to shape the conventions that underlie discourse, just as much as any other social practices.
- Although we tend to accept the way language is, and the way discourses operate, they are changing all the time.
- Forms of discourse receive their value according to the positions of their users in systems of power relations.
- Struggles over the control of discourse are the main ways in which power is obtained and exercised in modern societies. (Corson, 1999, p. 143–144)

Further, such concepts are manifested in efforts to promote social awareness of discourse, critical awareness of language variety, and practice for change. In short, it is clear that language policies can and do serve a variety of quite different ends. Language policies can serve as a tool for empowering groups and individuals, for creating and strengthening national bonds and ties, and for maximizing educational and economic development, but they can also be used (and often have been used) to maintain and perpetuate oppression, social class discrimination, and social and educational inequity (see Fairclough, 1989; Pennycook, 1994, 1998; Skutnabb-Kangas, 2000a, 2000b). Language policies, if they are to be defensible, must entail the active involvement and participation of those for whom they are intended. Only when emerging in such a context can language policies contribute to the creation of more just, humane, and legitimate social and educational policies. As James Tollefson argued quite powerfully, "the foundation for rights is *power* and . . . constant *struggle* is necessary to sustain language rights" (1991, p. 167). It is just such an understanding that we need to promote and encourage in our students.

QUESTIONS FOR REFLECTION AND DISCUSSION

1. James Cooper has argued that language policies are "deliberate efforts to influence the behavior of others with respect to the acquisition, structure, or functional allocation of their language codes." Doesn't this definition suggest that all second and foreign language education is in fact language policy being implemented in practice?
2. In this chapter, it is suggested that questions of language policy are often politically volatile. Why do you believe that this is the case? To what extent, and for what reasons, are such issues controversial in the U.S. context? To what extent, and why, are matters of language policy in the U.S. context sometimes *not* volatile?
3. Consider the articulated and implicit language policies in a school setting with which you are familiar. Using the four policy tests proposed by Donna Kerr, to what extent are these policies defensible? What kinds of changes might be appropriate?
4. Use the four policy tests proposed by Donna Kerr to critique the language policy of the Oakland Board of Education with respect to African American Vernacular English that was discussed in chapter 5. To what extent was that policy a good policy? How might the policy have been improved?
5. There is a great deal to be learned from the South African case. What are the similarities between the U.S. and South African cases? What are the differences?

FURTHER READING

There is an extensive literature dealing with issues of language policy and language planning. Among the best general works addressing this exciting and important field in recent years have been Robert Cooper's *Language Planning and Social Change* (1989), Robert Kaplan and Richard Baldauf's *Language Planning: From Practice to Theory* (1997), Tove Skutnabb-Kangas's masterful *Linguistic Genocide in Education—Or Worldwide Diversity and Human Rights?* (2000), and James Tollefson's *Planning Language, Planning Inequality: Language Policy in the Community* (1991) and his edited collection *Language Policies in Education: Critical Issues* (2002). For readers specifically interested in language policy in school contexts, see David Corson's *Language Policy in Schools: A Resource for Teachers and Administrators* (1999).

NOTES

1. I do not mean to suggest here that there has been no work on language policy in the U.S. context. In fact, there has been some outstanding work done (see, for example, Ricento & Burnaby, 1998). My concern, rather, is with the limited awareness of this literature, even among educators for whom it ought to be commonplace.

2. This section of the chapter is drawn largely from earlier works I have published on the topic of language policy and language planning in the South African context (see, for example, Reagan, 2001b).

3. It is interesting to note here that the decline in interest in studying the African languages in the South African context has been taking place even as there has been a dramatic improvement in the pedagogical quality of teaching materials and textbooks for many of these languages. This has been especially true in the cases of Xhosa (see Munnik, 1994; Pinnock, 1994; Zotwana, 1991) and Zulu (see Nxumalo & Cioran, 1996), although high quality Sesotho (see Mokoena, 1998) materials have also been developed and texts and materials for other languages are in production. In addition, multimedia programs are being produced, most notably by the Multimedia Education Project of the University of Cape Town (see Dowling, 1998).

4. Although the overwhelming majority of studies dealing with contemporary language policy in South Africa have viewed such developments favorably, there is at least one notable exception. Geneva Smitherman, who is well known for her work on African American Vernacular English in the U.S. context, has critiqued post-apartheid language policy on the grounds that it is too much of a compromise and that the continued hegemonic status of English and Afrikaans as official languages is problematic (see Smitherman, 2000, pp. 314–333; 2001). Although Smitherman, as I have suggested in this chapter, is right about the hegemonic power of English in particular, her alternatives—various ways of privileging African languages in the South African context—are also problematic on a number of grounds. In addition, although Smitherman draws an analogy between African American Vernacular English in the U.S. context and the African languages in the South African context, a more accurate analogy would be between African American Vernacular English in the United States and Cape Afrikaans (widely spoken by the so-called "Coloured" population) in South Africa.

Chapter 10

Critical Language Awareness in the Curriculum

It is hard to imagine how we might exaggerate the role of language in human life. In a wonderful essay titled, "How to Be the Centre of the Universe," the linguist Neil Smith has argued that

> Language makes us human. . . . Whatever we do, language is central to our lives, and the use of language underpins the study of every other discipline. Understanding language gives us insight into ourselves and a tool for the investigation of the rest of the universe. Proposing marriage, opposing globalization, composing a speech, all require the use of language; to buy a meal or sell a car involves communication, which is made possible by language; to be without language—as an infant, a foreigner or a stroke victim—is to be at a devastating disadvantage. Martians and dolphins, bonobos and bees, may be just as intelligent, cute, adept at social organization and morally worthwhile, but they don't share our language, they don't speak "human." (2002, p. 3)

If the centrality of language in human life is a given, this centrality must be even more true in the case of education. Leo van Lier has noted that

> There was a time, from the ancient Greeks to the late Middle Ages, when language was central in educational practices, in the form of the three branches of the *trivium*: grammar, logic, and rhetoric. Then, increasingly, language study became separated from other subjects . . . and became merely one other subject. . . . As a result, language lost its centrality and relevance as an educational focal point, and it became difficult to see how it connected to other parts of the curriculum. (1995, pp. 7–8)

Whether recognized or not, language has in fact continued to be the central element that not only makes education possible but plays a key role in the construction of knowledge for both the student and the teacher. Assumptions and beliefs about language, as well as attitudes toward it, function in important ways to color and set the parameters of the educational experience, and can, in the classroom and school contexts, serve either positive or negative ends (see Reagan, 2001a).

Language, Education, and Ideology has attempted, through a variety of lenses and the examination of a number of different aspects of language in society and in the curriculum, to begin the process of "mapping" the linguistic landscape of public schooling in the U.S. setting. It is intended to be a first step in a much longer journey. A necessary condition for the continuation of this journey—a journey that I believe to be essential to both the well-being of the language teaching professions and the establishment of social justice in our society—is the need for the development of critical language awareness not only in ourselves and among our colleagues, but even more, in our students. In this final chapter, we turn to a discussion of the nature and rationale for critical language awareness, as well as to an exploration of how such critical language awareness can be manifested in classroom practice, and how it overlaps and interfaces with critical pedagogy more broadly conceived.

WHAT IS CRITICAL LANGUAGE AWARENESS?

Critical language awareness actually constitutes a subset of "language awareness," a concept that gained increasing popularity in the language education professions in the 1980s and 1990s.[1] "Language awareness" had all of the characteristics of an educational slogan and buzzword throughout this period, and even to the present, and thus has been elusive with respect to any clear definition of its exact meaning. However, one reasonable attempt at defining the concept was made by a number of educational linguists in the early 1990s, and their working definition for the concept, which still has credibility I believe, was that language awareness involved "a person's sensitivity to and conscious awareness of the nature of language and its role in human life" (James & Garrett, 1992, p. 8). Such an awareness is certainly desirable and appropriate, but it is, in the view of many scholars, far from sufficient. As Norman Fairclough has suggested, *critical* language awareness is "an urgently needed element in language education [and] . . . coming to be a prerequisite for effective democratic citizenship, and should therefore be seen as an *entitlement* for citizens, especially children developing towards citizenship in the educational system" (1992, p. 3, emphasis in original). Fairclough also notes that critical language awareness

> presupposes and builds upon what is variously called "critical language study," "critical linguistics," or "critical discourse analysis." . . . It also presupposes a criti-

cal conception of education and schooling. . . . It is vital first of all to situate both critical language study and [critical language awareness] in their social and historical contexts. (1992, p. 2)

And what is it that makes language awareness critical? Ultimately, language awareness is critical when one is concerned with the social, political, economic, historical, and ideological contexts in which language is used, and in which language must be metalinguistically and metacognitively understood. In other words, critical language awareness involves the rejection of efforts and tendencies to reify or objectify language and linguistic discourse. Hywel Coleman, in a description of the implications of an ideological approach to the study of student and teacher behavior in the English language classroom, provides a powerful analysis that also applies to the case of critical language awareness. Coleman argues that among the implications emanating from an ideological perspective on language teaching are the following:

1. We should be aware that every manifestation of classroom practice may have meaning and value in its own context.
2. Before seeking to sweep away traditional modes of behaviour, therefore, we must examine them with care and seek to understand them.
3. When making recommendations for innovation in English language methodology, we must carry out the equivalent of an environmental audit of the impact of our proposed changes. In other words, we must seek to predict what the knock-on effect of methodological change is likely to be.
4. When making recommendations for innovation, we must explore the possibility—at least—of exploiting cultural patterns of behaviour as a way of achieving the desired change.
5. In particular, we must be alert to the possibility that learners are making effective use of learning opportunities in non-classroom contexts.
6. We must be very cautious in making evaluative judgments of current classroom practice, particularly if as observers we do not share the same ideology as the principal participants in the classroom event.
7. We must question whether there are universally appropriate ways of evaluating the success or otherwise of English language teaching projects.
8. We must learn to question the ideological origins of our own assumptions about all aspects of English language teaching in institutional contexts. (1996, p. 13)

Critical language awareness requires this same openness and flexibility. It also requires a fair degree of honesty about our own personal and institutional objectives, motives and motivations.

Beyond this, critical language awareness must also be understood to be not only an outgrowth of critical pedagogy but a necessary element of critical pedagogy in the foreign language context (see Osborn, 2000). As Catherine Wallace has suggested,

> A critical pedagogy presupposes an approach to language education in which learners and teachers aim to achieve some critical distance from language use in a range of spoken and written texts. Conversely, approaches under the broad umbrella of critical language awareness need to be located within a critical pedagogy if they are to have credibility as educational practice. . . . Critical understanding can be understood at two broad levels: first, in the cognitive sense of "conscious awareness"; secondly . . . a deeper sense of "critical" as the ability and willingness to critique the ideological bases of language choice and variation. (1997, p. 241)

Critical language awareness, like critical pedagogy in general, is in the final analysis concerned with empowerment. Empowerment involves not only helping students to recognize, understand, and question discourse, but also, as Norman Fairclough has pointed out, it "has a substantial 'shock' potential, and it can help people overcome their sense of impotence by showing them that existing orders of discourse are not immutable. The transformation of orders of discourse is a matter of the systemic de-structuring of existing orders and restructuring of new orders" (1989, p. 244). An important facet of this process of empowerment is recognizing that discourse is in fact negotiated between and among students and teachers. In short, as Karabel and Halsey observed in the late 1970s, "Teachers and pupils do not come together in a historical vacuum: the weight of precedent conditions the outcome of 'negotiation' over meaning at every turn" (1977, p. 58). Even the disempowered are not, after all, powerless.

WHY BE CRITICAL?

Why should language educators be concerned with being critical? Why, indeed, should any teacher be concerned with being critical in the sense in which the term is used in both critical pedagogy and critical language awareness? There are any number of ways in which these questions might be answered. We might, for instance, ground a response in the various "codes of ethics" that undergird the teaching profession (see Strike, Haller & Soltis, 1988; Strike & Soltis, 1992). We might, on the other hand, base a response of the role, place of functions of schooling and education in a democratic society, with especial emphasis on the development of meaningful critical thinking skills as a necessary preparation for the life of the citizen (see Gutmann, 1987; Soder, 1996). We could even address the questions by pointing out that the ability to generate a critical perspective is a key component in being an educated person—whether as a teacher, parent, citizen, or student. All of these are credible and valid responses, I believe, but perhaps the clearest and most forceful justification is that provided by Joan Wink for critical pedagogy in general:

> Why in the world does it matter? Kids matter. That's why. Our future matters. That's why. It is as simple as that. It is also something we all know. This is serious business we are talking about here. Students and teachers are hurting. We in education are a mirror of society that is more and more polarized. (2000, p. 165)

Precisely the same claims can be made for critical language awareness. Educators should be committed to encouraging the development of critical language awareness in our students because it is the right thing to do. It is a powerful way to promote social justice and the formation of a just, humane, and democratic society. It is also a way of helping individual children better understand the society in which they live, and better negotiate that society. It is, in essence, giving students the tools that they need to make their own decisions—and decisions not just about language but about every aspect of human life. This is why we should be critical and seek to promote the same in our students. Anything less is an abrogation of our duties as educators and as human beings.

MANIFESTATIONS OF CRITICAL LANGUAGE AWARENESS IN THE CLASSROOM

What would critical language awareness, properly conceived and conducted, look like in a typical language classroom? The most immediate answer that comes to mind is that it wouldn't look very much like a typical classroom at all; indeed, it could not do so and still be critical language awareness. What it would look like, though, is basically what some writers have called a "postmethod pedagogy." As Kumaravadivelu has explained, a postmodern pedagogy, which moves us beyond a simplistic transmission mode of instruction, would necessarily be one that

> Must (a) facilitate the advancement of a context-sensitive language education based on a true understanding of local linguistic, sociocultural, and political particularities; (b) rupture the reified role relationship between theorists and practitioners by enabling teachers to construct their own theory of practice; and (c) tap the sociopolitical consciousness that participants bring with them in order to aid their quest for identity formation and social transformation. (2001, p. 537)

This is not, to be sure, an easy thing to imagine, let alone to implement in practice. It is a pedagogy that is grounded in not only a rejection of, but also a critical sensitivity to, issues of linguicism[2] broadly conceived (see Phillipson, 1988). It is a pedagogy that seeks to help students construct not only knowledge of the subject matter but an understanding of the social, cultural, and ideological roles of the subject. In other words, it is ultimately a pedagogy that moves students and teachers far beyond simple models and conceptions of teaching, learning, and knowing.

TOWARD A CRITICAL SYNTHESIS

I have already argued in this chapter that critical language awareness needs to be understood not only as an outgrowth of critical pedagogy but also as a necessary element of critical pedagogy in the foreign language context. This is a start toward understanding the relationship between critical pedagogy and critical language awareness, but it is only a start. Pedagogy itself is a potentially problematic term; it has a long history and thus considerable baggage. Beyond this, it differs in important but not always recognized ways from "teaching." Roger Simon has provided a very clear way of thinking about pedagogy:

> Pedagogy is a more complex and extensive term than teaching, referring to the integration in practice of particular curriculum content and design, classroom strategies and techniques, a time and place for the practice of these . . . and evaluation purpose and methods. All of these aspects of educational practice come together in the realities of what happens in classrooms. Together they organize a view of how teachers' work within an institutional context specifies a particular version of what knowledge is of most worth, what it means to know something, and how we might construct representations of ourselves, others, and our physical and social environment. In other words, talk about pedagogy is simultaneously talk about details of what students and others might do together and the cultural politics such practices support. To propose a pedagogy is to propose a political vision . . . we cannot talk about teaching practices without talking about politics. (1987, p. 371)

If pedagogy is intrinsically political in nature, so too is language education—whether or not we seek it to be. Just as one can argue that moral education "comes with the territory" of public schooling, so must politics and ideology come with the territory. Thus, critical language awareness becomes not merely an option for the language educator but an imperative.

CONCLUSION

As I argued earlier in this book, beyond encouraging such sociolinguistic understanding, the foreign language classroom is also an ideal place to help students to begin to develop what can be called critical language awareness. The study of language needs to include not only the communicative and cultural aspects of language but also the political and ideological issues related to it. Students need to understand the ways in which language is used to convey and protect social status, as well as how it can be used to oppress and denigrate both individuals and groups. The foreign language classroom can either reinforce negative language attitudes and prejudices or be used to empower students to better understand the social roles of language in society. The choice is very much ours to make in our classrooms and in our interactions with our students. It is an important choice; perhaps among the most important choices that we can make as educators. I have every confidence that language educators will make the right choice.

QUESTIONS FOR REFLECTION AND DISCUSSION

1. Neil Smith is quoted in this chapter as saying that, "Language is what makes us human." Do you agree with this claim? To what extent is language the sine qua non for human identity? What are the implications of your answer for the complex issue of language rights?
2. This chapter has been concerned with critical language awareness. Is it possible, in your view, to talk about noncritical language awareness? What would such awareness look like, and how would it differ from critical language awareness?
3. What are the implications of the concept of an "environmental audit" for studying the culture of the foreign language classroom? What factors might one wish to include in such an audit? Why?
4. How do students negotiate meaning in the foreign language classroom? What does this tell us about the nature of language learning?
5. What does it mean to talk about critical language awareness as an "entitlement" for students, as Norman Fairclough does? In what ways might such an entitlement be (a) defined, and (b) justified?

FURTHER READING

Among the most influential writers on critical language awareness has been Norman Fairclough, and his works provide an excellent starting point for further explorations of the topic. Specifically, the works that will be of the greatest value to the reader, in my view at least, are his edited collection *Critical Language Awareness* (1992), and his *Language and Power* (1989) and *Critical Discourse Analysis* (1995). For a work that addresses the broader issues of critical reflection in foreign language education, see Osborn's *Critical Reflection and the Foreign Language Classroom* (2000).

NOTES

1. Among the best U.S. works that seek to raise issues of language awareness in general terms is Andrews (1998). Although I believe that this is an excellent work as far as it goes, it does not really move us to the level of critical language awareness.

2. As well as issues of racism, ethnocentrism, sexism, ageism, and so on, of course, all of which are, I would think, included under the broader term linguicism when linguistic and language-related matters are being discussed.

Bibliography

Abrahams, R., and R. Troike, eds. 1972. *Language and cultural diversity in American education*. Englewood Cliffs, NJ: Prentice-Hall.

Achard, P. 1993. *La sociologie du langage*. Paris: Presses Universitaires de France.

Afendras, E., and E. Kuo, eds. 1980. *Language and society in Singapore*. Singapore: University of Singapore Press.

African National Congress. 1994. *The reconstruction and development programme: A policy framework*. Johannesburg: African National Congress.

———. 1995. *A policy framework for education and training* (Discussion document). Braamfontein: Education Department, African National Congress.

Agnihotri, R., and A. Khanna. 1997. *Problematizing English in India*. New Delhi: Sage.

Aimard, P., and A. Morgon. 1985. *L'enfant sourd*. Paris: Presses Universitaires de France.

Alexander, N. 1989. *Language policy and national unity in South Africa/Azania*. Cape Town: Buchu Books.

———. 1990. The language question. In *Critical choices for South Africa*, ed. R. Schrire, 126–146. Cape Town: Oxford University Press.

———. 2001. Majority and minority languages in South Africa. In *The other languages of Europe*, ed. G. Extra and D. Gorter, 355–369. Clevedon: Multilingual Matters.

Alexander, R. 2000. *Intensive Bulgarian: A textbook and reference grammar*, Vol. 2. Madison: University of Wisconsin Press.

Allen, H., and M. Linn, eds. 1986. *Dialect and language variation*. Orlando, FL: Academic Press.

Allen, R. 1992. Teaching Arabic in the United States: Past, present, and future. In *The Arabic language in America*, ed. A. Rouchdy, 222–250. Detroit, MI: Wayne State University Press.

Almond, B. 1993. Rights. In *A companion to ethics*, ed. P. Singer, 259–269. Oxford: Basil Blackwell.

Altbach, P. 1984. The distribution of knowledge in the third world: A case study in neocolonialism. In *Education and the colonial experience,* ed. P. Altbach and G. Kelly, 229–251. New Brunswick, NJ: Transaction.

Altbach, P., G. Kelly, H. Petrie, and L. Weis, eds. 1991. *Textbooks in American society: Politics, policy, and pedagogy.* Albany: State University of New York Press.

Andersson, Y. 1990. The deaf world as a linguistic minority. In *Sign language research and application,* ed. S. Prillwitz and T. Vollhaber, 155–161. Hamburg: Signum Press.

———. 1994. Deaf people as a linguistic minority. In *Bilingualism in deaf education,* ed. I. Ahlgren and K. Hyltenstan, 9–13. Hamburg: Signum Press.

Andrews, D. 2000. Heritage learners in the Russian classroom: Where linguistics can help. *ADFL Bulletin* 31: 39–44.

Andrews, L. 1998. *Language exploration and awareness: A resource book for teachers.* 2d ed. Mahwah, NJ: Lawrence Erlbaum Associates.

Annamalai, E. 1986. Language rights and language planning. *New Language Planning Newsletter* 1: 1-3.

Anyon, J. 1979. Ideology and United States social studies textbooks. *Harvard Educational Review* 49: 361–386.

Appel, R., and P. Muysken. 1987. *Language contact and bilingualism.* London: Edward Arnold.

Apple, M. 1979. *Ideology and curriculum.* London: Routledge & Kegan Paul.

———. 1990. *Ideology and curriculum.* 2d ed. New York: Routledge.

———. 1995. *Education and power.* 2d ed. New York: Routledge.

———. 1996. *Cultural politics and education.* New York: Teachers College Press.

Apple, M., and L. Christian-Smith. 1991. The politics of the textbook. In *The politics of the textbook,* ed. M. Apple and L. Christian-Smith, 1–21. New York: Routledge.

Apple, M., and L. Weiss, eds. 1983. *Ideology and practice in schooling.* Philadelphia, PA: Temple University Press.

Appleton, N. 1983. *Cultural pluralism in education: Theoretical foundations.* New York: Longman.

Asante, M. 1988. *Afrocentricity.* Trenton, NJ: Africa World Press.

———. 1990. *Kemet, Afrocentricity, and knowledge.* Trenton, NJ: Africa World Press.

Asante, M., and K. Asante, eds. 1990. *African culture: Rhythms of unity.* Trenton, NJ: Africa World Press.

Ayalon, A. 1987. *Language and change in the Arab Middle East.* New York: Oxford University Press.

Baai, Z. 1992. Towards a more communicative approach to the teaching of African languages, particularly Xhosa, as second languages. *Southern African Journal of Applied Language Studies* 1: 60–68.

Bahan, B. 1992. American Sign Language literature: Inside the story. In *Deaf studies: What's up?—Conference proceedings,* 153–164. Washington, DC: College for Continuing Education, Gallaudet University.

Bailey, G., and N. Maynor. 1987. Decreolization? *Language in Society* 16: 449–473.

———. 1989. The divergence controversy. *American Speech* 64: 12–39.

Baker, C. 1993. *Foundations of bilingual education and bilingualism.* Clevedon: Multilingual Matters.

———. 2001. *Foundations of bilingual education and bilingualism.* 3rd ed. Clevedon: Multilingual Matters.

Baldauf, R. 1993. Fostering bilingualism and national development through school second language study. *Journal of Multilingual and Multicultural Development* 14: 121–134.

Baldwin, E. 1987. Theory vs. ideology in the practice of teacher education. *Journal of Teacher Education* 38: 16–19.

Ball, C. 1995. Providing comprehensible input in a dead foreign language: Two text-based strategies. In *Linguistics and the education of language teachers: Ethnolinguistic, psycholinguistic, and sociolinguistic aspects,* ed. J. Alatis, C. Straehle, B. Gallenberger, and M. Ronkin, 498–511. Washington, DC: Georgetown University Press.

Ball, R. 1997. *The French-speaking world: A practical introduction to sociolinguistic issues.* London: Routledge.

Ball, S., ed. 1990. *Foucault and education: Disciplines and knowledge.* London: Routledge.

Balme, M., and G. Lawall. 1990a. *Athenaze: An introduction to ancient Greek.* Rev. ed. New York: Oxford University Press.

———. 1990b. *Teacher's handbook—Athenaze: An introduction to ancient Greek.* Rev. ed. New York: Oxford University Press.

Bamgbose, A., A. Banjo, and A. Thomas, eds. 1997. *New Englishes: A west African perspective.* Trenton, NJ: Africa World Press.

Banks, J. 1991. A curriculum for empowerment, action, and change. In *Empowerment through multicultural education,* ed. C. Sleeter, 125–141. Albany: State University of New York Press.

———. 1994. *An introduction to multicultural education.* Boston: Allyn and Bacon.

Barker, M. 1972. *Español para el bilingüe.* Skokie, IL: National Textbook Company.

Barkhuizen, G., and D. Gough. 1996. Language curriculum development in South Africa: What place for English? *TESOL Quarterly* 30: 453–471.

Baron, D. 1990. *The English-only question: An official language for Americans?* New Haven: Yale University Press.

Barzun, J. 1954. *Teacher in America.* Garden City, NY: Doubleday Anchor Books.

Battison, R. 1978. *Lexical borrowing in American Sign Language.* Silver Spring, MD: Linstok Press.

———. 1980. Signs have parts: A simple idea. In *Sign language and the deaf community,* ed. C. Baker and R. Battison, 35–51. Silver Spring, MD: National Association of the Deaf.

Bauer, L., and P. Trudgill, eds. 1998. *Language myths.* New York: Penguin.

Baugh, J. 1988. Review of *Twice as less. Harvard Educational Review* 58: 395–404.

———. 1999. *Out of the mouths of slaves: African American language and educational malpractice.* Austin: University of Texas Press.

———. 2000. *Beyond Ebonics: Linguistic pride and racial prejudice.* Oxford: Oxford University Press.

Beard, M., and J. Henderson. 1995. *Classics: A very short introduction.* Oxford: Oxford University Press.

Beardsmore, H. 1993a. European models of bilingual education: Practice, theory and development. *Journal of Multilingual and Multicultural Development* 14: 103–120.

———, ed. 1993b. *European models of bilingual education.* Clevedon: Multilingual Matters.

Bekerie, A. 1997. *Ethiopic: An African writing system, its history and principles.* Lawrenceville, NJ: Red Sea Press.

Belka, R. 2000. Is American Sign Language a 'foreign' language? *Northeast Conference on the Teaching of Foreign Languages Review* 48: 45–52.

Bennet, J. 1996. Administration rejects Black English as a second language. *New York Times* (25 December), A–22.

Bennett, C. 1995. *Comprehensive multicultural education: Theory and practice.* 3rd ed. Boston: Allyn and Bacon.

Bennett, W., ed. 1993. *The book of virtues: A treasure of moral stories.* New York: Simon & Schuster.

———, ed. 1995. *The moral compass: A companion to the Book of Virtues.* New York: Simon & Schuster.

Berlinerblau, J. 1999. *Heresy in the university: The Black Athena controversy and the responsibilities of American intellectuals.* New Brunswick, NJ: Rutgers University Press.

Bermel, N., and O. Kagan, 2000. The maintenance of written Russian in heritage speakers. In *The learning and teaching of Slavic languages and cultures,* ed. O. Kagan and B. Rifkin, 405–436. Bloomington, IN: Slavica.

Bernal, M. 1987. *Black Athena: The Afroasiatic roots of classical civilization, Volume I—The fabrication of ancient Greece, 1785–1985.* New Brunswick, NJ: Rutgers University Press.

———. 1991. *Black Athena: The Afroasiatic roots of classical civilization, Volume II—The archeological and documentary evidence.* New Brunswick, NJ: Rutgers University Press.

———. 2001. *Black Athena writes back: Martin Bernal responds to his critics.* Durham, NC: Duke University Press.

Berreman, G. 1999. Race, caste, and other invidious distinctions in social stratification. In *Majority and minority: The dynamics of race and ethnicity in American life,* ed. N. Yetman, 39–56. Boston: Allyn and Bacon.

Beukes, A. 1991a. Language teaching and the politics of language. *Journal for Language Teaching* 25: 89–100.

———. 1991b. The politics of language in formal education: The position of Afrikaans. *Journal for Language Teaching* 25: 64–78.

———. 1992. Moedertaalonderrig in 'n demokratiese Suid-Afrika. *Per Linguam* 8: 42–51.

———. 1996. New horizons in language laws and language rights: Multilingualism in the new South Africa. In *XIV World Congress of the Fédération Internationale des Traducteurs Proceedings, Volume 2,* 609–622. Melbourne: The Australian Institute of Interpreters and Translators.

Beukes, A., and M. Barnard, eds. 1994. *Proceedings of the 'Languages for All' Conference: Towards a Pan South African language board.* Pretoria: CSIR Conference Centre.

Birckbichler, D., ed. 1990. *New perspectives and new directions in foreign language education.* Lincolnwood, IL: National Textbook Company, in conjunction with the American Council on the Teaching of Foreign Languages.

Blackledge, A. 2000. *Literacy, power, and social justice.* London: Trentham.

Blackshire-Belay, C. 1996. The location of Ebonics within the framework of the Africological paradigm. *Journal of Black Studies* 27: 5–23.

Blommaert, J. 1996. Language planning as a discourse on language and society: The linguistic ideology of a scholarly tradition. *Language Problems and Language Planning* 20: 199–222.

Bloom, A. 1987. *The closing of the American mind: How higher education has failed democracy and impoverished the souls of today's students.* New York: Simon and Schuster.

Boseker, B. 1994. The disappearance of American Indian languages. *Journal of Multilingual and Multicultural Development* 15: 147–160.

Bowers, C., and D. Flinders. 1990. *Responsive teaching: An ecological approach to classroom patterns of language, culture, and thought.* New York: Teachers College Press.

Bragg, L., ed. 2001. *DEAF-WORLD: A historical reader and primary sourcebook.* New York: New York University Press.

Brandeis, L. 1954. True Americanism. In *American thought: Civil War to World War I,* ed. P. Miller, 340–341. New York: Holt, Rinehard and Winston.

Brandt, R. 1961. *Value and obligation.* New York: Harcourt, Brace & World.

Brecht, R., and A. Walton. 1994. National strategic planning in the less commonly taught languages. In *Foreign language policy,* ed. R. Lambert, 190–212. Thousand Oaks, CA: Sage.

Brink, A. 1984. The future of Afrikaans. *Leadership SA* 3: 29–36.

Brisk, M. 1998. *Bilingual education: From compensatory to quality schooling.* Mahwah, NJ: Lawrence Erlbaum Associates.

Brooks, J., and M. Brooks. 1993. *The case for constructivist classrooms.* Alexandria, VA: Association for Supervision and Curriculum Development.

Bullivant, B. 1981. *The pluralist dilemma in education: Six case studies.* Sydney: George Allen & Unwin.

Bunge, R. 1992. Language: The psyche of a people. In *Language loyalties,* ed. J. Crawford, 376–380. Chicago: The University of Chicago Press.

Burchfield, R. 1985. *The English language.* Oxford: Oxford University Press.

Burkert, W. 1992. *The orientalizing revolution: Near eastern influence on Greek culture in the early archaic age.* Cambridge, MA: Harvard University Press.

Butters, R. 1989. *The death of Black English: Divergence and convergence in black and white vernaculars.* Frankfort: Peter Lang.

Byram, M. 1989. *Cultural studies in foreign language education.* Clevedon: Multilingual Matters.

Byram, M., C. Morgan, and colleagues. 1994. *Teaching-and-learning language-and-culture.* Clevedon: Multilingual Matters.

Cairns, D. 1993. *Aidōs: The psychology and ethics of honour and shame in ancient Greek literature.* Oxford: Clarendon Press.

Cameron, D. 1995. *Verbal hygiene.* London: Routledge.

Cardonna, G. 1990. Sanskrit. In *The world's major languages,* ed. B. Comrie, 448–469. Oxford: Oxford University Press.

Carter, R., ed. 1990. *Knowledge about language and the curriculum: The LINC reader.* London: Hodder & Stoughton.

Cartledge, P. 1995. 'We are all Greeks'? Ancient (especially Herodotean) and modern contestations of Hellenism. *Bulletin of the Institute of Classical Studies*, 40, Institute of Classical Studies, University of London: 75–82.

Cenoz, J., and F. Genesee. 1998. Psycholinguistic perspectives on multilingualism and multilingual education. In *Beyond bilingualism: Multilingualism and multilingual education,* ed. J. Cenoz and F. Genesee, 16–32. Clevedon: Multilingual Matters.

Chambers, J., and P. Trudgill. 1980. *Dialectology.* Cambridge: Cambridge University Press.

Charlton, J. 1998. *Nothing about us without us: Disability oppression and empowerment.* Berkeley: University of California Press.

Chastain, K. 1976. *Developing second-language skills: Theory to practice.* 2d ed. Chicago: Rand McNally.

Chejne, A. 1969. *The Arabic language: Its role in history.* Minneapolis: University of Minnesota Press.

Chen, Ping. 1999. *Modern Chinese: History and sociolinguistics.* Cambridge: Cambridge University Press.

Cheshire, J., ed. 1991. *English around the world: Sociolinguistic perspectives.* Cambridge, MA: Cambridge University Press.

Chick, J. 1992. Language policy in education. In *McGregor's education alternatives,* ed. R. McGregor and A. McGregor, 271–292. Kenwyn: Juta.

Chick, J., and R. Wade. 1997. Restandardisation in the direction of a new English: Implications for access and equity. *Journal of Multilingual and Multicultural Development* 18: 271–284.

Chisanga, T., and N. Kamwangamalu. 1997. Owning the other tongue: The English language in Southern Africa. *Journal of Multilingual and Multicultural Development* 18: 89–99.

Chomsky, N. 1988. *Language and problems of knowledge: The Managua lectures.* Cambridge: MIT Press.

Christian, D. 1988. Language planning: The view from linguistics. In *Linguistics: The Cambridge survey, Volume 4,* ed. F. Newmeyer, 193–209. Cambridge: Cambridge University Press.

Christie, F. 1989. *Language education.* Oxford: Oxford University Press.

Cleary, L., and M. Linn, eds. 1993. *Linguistics for teachers.* New York: McGraw-Hill.

Cluver, A. 1992. Language planning models for a post-apartheid South Africa. *Language Problems and Language Planning* 16: 105–136.

———. 1993a. The decline of Afrikaans. *Language Matters: Studies in the Languages of Southern Africa* 24: 15–46.

———. 1993b. *A dictionary of language planning terms.* Pretoria: University of South Africa.

Cobarrubias, J. 1983a. Ethical issues in status planning. In *Progress in language planning,* ed. J. Cobarrubias and J. Fishman, 41–85. Berlin: Mouton.

———. 1983b. Language planning: The state of the art. In *Progress in language planning,* ed. J. Cobarrubias and J. Fishman, 3–26. Berlin: Mouton.

Cobarrubias, J., & J. Fishman, eds. 1983. *Progress in language planning: International perspectives.* Berlin: Mouton.

Cohen, L. 1994. *Train go sorry: Inside a deaf world.* Boston: Houghton Mifflin.

Coleman, H. 1996. Autonomy and ideology in the English language classroom.

In *Society and the language classroom,* ed. H. Coleman, 1–15. Cambridge: Cambridge University Press.

Coles, G. 2000. *Misreading reading: The bad science that hurts children.* Portsmouth, NH: Heinemann.

Collier, V. 1992. A synthesis of studies examining long-term language minority student data on academic achievement. *Bilingual Research Journal* 16: 187–212.

Combrink, J. 1991. Die toekomstige status en funksies van Afrikaans. *Tydskrif vir Geesteswetenskappe* 31: 101–112.

Constitutional Assembly. 1997. *The constitution of the Republic of South Africa, 1996: Annotated version.* Wynburg: Author.

Cook, V. 1996. *Second language learning and language teaching.* 2d ed. London: Arnold.

Cooper, R. 1989. *Language planning and social change.* Cambridge: Cambridge University Press.

Co-ordinating Committee on the National Action Plan. 1998. *The National Action Plan for the Promotion and Protection of Human Rights.* Houghton: Author.

Cordeiro, P., T. Reagan, and L. Martinez. 1994. *Multiculturalism and TQE: Addressing cultural diversity in schools.* Thousand Oaks, CA: Corwin Press.

Corson, D. 1999. *Language policy in schools: A resource for teachers and administrators.* Mahwah, NJ: Lawrence Erlbaum Associates.

———. 2001. *Language diversity and education.* Mahwah, NJ: Lawrence Erlbaum Associates.

Coulombe, P. 1993. Language rights, individual and communal. *Language Problems and Language Planning* 17: 140–152.

Craig, B. 1995. Boundary discourse and the authority of language in the second-language classroom: A social-constructionist approach. In *Georgetown University Round Table on Languages and Linguistics 1995: Linguistics and the education of language teachers,* ed. J. Alatis, C. Straehle, B. Gallenberger, and M. Ronkin, 40–54. Washington, DC: Georgetown University Press.

Crandall, J., ed. 1987. *ESL through content area instruction: Mathematics, science, social studies.* Englewood Cliffs, NJ: Prentice Hall.

Crawford, J. 1992a. *Hold your tongue: Bilingualism and the politics of 'English only.'* Reading, MA: Addison-Wesley.

———. 2000. *At war with diversity: U.S. language policy in an age of anxiety.* Clevedon: Multilingual Matters.

Crawford, J., ed. 1992b. *Language loyalties: A source book on the official English controversy.* Chicago: University of Chicago Press.

Crookes, G., R. Sakka, S. Shiroma, and Lei Ye. 1991. *Towards a generic curriculum for the less commonly taught languages* (Research Note #1). Honolulu: University of Hawai'i, Second Language Teaching and Curriculum Center.

Crystal, D. 1991. *A dictionary of linguistics and phonetics.* 3rd ed. Oxford: Basil Blackwell.

———. 1997a. *The Cambridge encyclopedia of language.* 2d ed. Cambridge: Cambridge University Press.

———. 1997b. *English as a global language.* Cambridge: Cambridge University Press.

———. 2000. *Language death.* Cambridge: Cambridge University Press.

Cubberley, E. 1909. *Changing conceptions of education.* Boston: Houghton Mifflin.

Cummins, J. 1996. *Negotiating identities: Education for empowerment in a diverse society.* Ontario: California Association for Bilingual Education.

———. 2000. *Language, power and pedagogy: Bilingual children in the crossfire.* Clevedon: Multilingual Matters.

Cunningham-Andersson, U., and S. Andersson. 1999. *Growing up with two languages: A practical guide.* New York: Routledge.

Cuppy, W. 1941. *How to become extinct.* New York: Farrer & Rinehart.

Curtain, H., and C. Pesola. 1994. *Languages and children, making the match: Foreign language instruction for an early start, grades K-8.* 2d ed. White Plains, NY: Longman.

Davis, L. 1995. *Enforcing normalcy: Disability, deafness, and the body.* New York: Verso.

———, ed. 1997. *The disability studies reader.* New York: Routledge.

de Kadt, E. 1996. Language and apartheid: The power of minorities. *Alternation: Journal of the Centre for the Study of Southern Africa* 3: 184–194.

de Klerk, V., and G. Barkhuizen. 1998. Language policy in the SANDF: A case of biting the bullet? *Language Problems and Language Planning* 22: 215–236.

Department of Arts, Culture, Science and Technology. 1997. *Standardising the designation of government departments* (Language Planning Report # 5.5). Pretoria: Government Printer.

———. 1999. *Marketing linguistic human rights* (Language Planning Report # 5.7). Pretoria: Government Printer.

Department of Education and Culture, House of Assembly. 1992. *An investigation into the position of French and German in the Republic of South Africa.* Pretoria: Government Printer.

Department of National Education. 1997. *South Africa's new language policy: The facts.* Pretoria: Government Printer.

Desai, Z. 1991. Democratic language planning and the transformation of education in post-apartheid South Africa. In *Education in a future South Africa,* ed. E. Unterhalter, H. Wolpe, and T. Botha, 112–122. Houghton: Heinemann.

———. 1994. Praat or speak but don't theta: On language rights in South Africa. In *Sustaining local literacies,* ed. D. Barton, 19–29. Clevedon: Multilingual Matters.

Deurr, H., ed. 1980. *Versuchungen Aufsätze zur Philosophie Paul Feyerabends: I.* Frankfort am Main: Suhrkamp Verlag.

———, ed. 1981. *Versuchungen Aufsätze zur Philosophie Paul Feyerabends: II.* Frankfort am Main: Suhrkamp Verlag.

Dicker, S. 1996. *Languages in America: A pluralist view.* Clevedon: Multilingual Matters.

DiPietro, R. 1971. *Language structures in contrast.* Rowley, MA: Newbury House.

Dixon, R. 1997. *The rise and fall of languages.* Cambridge: Cambridge University Press.

Dobson, J. 1993. *Learn New Testament Greek.* 2d ed. Grand Rapids, MI: Baker Books.

Dolnick, E. 1993. Deafness as culture. *Atlantic Monthly* 272: 37–53.

Dorian, N. 1981. *Language death: The life cycle of a Scottish Gaelic dialect.* Philadelphia: University of Pennsylvania Press.

Dowling, T. 1998. *Speak Xhosa with us / Thetha isiXhosa Nathi* (CD-ROM program). Cape Town: Mother Tongues Multimedia Development, in association with the University of Cape Town Multimedia Education Project.

Draper, J., and J. Hicks. 1996. Foreign language enrollments in public secondary schools, fall 1994: Summary report. *Foreign Language Annals* 29: 303–314.

D'Souza, D. 1991. *Illiberal education: The politics of race and sex on campus*. New York: Free Press.

duBois, P. 2001. *Trojan horses: Saving the classics from conservatives*. New York: New York University Press.

Eastman, C. 1983. *Language planning: An introduction*. San Francisco, CA: Chandler & Sharp.

Edmondson, W., and F. Karlsson, eds. 1990. *SLR '87: Papers from the Fourth International Symposium on Sign Language Research*. Hamburg: Signum Press.

Edwards, J. 1994. *Multilingualism*. New York: Routledge.

Elgin, S. 2000. *The language imperative*. Cambridge, MA: Perseus.

Emmorey, K., and J. Reilly, eds. 1995. *Language, gesture, and space*. Hillsdale, NJ: Lawrence Erlbaum Associates.

Ennis, R. 1969. *Logic in teaching*. Englewood Cliffs, NJ: Prentice-Hall.

Ervin, G., ed. 1991. *International perspectives on foreign language teaching*. Lincolnwood, IL: National Textbook Company, in conjunction with the American Council on the Teaching of Foreign Languages.

Everson, M. 1993. Research in the less commonly taught languages. In *Research in language learning*, ed. A. Omaggio Hadley, 198–228. Lincolnwood, IL: National Textbook Company, in conjunction with the American Council on the Teaching of Foreign Languages.

Fairclough, N. 1989. *Language and power*. London: Longman.

———. 1995. *Critical discourse analysis: The critical study of language*. London: Longman.

Fairclough, N., ed. 1992. *Critical language awareness*. London: Longman.

Falkner, T., and J. de Luce, eds. 1989. *Old age in Greek and Latin literature*. Albany: State University of New York Press.

Farrell, J. 2001. *Latin language and Latin culture: From ancient to modern times*. Cambridge: Cambridge University Press.

Fenstermacher, G. 1997. *On knowledge and its relation to the human conversation* (Work in Progress Series, No. 6). Seattle, WA: Institute for Educational Inquiry.

Ferguson, C. 1982. Foreword. In *The other tongue: English across cultures*, ed. B. Kachru, vii–xi. Oxford: Pergamon Press.

Ferguson, C., and S. Heath, eds. 1981. *Language in the USA*. Cambridge: Cambridge University Press.

Fettes, M. 1992. *A guide to language strategies for First Nations communities*. Ottawa: Assembly of First Nations.

———. 1994. Linguistic rights in Canada: Collisions or collusions? A conference report. *Bulletin of the Canadian Centre for Linguistic Rights* 1: 18–20.

———. 1998. Life on the edge: Canada's aboriginal languages under official bilingualism. In *Language and politics in the United States and Canada*, ed. T. Ricento and B. Burnaby, 117–149. Mahwah, NJ: Lawrence Erlbaum Associates.

Feyerabend, P. 1975. *Against method: Outline of an anarchistic theory of knowledge.* London: Verso.

———. 1981a. *Philosophical papers, Volume I: Realism, rationalism and scientific method.* Cambridge: Cambridge University Press.

———. 1981b. *Philosophical papers, Volume II: Problems of empiricism.* Cambridge: Cambridge University Press.

———. 1987. *Farewell to reason.* London: Verso.

———. 1991. *Three dialogues on knowledge.* Cambridge, MA: Basil Blackwell.

———. 1993. *Against method.* 3rd ed. London: Verso.

———. 1995. *Killing time: The autobiography of Paul Feyerabend.* Chicago: University of Chicago Press.

———. 1999. *Conquest of abundance: A tale of abstraction versus the richness of being.* Chicago: University of Chicago Press.

Finchilescu, G., and G. Nyawose. 1998. Talking about language: Zulu students' views on language in the new South Africa. *South African Journal of Psychology* 28: 53–61.

Fischer, R., and H. Lane, eds. 1993. *Looking back: A reader on the history of deaf communities and their sign languages.* Hamburg: Signum Press.

Fischer, S., and S. Siple, eds. 1990. *Theoretical issues in sign language research: Volume 1, Linguistics.* Chicago: University of Chicago Press.

Fishman, J. 1991. *Reversing language shift: Theoretical and empirical foundations of assistance to threatened languages.* Clevedon: Multilingual Matters.

———, ed. 2001. *Can threatened languages be saved? Reversing language shift, revisited: A 21st century perspective.* Clevedon: Multilingual Matters.

Fosnot, C. 1993. Preface. In *The case for constructivist classrooms,* J. Grennon Brooks and M. Brooks, vii–viii. Alexandria, VA: Association for Supervision and Curriculum Development.

Friedman, L., ed. 1977. *On the other hand: New perspectives on American Sign Language.* New York: Academic Press.

Frishberg, N. 1988. Signers of tales: The case for literary status of an unwritten language. *Sign Language Studies,* 59, 149–170.

Fullinwider, R., ed. 1996. *Public education in a multicultural society: Policy, theory, critique.* Cambridge: Cambridge University Press.

Gaganakis, M. 1992. Language and ethnic group relations in non-racial schools. *English Academy Review* 9: 46–55.

Gándara, P., and J. Fish. 1994. Year round schooling as an avenue to major structural reform. *Educational Evaluation and Policy Analysis* 16: 67–86.

Gao, M. 2000. *Mandarin Chinese: An introduction.* Oxford: Oxford University Press.

García, O., and C. Baker, eds. 1995. *Policy and practice in bilingual education: Extending the foundations.* Clevedon: Multilingual Matters.

Gay, G. 1995. Mirror images on common issues: Parallels between multicultural education and critical pedagogy. In *Multicultural education, critical pedagogy, and the politics of difference,* ed. C. Sleeter and P. McLaren, 155–189. Albany: State University of New York Press.

Gee, J. 1996. *Social linguistics and literacies: Ideology in discourse.* 2d ed. London: Taylor & Francis.

Gibson, M., and J. Ogbu, eds. 1991. *Minority status and schooling: A comparative study of immigrant and involuntary minorities.* New York: Garland.

Giliomee, H., and H. Adam. 1981. *Afrikanermag: Opkoms en toekoms*. Stellenbosch: Universiteitsuitgewers en Boekhandelaars.
Gill, C. 1996. *Personality in Greek epic, tragedy, and philosophy: The self in dialogue*. Oxford: Clarendon Press.
Giroux, H. 1983. *Theory and resistance in education: A pedagogy for the opposition*. South Hadley, MA: Bergin & Garvey.
———, ed. 1991. *Postmodernism, feminism, and cultural politics: Redrawing educational boundaries*. Albany: State University of New York Press.
———. 1997. *Pedagogy and the politics of hope: Theory, culture, and schooling*. Boulder, CO: Westview Press.
Glenny, M. 1996. *The fall of Yugoslavia: The third Balkan war*. 3rd ed. New York: Penguin.
Gollnick, D., and P. Chinn. 1994. *Multicultural education in a pluralistic society*. 4th ed. New York: Merrill.
Gomes de Matos, F. 1985. The linguistic rights of language learners. *Language Planning Newsletter* 11: 1–2.
González, R., with I. Melis, eds. 2001a. *Language ideologies: Critical perspectives on the Official English Movement, Volume I, Education and the social implications of official language*. Mahwah, NJ: Lawrence Erlbaum Associates.
———, eds. 2001b. *Language ideologies: Critical perspectives on the Official English Movement, Volume II, History, theory, and policy*. Mahwah, NJ: Lawrence Erlbaum Associates.
Graddol, D. 1997. *The future of English? A guide to forecasting the popularity of the English language in the 21st century*. London: British Council.
Green, T. 1966. *Education and pluralism: Ideal and reality*. Syracuse, NY: Syracuse University Press.
Grenoble, L., and L. Whaley, eds. 1998. *Endangered languages: Current issues and future prospects*. Cambridge: Cambridge University Press.
Gupta, A., and J. Ferguson, eds. 1997. *Culture, power, place: Explorations in critical anthropology*. Durham, NC: Duke University Press.
Guthrie, G. 1985. *A school divided: An ethnography of bilingual education in a Chinese community*. Hillsdale, NJ: Lawrence Erlbaum Associates.
Gutmann, A. 1987. *Democratic education*. Princeton, NJ: Princeton University Press.
Habermas, J. 1968. *Erkenntnis und Interesse*. Frankfort am Main: Suhrkamp Verlag.
———. 1970. *Toward a rational society*. Boston: Beacon Press.
———. 1971. *Knowledge and human interests*. Boston: Beacon Press.
———. 1984. *The theory of communicative action: Volume I. Reason and the rationalization of society*. Boston: Beacon Press.
Hadley, A. 1993. *Teaching language in context*. 2d ed. Boston: Heinle & Heinle.
Hakuta, K., and L. Gould. 1987. Synthesis of research on bilingual education. *Educational Leadership* 44: 38–45.
Hale, T. 1999. Francophone African literature and the hexagon: Building bridges for the new millennium. *The French Review* 72: 444–455.
Hall, E. 1989. *Inventing the barbarian: Greek self-definition through tragedy*. Oxford: Clarendon Press.
Hall, J., and W. Eggington, eds. 2000. *The sociopolitics of English language teaching*. Clevedon: Multilingual Matters.
Hamel, E. 1995a. Indigenous education in Latin America: Policies and legal

frameworks. In *Linguistic human rights,* ed. T. Skutnabb-Kangas and R. Phillipson, 271–287. Berlin: Mouton de Gruyter.

———. 1995b. Linguistic rights for Amerindian peoples in Latin America. In *Linguistic human rights,* ed. T. Skutnabb-Kangas and R. Phillipson, 289–303. Berlin: Mouton de Gruyter.

Hamilton, E. 1958. *The Greek way.* New York: W. W. Norton.

Hansen, M. 1997. One hundred and sixty theses about Athenian democracy. *Classica et Mediaevalia: Revue Danoise de Philologie et d'Histoire* 48: 205–265.

Hanson, V., and J. Heath. 2001. *Who killed Homer? The demise of classical education and the recovery of Greek wisdom.* San Francisco: Encounter.

Hanson, V., J. Heath, and B. Thornton. 2001. *Bonfire of the humanities: Rescuing the classics in an impoverished age.* Wilmington, DE: ISI Books.

Harrington, K. 1997. *Medieval Latin.* 2d ed., rev. by J. Pucci. Chicago: University of Chicago Press.

Harris, J. 1992. *Against relativism: A philosophical defense of method.* LaSalle, IL: Open Court.

Hartshorne, K. 1987. Language policy in African education in South Africa, 1910–1985, with particular reference to the issue of medium of instruction. In *Bridging the gap between theory and practice in English second language teaching,* ed. D. Young, 62–81. Cape Town: Maskew Miller Longman.

———. 1992. *Crisis and challenge: Black education, 1910–1990.* Cape Town: Oxford University Press.

Hawkesworth, C. 1998. *Colloquial Croatian and Serbian: The complete course for beginners.* London: Routledge.

Hawkins, E. 1981. *Modern languages in the curriculum.* Cambridge: Cambridge University Press.

Heath, S. B. 1983. *Ways with words: Language, life, and work in communities and classrooms.* Cambridge: Cambridge University Press.

Hedberg, T. 1994. Name signs in Swedish Sign Language: Their formation and use. In *The deaf way: Perspectives from the international conference on deaf culture,* ed. C. Erting, R. Johnson, D. Smith, and B. Snider, 416–424. Washington, DC: Gallaudet University Press.

Heine, B., and D. Nurse, eds. 2000. *African languages: An introduction.* Cambridge: Cambridge University Press.

Hernandez, R. 1996. Never mind teaching Ebonics: Teach proper English. *The Hartford Courant* (26 December), A–21.

Hernández-Chávez, E. 1995. Language policy in the United States: A history of cultural genocide. In *Linguistic human rights,* ed. T. Skutnabb-Kangas and R. Phillipson, 141–158. Berlin: Mouton de Gruyter.

Herriman, M., and B. Burnaby, eds. 1996. *Language policies in English-dominant countries.* Clevedon: Multilingual Matters.

Heugh, K. 1985. The relationship between nationalism and language in education in the South African context. In *UCT papers in language education,* ed. D. Young, 35–70. Cape Town: University of Cape Town, Language Education Unit, Department of Education.

———. 1987. Trends in language medium policy for a post-apartheid South Africa. In *Language: Planning and medium in education,* ed. D. Young, 206–220. Rondebosch: Language Education Unit (UCT) and SAALA.

———. 1993. The place of English in relation to other languages in South Africa. *Per Linguam* 9: 210.

———. 1995. Disabling and enabling: Implications of language policy trends in South Africa. In *Language and social history,* ed. R. Mesthrie, 329–350. Cape Town: David Philip.

Heugh, K., A. Siegrühn, and P. Plüddemann, eds. 1995. *Multilingual education for South Africa.* Johannesburg: Heinemann.

Hirsch, E. D. 1987. *Cultural literacy: What every American needs to know.* New York: Random House.

Hoffmeister, R. 1990. ASL and its implications for education. In *Manual communication,* ed. H. Bornstein, 81–107. Washington, DC: Gallaudet University Press.

Holborow, M. 1999. *The politics of English.* Thousand Oaks, CA: Sage.

Hollins, E. 1996. *Culture in school learning: Revealing the deep meaning.* Mahwah, NJ: Lawrence Erlbaum Associates.

Holmes, S. 1996. Voice of inner city streets is defended and criticized. *The New York Times* (30 December), A–9.

Horrocks, G. 1997. *Greek: A history of the language and its speakers.* New York: Longman.

Howe, S. 1998. *Afrocentrism: Mythical pasts and imagined homes.* London: Verso.

Hudson, R. 1996. *Sociolinguistics.* 2d ed. Cambridge: Cambridge University Press.

Hymes, D. 1996. *Ethnography, linguistics, narrative inequality: Toward an understanding of voice.* London: Taylor and Francis.

Ihde, T. 1997. Teacher certification and less commonly taught languages. *Journal of Celtic Language Learning* 3: 41–50.

Irwin, J. 1996. *Empowering ourselves and transforming schools: Educators making a difference.* Albany: State University of New York Press.

Jacobowitz, E. 1992. American Sign Language literature: Curriculum considerations. In *Deaf studies for educators: Conference proceedings,* 76–82. Washington, DC: College for Continuing Education, Gallaudet University.

Jacobs, R. 1996. Just how hard is it to learn ASL? The case for ASL as a truly foreign language. In *Multicultural aspects of sociolinguistics in deaf communities,* ed. C. Lucas, 183–226. Washington, DC: Gallaudet University Press.

Jaeger, W. 1971a. *Paideia: The ideals of Greek culture, Volume II—In search of the divine centre.* New York: Oxford University Press.

———. 1971b. *Paideia: The ideals of Greek culture, Volume III—The conflict of cultural ideals in the age of Plato.* New York: Oxford University Press.

———. 1973. *Paideia: The ideals of Greek culture, Volume I—Archaic Greece, the mind of Athens.* 2d ed. New York: Oxford University Press.

James, C. 1979. Foreign languages in the school curriculum. In *Foreign languages in education,* ed. G. Perren, 7–28. London: CILT.

James, C., and P. Garrett. 1992. *Language awareness in the classroom.* London: Longman.

Janks, H. 1991. A critical approach to the teaching of language. *Educational Review* 43: 191–199.

———. 1997. Critical discourse analysis as a research tool. *Discourse: Studies in the Politics of Education* 18: 329–342.

Janks, H., and R. Ivanič. 1992. Critical language awareness. In *Critical language awareness,* ed. N. Fairclough, 305–331. London: Longman.

Jansen, J., ed. 1991. *Knowledge and power in South Africa: Critical perspectives across the disciplines.* Johannesburg: Skotaville.

Jarvis, G. 1980. The value of second-language learning. In *Learning a second language: Seventy-ninth yearbook of the National Society for the Study of Education, Part II,* ed. F. Grittner, 26–43. Chicago, IL: National Society for the Study of Education, distributed by the University of Chicago Press.

Johnson, S. 1998. *Exploring the German language.* London: Arnold.

Jones, R. F. 1953. *The triumph of the English language.* Stanford, CA: Stanford University Press.

Jordan, E., and R. Walton. 1987. Truly foreign languages: Instructional challenges. *Annals of the American Academy of Social and Political Science* 490: 110–124.

Joseph, J., and T. Taylor, eds. 1990. *Ideologies of language.* London: Routledge.

Kachru, B., ed. 1982. *The other tongue: English across cultures.* Oxford: Pergamon Press.

Kamwangamalu, N. 1997. Multilingualism and education policy in post-apartheid South Africa. *Language Problems and Language Planning* 21: 234–253.

———. 1998. 'We-codes', 'they-codes', and 'codes-in-between': Identities of English and codeswitching in post-apartheid South Africa. *Multilingua: Journal of Cross-Cultural and Interlanguage Communication* 17: 277–296.

Kanpol, B. 1994. *Critical pedagogy: An introduction.* Westport, CT: Bergin & Garvey.

Kaplan, R., and R. Baldauf. 1997. *Language planning: From theory to practice.* Clevedon: Multilingual Matters.

Karabel, J., and A. Halsey, eds. 1977. *Power and ideology in education.* New York: Oxford University Press.

Karmani, S. 1995. Islam, politics, and English language teaching. *Muslim Education Quarterly* 13: 12–32.

Kaschula, R., and C. Anthonissen. 1995. *Communicating across cultures in South Africa: Toward a critical language awareness.* Johannesburg: Witwatersrand University Press.

Kashoki, M. 1993. Some thoughts on future language policy for South Africa. *African Studies* 52: 141–162.

Katz, M. 1999. Women and democracy in ancient Greece. In *Contextualizing classics,* ed. T. Falkner, N. Felson, and D. Konstan, 41–68. Lanham, MD: Rowman & Littlefield.

Kaye, A. 1990. Arabic. In *The world's major languages,* ed. B. Comrie, 664–685. Oxford: Oxford University Press.

Kazmi, Y, 1997. The hidden political agenda of teaching English as an international language. *Muslim Education Quarterly* 15: 45–59.

Kennedy, C., ed. 1983. *Language planning and language education.* London: George Allen & Unwin.

Kerr, D. 1976. *Educational policy: Analysis, structure, and justification.* New York: David McKay.

King, M., and O. van den Berg. 1992. *One nation, many languages: What policy for schools?* Pietermaritzburg: Centaur Publications, in association with the Independent Examinations Board.

Klee, C. 1998. Communication as an organizing principle in the national standards: Sociolinguistic aspects of Spanish language teaching. *Hispania* 81: 339–351.

Klemke, E., R. Hollinger, and D. Rudge, with A. Kline, eds. 1998. *Introductory readings in the philosophy of science.* 3rd ed. Amherst, NY: Prometheus.

Klima, E., and U. Bellugi. 1979. *The signs of language.* Cambridge, MA: Harvard University Press.

Kloss, H. 1978. *Problems of language policy in South Africa.* Vienna: Wilhelm Braumüller.

Kopff, E. 2001. *The devil knows Latin: Why America needs the classical tradition.* Wilmington, DE: Isi Books.

Kouzmin, L. 1982. Grammatical interference in Australian Russian. In *The Slavic languages in émigré communities,* ed. R. Sussex, 73–87. Edmonton: Linguistic Research.

Kramer, C. 1999a. *Macedonian: A course for beginning and intermediate students.* Madison: University of Wisconsin Press.

———. 1999b. Official language, minority language, no language at all: The history of Macedonian in primary education in the Balkans. *Language Problems and Language Planning* 23: 233–250.

Krashen, S. 1996. *Under attack: The case against bilingual education.* Culver City, CA: Language Education Associates.

Krauss, M. 1992. The world's languages in crisis. *Language* 68: 4–10.

Kress, G., and R. Hodge. 1979. *Language as ideology.* London: Routledge & Kegan Paul.

Kriel, M. 1998. Taal en identiteitskrisis, en die alternatiewe Afrikaans musiekbeweging. *South African Journal of Linguistics* 16: 16–26.

Krishnaswamy, N., and A. Burde. 1998. *The politics of Indians' English: Linguistic colonialism and the expanding English empire.* Delhi: Oxford University Press.

Kroll, S., and D. Zahirovič. 1998. *Bosnian-English / English-Bosnian dictionary.* New York: Hippocrene.

Kuhn, T. 1970. *The structure of scientific revolutions.* 2d ed. enlarged. Chicago: University of Chicago Press.

———. 1977. *The essential tension: Selected studies in scientific tradition and change.* Chicago: University of Chicago Press.

Kumaravadivelu, B. 2001. Toward a postmethod pedagogy. *TESOL Quarterly* 35: 537–560.

Kyle, J. 1990. The deaf community: Custom, culture and tradition. In *Sign language research and application,* ed. S. Prillwitz and T. Vollhaber, 175–185. Hamburg: Signum Press.

Kyle, J., and B. Woll, eds. 1983. *Language in sign: An international perspective on sign language.* London: Croom Helm.

———. 1985. *Sign language: The study of deaf people and their language.* Cambridge: Cambridge University Press.

Labov, W. 1972a. *Language in the inner city: Studies in the Black English vernacular.* Philadelphia: University of Pennsylvania Press.

———. 1972b. *Sociolinguistic patterns.* Philadelphia: University of Pennsylvania Press.

———. 1978. *The study of nonstandard English.* Urbana, IL: National Council of Teachers of English.

———. 1993. Recognizing Black English in the classroom. In *Linguistics for teachers,* ed. L. Cleary and M. Linn, 149–173. New York: McGraw-Hill.

Lafayette, R., ed. 1996. *National standards: A catalyst for reform.* Lincolnwood, IL: National Textbook Co., in conjunction with the American Council on the Teaching of Foreign Languages.

LaFleur, R. 1992. Latin and classics in the college curriculum: Something new under the sun. In *Teaching languages in college: Curriculum and content,* ed. W. Rivers, 157–197. Lincolnwood, IL: National Textbook Company.

Lakatos, I., and A. Musgrave, eds. 1970. *Criticism and the growth of knowledge.* Cambridge: Cambridge University Press.

Lambert, R. 1990. *Language policy: An international perspective.* Washington, DC: Johns Hopkins University, National Foreign Language Center.

———, ed. 1994. *Foreign language policy: An agenda for change.* Thousand Oaks, CA: Sage.

Lampe, J. 2000. *Yugoslavia as history: Twice there was a country.* 2d ed. Cambridge: Cambridge University Press.

Lane, H. 1992. *The mask of benevolence: Disabling the deaf community.* New York: Alfred A. Knopf.

Lane, H., R. Hoffmeister, and B. Bahan. 1996. *A journey into the DEAF-WORLD.* San Diego, CA: DawnSign Press.

Lanehart, S. 1998. African American Vernacular English and education: The dynamics of pedagogy, ideology and identity. *Journal of English Linguistics* 26: 122–136.

———. 1999. African American Vernacular English. In *Handbook of language and ethnic identity,* ed. J. Fishman, 211–225. Oxford: Oxford University Press.

Language Plan Task Group. 1996. *Towards a national language plan for South Africa: Final report of the Language Plan Task Group (LANGTAG).* Pretoria: Government Printer.

Lardinois, A., and L. McClure, eds. 2001. *Making silence speak: Women's voices in Greek literature and society.* Princeton, NJ: Princeton University Press.

Larsen-Freeman, D. 1986. *Techniques and principles in language teaching.* New York: Oxford University Press.

Larson, C., and C. Ovando. 2001. *The color of bureaucracy: The politics of equity in multicultural school communities.* Belmont, CA: Wadsworth.

Lee, P. 1996. *The Whorf theory complex: A critical reconstruction.* Philadelphia, PA: John Benjamins.

Lefkowitz, M. 1996a. Ancient history, modern myths. In *Black Athena revisited,* ed. M. Lefkowitz and G. Rogers, 3–23. Chapel Hill: University of North Carolina Press.

———. 1996b. *Not out of Africa: How Afrocentrism became an excuse to teach myth as history.* New York: Basic Books.

Lefkowitz, M., and G. Rogers, eds. 1996. *Black Athena revisited.* Chapel Hill: University of North Carolina Press.

Levesque, J. 2001. Let's return ASL to deaf ownership. In *DEAF-WORLD: A historical reader and primary sourcebook,* ed. L. Bragg, 116–117. New York: New York University Press.

Liddell, S. 1980. *American Sign Language syntax.* The Hague: Mouton.

Lillo-Martin, D. 1991. *Universal grammar and American Sign Language: Setting the null argument parameters.* Dordrecht: Kluwer.

Lindholm, K. 1987. *Directory of bilingual immersion programs: Two way bilingual education for language minority and majority students.* Los Angeles, CA: Center for Language Education and Research.

Linton, S. 1998. *Claiming disability: Knowledge and identity.* New York: New York University Press.

Lippi-Green, R. 1997. *English with an accent: Language, ideology, and discrimination in the United States.* London: Routledge.

Lipton, G. 1992. *Practice handbook to elementary foreign language programs.* 2d ed. Lincolnwood, IL: National Textbook Company.

Liskin-Gasparro, J. 1982. *ETS oral proficiency testing manual.* Princeton, NJ: Educational Testing Service.

Littlewood, W. 1984. *Foreign and second language learning: Language acquisition research and its implications for the classroom.* Cambridge: Cambridge University Press.

Louw-Potgieter, J., and J. Louw. 1991. Language planning: Preferences of a group of South African students. *South African Journal of Linguistics* 9: 96–99.

Low, W. 1992. Colors of ASL . . . A world expressed: ASL poetry in the curriculum. In *Deaf studies for educators: Conference proceedings,* 53–59. Washington, DC: College for Continuing Education, Gallaudet University.

Lowenberg, P. 1995. Language and the institutionalization of ethnic inequality: Malay and English in Malaysia. In *Language and peace,* ed. C. Schäffner and A. Wenden, 161–172. Amsterdam: Harwood Academic Publishers.

Lubiner, E. 1996. *Learning about languages: A comprehensive FLEX activity book.* Lincolnwood, IL: National Textbook Company.

Lucas, C., ed. 1989. *The sociolinguistics of the deaf community.* San Diego, CA: Academic Press.

———, ed. 1990. *Sign language research: Theoretical issues.* Washington, DC: Gallaudet University Press.

———, ed. 1995. *Sociolinguistics in deaf communities.* Washington, DC: Gallaudet University Press.

———, ed. 1996. *Multicultural aspects of sociolinguistics in deaf communities.* Washington, DC: Gallaudet University Press.

———, ed. 2001. *The sociolinguistics of sign languages.* Cambridge: Cambridge University Press.

Lucas, C., R. Bayley, and C. Valli. 2001. *Sociolinguistic variation in American Sign Language.* Washington, DC: Gallaudet University Press.

Lucas, C., and C. Valli. 1992. *Language contact in the American deaf community.* San Diego, CA: Academic Press.

Lucas, T., R. Henze, and R. Donato. 1990. Promoting the success of Latino language minority students: An exploratory study of six high schools. *Harvard Educational Review* 60: 315–340.

Luke, A. 1988. *Literacy, textbooks and ideology.* Philadelphia, PA: Falmer Press.

Maartens, J. 1994. Teaching Afrikaans as emancipatory discourse. In *Taalwetenskap vir die taalprofessies/Linguistics for the language professions, 2,* ed. R. Botha, M. Kemp, C. le Roux, and W. Winckler, 298–208. Stellenbosch: Department of General Linguistics, University of Stellenbosch.

Macedo, D. 2000. The colonialism of the English Only Movement. *Educational Researcher* 29: 15–24.

MacMillan, M. 1982. Henri Bourassa on the defence of language rights. *Dalhousie Review* 62: 413–430.

Mamdani, M., ed. 2000. *Beyond rights talk and culture talk.* Cape Town: David Philip.

Mansoor, S. 1993. *Punjabi, Urdu, English in Pakistan: A sociolinguistic study.* Lahore, Pakistan: Vanguard.

Mansour, G. 1993. *Multilingualism and nation-building.* Clevedon: Multilingual Matters.

Marcus, G., and M. Fischer. 1999. *Anthropology as cultural critique.* 2d ed. Chicago: University of Chicago Press.

Marivate, C. 1993. Language and education, with special reference to the mother-tongue policy in African schools. *Language Matters: Studies in the Languages of Southern Africa* 24: 91–105.

Mar-Molinero, C. 1997. *The Spanish-speaking world: A practical introduction to sociolinguistic issues.* London: Routledge.

———. 2000. *Politics of language in the Spanish-speaking world.* London: Routledge.

Martin-Jones, M., and S. Romaine. 1986. Semilingualism: A half-baked theory of communicative competence. *Applied Linguistics* 7: 26–38.

Mastronarde, D. 1993. *Introduction to Attic Greek.* Berkeley: University of California Press.

Mawasha, A. 1996. Teaching African languages to speakers of other South African languages: Operationalising the new democratic language policy in South Africa. *Journal for Language Teaching* 30: 35–41.

Maxwell, B. 1997. Miss Bonaparte wouldn't approve! *The New Britain Herald* (2 January), B–2.

Mazrui, A. 2000. The World Bank, the language question, and the future of African education. In *A thousand flowers: Social struggles against structural adjustment in African universities,* ed. S. Federici, G. Caffentzis, and O. Alidou, 43–59. Trenton, NJ: Africa World Press.

Mazrui, A., and A. Mazrui. 1998. *The power of Babel: Language and governance in the African experience.* Oxford: James Currey.

McArthur, T. 1998. *The English languages.* Cambridge: Cambridge University Press.

McDade, L. 1987. The difference-deficit debate: Theoretical smokescreen for a conservative ambush. In *Philosophical studies in education: Proceedings of the Ohio Valley Philosophy of Education Society, 1987–1988,* ed. F. Estes, 65–79. Terre Haute, IN: Ohio Valley Philosophy of Education Society.

McKay, S. 1993. *Agendas for second language literacy.* Cambridge: Cambridge University Press.

McKee, R., and D. McKee. 2000. Name signs and identity in New Zealand Sign Language. In *Bilingualism and identity in deaf communities,* ed. M. Metzger, 3–40. Washington, DC: Gallaudet University Press.

McKeon, D., and L. Malarz. 1991. *School based management: What bilingual and ESL program directors should know.* Washington, DC: National Clearinghouse for Bilingual Education.

McLaren, P. 1989. *Life in schools: An introduction to critical pedagogy in the foundations of education.* New York: Longman.

McLaren, P., and J. Muñoz. 2000. Contesting whiteness: Critical perspectives on the struggle for social justice. In *The politics of multiculturalism in bilingual education: Students and teachers in the cross fire,* ed. C. Ovando and P. McLaren, 22–49. Boston: McGraw-Hill.

McLaughlin, B. 1992. *Myths and misconceptions about second language learning: What every teacher needs to unlearn.* Santa Cruz, CA: National Center for Research on Cultural Diversity and Second Language Learning.

McManus, B. 1997. *Classics and feminism: Gendering the classics.* New York: Twayne.

McNeil, L. 2000. *Contradictions of school reform: Educational costs of standardized testing.* New York: Routledge.

McRae, K. 1978. Bilingual language districts in Finland and Canada: Adventures in the transplanting of an institution. *Canadian Public Policy* 4: 331–351.

McWhorter, J. 1998. *The word on the street: Fact and fable about American English.* New York: Plenum.

———. 2001. *Losing the race: Self-sabotage in black America.* New York: Perennial.

Meadow, K. 1977. Name signs as identity symbols in the deaf community. *Sign Language Studies* 16: 237–246.

Meier, D. 2000. *Will standards save public education?* Boston: Beacon Press.

Met, M., and V. Galloway. 1992. Research in foreign language curriculum. In *Handbook of research on curriculum,* ed. P. Jackson, 852–890. New York: Macmillan.

Milroy, J., and L. Milroy. 1985. *Authority in language: Investigating language prescription and standardisation.* London: Routledge & Kegan Paul.

Minicucci, C., and L. Olsen. 1992. *Programs for secondary LEP students: A California study.* Washington, DC: National Clearinghouse for Bilingual Education.

Mokoena, A. 1998. *Sesotho made easy.* Pretoria: J. L. van Schaik.

Mounce, W. 1993. *Basics of biblical Greek grammar.* Grand Rapids, MI: Zondervan.

Msimang, C. 1992. The future status and function of Zulu in the new South Africa. *South African Journal of African Languages* 12: 139–143.

Mtintsilana, P., and R. Morris. 1988. Terminology in African languages in South Africa. *South African Journal of African Languages* 8: 109–113.

Mtuze, M. 1993. The language practitioner in a multilingual South Africa. *South African Journal of African Languages* 13: 47–52.

Mufwene, S., J. Rickford, J. Bailey, and J. Baugh, eds. 1998. *African-American English: Structure, history and use.* London: Routledge.

Muir, F., ed. 1976. *An irreverent and thoroughly incomplete social history of almost everything.* New York: Stein and Day.

Munnik, A. 1994. *Learn Xhosa.* Pietermaritzburg: Shuter & Shooter.

Musker, P., ed. 1997. *Multilingual learning: Working in multilingual classrooms.* Cape Town: Maskew Miller Longman.

Mutasa, D. 1996. Constraints on the promotion of African languages to the level of English, French and Portuguese. *South African Journal of Linguistics* (Suppl. 32): 23–34.

Nahir, M. 1977. The five aspects of language planning. *Language Problems and Language Planning* 1: 107–124.

Nash, G., C. Crabtree, and R. Dunn. 1997. *History on trial: Culture wars and the teaching of the past.* New York: Alfred A. Knopf.

National Education Policy Investigation. 1992a. *Post-secondary education.* Cape Town: Oxford University Press.

———. 1992b. *Report of the National Educational Policy Investigation Language Research Group.* Cape Town: Oxford University Press.

———. 1993a. *Education planning, systems, and structure.* Cape Town: Oxford University Press.

———. 1993b. *The Framework Report.* Cape Town: Oxford University Press.

National Standards in Foreign Language Education Project. 1996. *Standards for foreign language learning: Preparing for the 21st century.* Lawrence, KS: Allen Press.

———. 1999. *Standards for foreign language learning in the 21st century: Including Chinese, Classical languages, French, German, Italian, Japanese, Portuguese, Russian, and Spanish.* Lawrence, KS: Allen Press.

Natsis, J. 1999. Legislation and language: The politics of speaking French in Louisiana. *The French Review* 73: 325–331.

Ndebele, N. 1987. The English language and social change in South Africa. *The English Academy Review* 4: 1–16.

Neisser, A. 1983. *The other side of silence: Sign language and the deaf community in America.* New York: Alfred A. Knopf.

Nettle, D. 1999. *Linguistic diversity.* Oxford: Oxford University Press.

Nettle, D., and S. Romaine. 2000. *Vanishing voices: The extinction of the world's languages.* Oxford: Oxford University Press.

Nikel, R., ed. 1974. *Didaktik des Altsprachlichen Unterrichts.* Darmstad: Wissenschaftliche Buchgesellschaft.

Nieto, S. 2000. *Affirming diversity: The sociopolitical context of multicultural education.* 3rd ed. New York: Longman.

Norris, D. 1993. *Serbo-Croat: A complete course for beginners.* London: Hodder Headline.

Nunan, D. 1995. *Language teaching methodology: A textbook for teachers.* New York: Phoenix ELT.

Nxumalo, T., and S. Cioran. 1996. *Funda IsiZulu!/Learn Zulu! An introduction to Zulu.* Cape Town: Juta & Company.

Office of the Deputy President (T. M. Mbeki). 1997. *White Paper on an Integrated National Disability Strategy.* Pretoria: Author.

Ogbu, J. 1978. *Minority education and caste: The American system in cross-cultural perspective.* New York: Academic Press.

———. 1987. Variability in minority school performance: A problem in search of an explanation. *Anthropology and Education Quarterly* 18: 312–334.

———. 1988. Class stratification, racial stratification, and schooling. In *Class, race and gender in American education,* ed. L. Weis, 106–125. Albany: State University of New York Press.

———. 1992. Understanding cultural diversity and learning. *Educational Researcher* 21: 5–14.

O'Hear, A. 1989. *An introduction to the philosophy of science.* Oxford: Clarendon Press.

Olivier, P. 1993. Language rights and human rights. In *Language, law and equality,* ed. K. Prinsloo, Y. Peeters, J. Turi , and C. van Rensburg, 128–137. Pretoria: University of South Africa.

Olszewski, L. 1996. Oakland schools OK Black English: Ebonics to be regarded as different, not wrong. *The San Francisco Chronicle* (19 December), A–1, A–19.

Orr, E. 1987. *Twice As less: Black English and the performance of black students in mathematics and science.* New York: Norton.

Ortega, L. 1999. Language and equality: Ideological and structural constraints in foreign language education in the U.S. In *Sociopolitical perspectives on language policy and planning in the USA,* ed. T. Huebner and K. Davis, 243–266. Amsterdam: John Benjamins.

Ortiz de Montellano, B. 1995. Multiculturalism, cult archaeology, and pseudoscience. In *Cult archaeology and creationism,* ed. F. Harrold and R. Eve, 134–151. Iowa City: University of Iowa Press.

Osborn, T. 1998. *The concept of "foreignness" in U.S. secondary language curricula: A critical philosophical analysis.* (Ph.D. diss., University of Connecticut.)

———. 2000. *Critical reflection and the foreign language classroom.* Westport, CT: Bergin & Garvey.

———. 2001. A critical historical overview of language requirements in graduate education: Where, and why, we went wrong. Paper presented at the annual meeting of the Northeastern Educational Research Association in Kerhonkson, New York, 25 October.

———, ed. 2002. *The future of foreign language education in the United States.* Westport, CT: Bergin & Garvey.

Osborn, T., and T. Reagan. 1998. Why Johnny can't *hablar, parler* or *sprechen:* Foreign language education and multicultural education. *Multicultural Education* 6: 2–9.

Ovando, C. 1993. Language diversity and education. In *Multicultural education: Issues and perspectives,* ed. J. Banks and C. Banks, 215–235. Boston: Allyn and Bacon.

Padden, C., and T. Humphries. 1988. *Deaf in America: Voices from a culture.* Cambridge, MA: Harvard University Press.

Pai, Y., and S. Adler. 2001. *Cultural foundations of education.* 3rd ed. Columbus, OH: Merrill/Prentice-Hall.

Partridge, M. 1972. *Serbo-Croat: Practical grammar and reader.* Belgrade: Izdavački Zavod Jugoslavija.

Paul, P., and D. Jackson. 1993. *Toward a psychology of deafness: Theoretical and empirical perspectives.* Boston: Allyn and Bacon.

Pease-Alvarez, L., E. García, and P. Espinosa. 1991. Effective instruction for language minority students: An early childhood case study. *Early Childhood Research Quarterly* 6: 347–361.

Peirce, B. 1989. Toward a pedagogy of possibility in the teaching of English internationally: People's English in South Africa. *TESOL Quarterly* 23: 401–420.

Penn, C. 1992. The sociolinguistics of South African Sign Language. In *Language and society in Africa,* ed. R. Herbert, 277–284. Johannesburg: Witwatersrand University Press.

———. 1993. Signs of the times: Deaf language and culture in South Africa. *South African Journal of Communication Disorders* 31: 6–11.

Penn, C., and T. Reagan. 1990. How do you sign 'apartheid'? The politics of South African Sign Language. *Language Problems and Language Planning* 14: 91–103.

———. 1995. On the other hand: Implications of the study of South African Sign Language for the education of the deaf in South Africa. *South African Journal of Education* 15: 92–96.

———. 1999. Linguistic, social and cultural perspectives on sign language in South Africa. *Indian Journal of Applied Linguistics* 25: 49–69.

Pennycook, A. 1994. *The cultural politics of English as an international language.* London: Longman.

———. 1998. *English and the discourses of colonialism.* London: Routledge.

———. 2000. The social politics and cultural politics of language classrooms. In *The sociopolitics of English language teaching,* ed. J. Hall and W. Eggington, 89–103. Clevedon: Multilingual Matters.

Pérez, B., ed. 1998. *Sociocultural contexts of language and literacy.* Mahwah, NJ: Lawrence Erlbaum Associates.

Perry, T., and L. Delpit, eds. 1998. *The real Ebonics debate: Power, language, and the education of African-American children.* Boston: Beacon Press.

Peters, C. 2000. *Deaf American literature: From carnival to the canon.* Washington, DC: Gallaudet University Press.

Phillips, J., ed. 1999. *Foreign language standards: Linking research, theories, and practices.* Lincolnwood, IL: National Textbook Co., in conjunction with the American Council on the Teaching of Foreign Languages.

Phillipson, R. 1988. Linguicism: Structures and ideologies in linguistic imperialism. In *Minority education: From shame to struggle,* ed. T. Skutnabb-Kangas and J. Cummins, 339–358. Clevedon: Multilingual Matters.

———. 1992. *Linguistic imperialism.* Oxford: Oxford University Press.

———. 1998. Language policies: Towards a multidisciplinary approach. In *Al lingva demokratio/Towards linguistic democracy/Vers la démocratie linguistique: Proceedings of the Nitobe Symposium of International Organizations,* ed. M. Fettes and S. Bolduc, 95–97. Rotterdam: Universala Esperanto-Asocio.

———, ed. 2000. *Rights to language: Equity, power, and education.* Mahwah, NJ: Lawrence Erlbaum Associates.

Phillipson, R., M. Rannut, and T. Skutnabb-Kangas. 1995. Introduction. In *Linguistic human rights,* ed. T. Skutnabb-Kangas and R. Phillipson, in conjunction with M. Rannut, 1–22. Berlin: Mouton de Gruyter.

Phillipson, R., and T. Skutnabb-Kangas. 1995. Linguistic rights and wrongs. *Applied Linguistics* 16: 483–504.

———. 1996. English only worldwide or language ecology? *TESOL Quarterly* 30: 429–452.

Pieterse, H. 1991. Taalbeplanningsmodelle vir Suid-Afrika: 'n oorsig en voorlopige sintese. *Tydskrif vir Geesteswetenskappe* 31: 87–100.

Pinnock, P. 1994. *Xhosa: A cultural grammar for beginners.* Cape Town: African Sun Press.

Polinsky, M. 1996. Russian in the U.S.: An endangered language? Unpublished ms.

Poon, A. 2000. *Medium of instruction in Hong Kong: Policy and practice.* Lanham, MD: University Press of America.

Popper, K. 1959. *The logic of scientific discovery.* New York: Harper & Row.

Porter, R. 1990. *Forked tongue: The politics of bilingual education.* New York: Basic Books.

Posner, R. 1996. *The Romance languages.* Cambridge: Cambridge University Press.

Poulos, G., and C. Msimang. 1998. *A linguistic analysis of Zulu.* Cape Town: Via Afrika.

Pratte, R. 1977. *Ideology and education.* New York: David McKay.

———. 1979. *Pluralism in education.* Springfield, IL: Charles C. Thomas.

Pretorius, F., and E. Lemmer, eds. 1998. *South African education and training: Transition in a democratic era.* Johannesburg: Hodder & Stoughton.

Prillwitz, S., and T. Vollhaber, eds. 1990a. *Current trends in European sign language research.* Hamburg: Signum Press.

———, eds. 1990b. *Sign language research and application.* Hamburg: Signum Press.

Prinsloo, K., and C. Malan. 1988. Cultures in contact: Language and the arts in South Africa. In *South Africa,* ed. H. Marais, 257–281. Pinetown: Owen Burgess.

Prinsloo, K., Y. Peeters, J. Turi, and C. van Rensburg, eds. 1993. *Language, law and equality: Proceedings of the Third International Conference of the International Academy of Language Law.* Pretoria: University of South Africa.

Prinsloo, M., and M. Breier, eds. 1996. *The social uses of literacy: Theory and practice in contemporary South Africa.* Amsterdam: John Benjamins.

Pullum, G. 1991. *The great Eskimo vocabulary hoax and other irreverent essays on the study of language.* Chicago: University of Chicago Press.

Quintela, D., I. Ramírez, X. Robertson, and A. Pérez. 1997. ¿Por qué una educación bicultural bilingüe para las personas sordas? *Revista de la Universidad Metropolitana de Ciencias de la Educación* 3: 43–52.

Rahman, T. 1996. British language policies and imperialism in India. *Language Problems and Language Planning* 20: 91–115.

———. 1998. *Language and politics in Pakistan.* Karachi, Pakistan: Oxford University Press.

Ramanathan, V. 1999. 'English is here to stay': A critical look at institutional and educational practices in India. *TESOL Quarterly* 33: 211–231.

Ramirez, J., S. Yuen, D. Ramey, D. Pasta, and D. Billings. 1991. *Longitudinal study of structured English immersion strategy, early-exit and late-exit transitional bilingual education programs for language minority students.* Washington, DC: U.S. Office of Policy and Planning.

Reagan, T. 1983. The economics of language: Implications for language planning. *Language Problems and Language Planning* 7: 148–161.

———. 1984. Language policy, politics and ideology: The case of South Africa. *Issues in Education* 2: 155–164.

———. 1985. 'Taalideologie' en taalbeplanning. *South African Journal of Linguistics* 3: 45–59.

———. 1986a. Considerations on liberation and oppression: The place of English in black education in South Africa. *Journal of Thought* 21: 91–99.

———. 1986b. 'Language ideology' in the language planning process: Two African case studies. *South African Journal of African Languages* 6: 94–97.

———. 1986c. The role of language policy in South African education. *Language Problems and Language Planning* 10: 1–13.
———. 1986d. Taalbeplanning in die Suid-Afrikaanse onderwys: 'n oorsig. *South African Journal of Linguistics* 4: 32–55.
———. 1987a. Ideology and language policy in education: The case of Afrikaans. In *Afrikaans en taalpolitiek,* ed. H. du Plessis and T. du Plessis, 132–139. Pretoria: Haum.
———. 1987b. The politics of linguistic apartheid: Language policies in black education in South Africa. *Journal of Negro Education* 56: 299–312.
———. 1989. Nineteenth-century conceptions of deafness: Implications for contemporary educational practice. *Educational Theory* 39: 39–46.
———. 1990a. Cultural considerations in the education of deaf children. In *Research in educational and developmental aspects of deafness,* ed. D. Moores and K. Meadow-Orlans, 74–84. Washington, DC: Gallaudet University Press.
———. 1990b. The development and reform of sign languages. In *Language reform: History and future,* vol. 5, ed. I. Fodor and C. Hagège, 253–267. Hamburg: Buske Verlag.
———. 1990c. Responding to linguistic diversity in South Africa: The contribution of language planning. *South African Journal of Linguistics* 8: 178–184.
———. 1992a. The comparative analysis of sign languages: Issues and challenges. In *Language as barrier and bridge,* ed. K. Müller, 103–114. Lanham, MD: University Press of America and the Center for Research and Documentation on World Language Problems.
———. 1992b. The deaf as a linguistic minority: Educational considerations. In *Special education at the century's end,* ed. T. Hehir and T. Latus, 305–320. Cambridge, MA: Harvard Educational Review.
———. 1995a. A sociocultural understanding of deafness: American Sign Language and the culture of deaf people. *International Journal of Intercultural Relations* 19: 239–251.
———. 1995b. Language planning and language policy in South Africa: A perspective on the future. In *Language and social history: Studies in South African sociolinguistics,* ed. R. Mesthrie, 315–328. Cape Town: David Philip.
———. 1995c. "Neither easy to understand nor pleasing to see": The development of manual sign codes as language planning activity. *Language Problems and Language Plannning* 19: 133–150.
———. 1996. The contribution of language planning and language policy to the reconciliation of unity and diversity in the post-Cold War era. In *Language status in the post-Cold War era,* ed. K. Müller, 59–66. Lanham, MD: University Press of America and the Center for Research and Documentation on World Language Problems.
———. 1997a. The case for applied linguistics in teacher education. *Journal of Teacher Education* 48: 185–195.
———. 1997b. When is a language not a language? Challenges to 'linguistic legitimacy' in educational discourse. *Educational Foundations* 11: 5–28.
———. 1998a. A rejoinder to Donald Vandenberg. *Educational Foundations* 12: 87–90.
———. 1998b. Multilingualism and language competition in contemporary South Africa: A case study of the role of language rights in nation-building. In

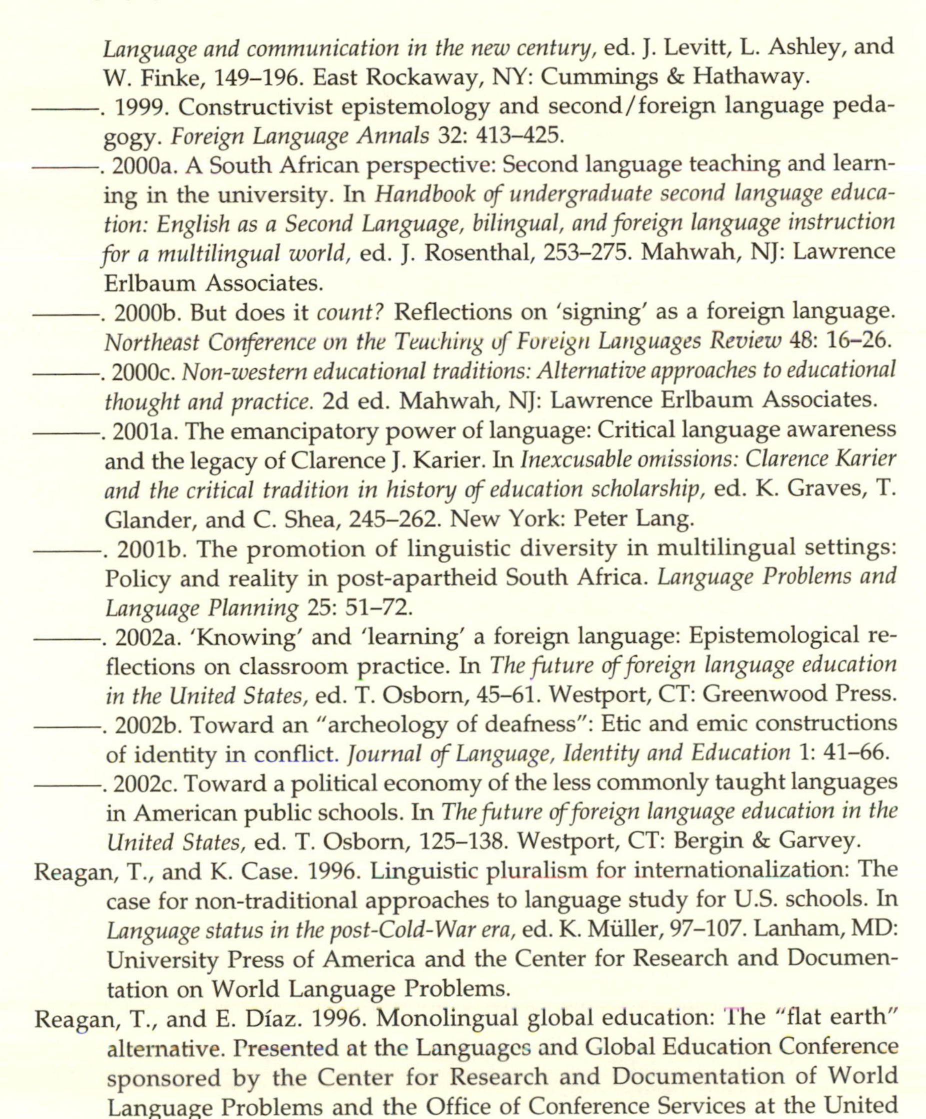

Language and communication in the new century, ed. J. Levitt, L. Ashley, and W. Finke, 149–196. East Rockaway, NY: Cummings & Hathaway.

———. 1999. Constructivist epistemology and second/foreign language pedagogy. *Foreign Language Annals* 32: 413–425.

———. 2000a. A South African perspective: Second language teaching and learning in the university. In *Handbook of undergraduate second language education: English as a Second Language, bilingual, and foreign language instruction for a multilingual world,* ed. J. Rosenthal, 253–275. Mahwah, NJ: Lawrence Erlbaum Associates.

———. 2000b. But does it *count?* Reflections on 'signing' as a foreign language. *Northeast Conference on the Teaching of Foreign Languages Review* 48: 16–26.

———. 2000c. *Non-western educational traditions: Alternative approaches to educational thought and practice.* 2d ed. Mahwah, NJ: Lawrence Erlbaum Associates.

———. 2001a. The emancipatory power of language: Critical language awareness and the legacy of Clarence J. Karier. In *Inexcusable omissions: Clarence Karier and the critical tradition in history of education scholarship,* ed. K. Graves, T. Glander, and C. Shea, 245–262. New York: Peter Lang.

———. 2001b. The promotion of linguistic diversity in multilingual settings: Policy and reality in post-apartheid South Africa. *Language Problems and Language Planning* 25: 51–72.

———. 2002a. 'Knowing' and 'learning' a foreign language: Epistemological reflections on classroom practice. In *The future of foreign language education in the United States,* ed. T. Osborn, 45–61. Westport, CT: Greenwood Press.

———. 2002b. Toward an "archeology of deafness": Etic and emic constructions of identity in conflict. *Journal of Language, Identity and Education* 1: 41–66.

———. 2002c. Toward a political economy of the less commonly taught languages in American public schools. In *The future of foreign language education in the United States,* ed. T. Osborn, 125–138. Westport, CT: Bergin & Garvey.

Reagan, T., and K. Case. 1996. Linguistic pluralism for internationalization: The case for non-traditional approaches to language study for U.S. schools. In *Language status in the post-Cold-War era,* ed. K. Müller, 97–107. Lanham, MD: University Press of America and the Center for Research and Documentation on World Language Problems.

Reagan, T., and E. Díaz. 1996. Monolingual global education: The "flat earth" alternative. Presented at the Languages and Global Education Conference sponsored by the Center for Research and Documentation of World Language Problems and the Office of Conference Services at the United Nations, 3 May.

Reagan, T., and I. Ntshoe. 1987. Language policy and black education in South Africa. *Journal of Research and Development in Education* 20: 1–18.

Reagan, T., and T. Osborn. 1998. Power, authority, and domination in foreign language education: Toward an analysis of educational failure. *Educational Foundations* 12: 45–62.

———. 2002. *The foreign language educator in society: Toward a critical pedagogy.* Mahwah, NJ: Lawrence Erlbaum Associates.

Reagan, T., and C. Penn. 1997. Language policy, South African Sign Language, and the deaf: Social and educational implications. *Southern African Journal of Applied Language Studies* 5: 1–13.

Reagan, T., and J. Vorster. 2000. Die politiek van vergetelheid: Stand van die minder-algemeen-onderrigte tale. *Language Problems and Language Planning* 24: 55–76.

Ricento, T., and B. Burnaby, eds. 1998. *Language and politics in the United States and Canada: Myths and realities.* Mahwah, NJ: Lawrence Erlbaum Associates.

Richard-Amato, P. 1988. *Making it happen: Interaction in the second language classroom.* Reading, MA: Addison-Wesley.

Richards, J., and T. Rodgers. 2001. *Approaches and methods in language teaching.* 2d ed. New York: Cambridge University Press.

Rickford, J., and R. Rickford. 2000. *Spoken soul: The story of Black English.* New York: John Wiley & Sons.

Ridge, S. 1996. Language policy in a democratic South Africa. In *Language policies in English-dominant countries,* ed. M. Herrman and B. Burnaby, 15–34. Clevedon: Multilingual Matters.

Robinson, C. 1996. Winds of change in Africa: Fresh air for African languages? Some preliminary reflections. In *Change and language,* ed. H. Coleman and L. Cameron, 166–182. Clevedon: Multilingual Matters, in association with the British Association for Applied Linguistics.

Romaine, S. 2000. *Language in society: An introduction to sociolinguistics.* 2d ed. Oxford: Oxford University Press.

Rose, P. 1999. Theorizing Athenian imperialism and the Athenian state. In *Contextualizing classics,* ed. T. Falkner, N. Felson, and D. Konstan, 19–39. Lanham, MD: Rowman & Littlefield.

Rotberg, R. 1987. The ascendancy of Afrikanerdom. In *The anti-apartheid reader: South Africa and the struggle against white racist rule,* ed. D. Mermelstein, 78–91. New York: Grove Press.

Rouchette, B. 1997. *Le latin dans le monde grec.* Bruxelles: Latomus Revue d'Études Latines.

Rousseau, P. 1995. 'Learned women' and the development of a Christian culture in late antiquity. *Symbolae Osloensesm* 70: 116–147.

Rubin, J., and B. Jernudd, eds. 1971. *Can language be planned? Sociolinguistic theory and practice for developing nations.* Honolulu: University Press of Hawaii.

Ruíz, R. 1991. The empowerment of language minority students. In *Empowerment through multicultural education,* ed. C. Sleeter, 217–227. Albany: State University of New York Press.

Rutherford, S. 1993. *A study of American deaf folklore.* Silver Spring, MD: Linstok Press.

Ryazanova-Clarke, L., and T. Wade. 1999. *The Russian language today.* London: Routledge.

Ryding, K. C. 1989. Less commonly taught languages: The current situation. In *Language teaching, testing, and technology,* ed. J. Alatis, 114–121. Washington, DC: Georgetown University Press.

Sacks, O. 1989. *Seeing voices: A journey into the world of the deaf.* Berkeley: University of California Press.

Saffire, P., and C. Freis. 1999. *Ancient Greek alive.* 3rd ed. Chapel Hill: University of North Carolina Press.

Samway, K. D., and D. McKeon. 1999. *Myths and realities: Best practices for language minority students.* Portsmouth, NH: Heinemann.

Sánchez, R. 1981. Spanish for native speakers at the university: Suggestions. In *Teaching Spanish to the hispanic bilingual,* ed. G. Valdés, A. Lozano, and R. García-Moya, 91–99. New York: Teachers College Press.

Sarinjeive, D. 1997. Realities and ideologies of English and 'other' Englishes. *Journal for Language Teaching* 31: 68–76.

———. 1999. The mother-tongue, English and student aspirations and realities. *Journal for Language Teaching* 33: 128–140.

Schein, J. 1984. *Speaking the language of sign: The art and science of signing.* Garden City, NY: Doubleday.

———. 1989. *At home among strangers: Exploring the deaf community in the United States.* Washington, DC: Gallaudet University Press.

Schein, J., and D. Stewart. 1995. *Language in motion: Exploring the nature of sign.* Washington, DC: Gallaudet University Press.

Schiffman, H. 1996. *Linguistic culture and language policy.* New York: Routledge.

Schlesinger, I., and L. Namir, eds. 1978. *Sign language of the deaf: Psychological, linguistic and sociological perspectives.* New York: Academic Press.

Schmied, J. 1991. *English in Africa: An introduction.* New York: Longman.

Schneider, E. 1989. *American earlier Black English: Morphological and syntactic variables.* Tuscaloosa, AL: The University of Alabama Press.

Schorr, J. 1997. Give Oakland's schools a break. *The New York Times* (2 January), A–19.

Schuring, G. 1991. Language policies in Africa and their relevance to a future South Africa. In *South Africa in the nineties,* ed. D. van Vuuren, N. Wiehahn, N. Rhoodie, and M. Wiechers, 617–647. Pretoria: Human Sciences Research Council.

Scott, J. 1998. The serious side of Ebonics humor. *Journal of English Linguistics* 26: 137–155.

Searle, C. 1983. A common language. *Race and Class* 34: 45–54.

Shapiro, M., and H. Schiffman. 1981. *Language and society in South Asia.* Columbia, MO: South Asia Books.

Shinagawa, L., and M. Jang. 1998. *Atlas of American diversity.* Walnut Creek, CA: Altamira Press.

Shopen, T., ed. 1979a. *Languages and their speakers.* Philadelphia: University of Pennsylvania Press.

———, ed. 1979b. *Languages and their status.* Philadelphia: University of Pennsylvania Press.

Sign language: A way to talk, but is it foreign? 1992. *The New York Times* (7 January).

Simon, P. 1980. *The tongue-tied American: Confronting the foreign language crisis.* New York: Continuum.

Simon, R. 1987. Empowerment as a pedagogy of possibility. *Language Arts* 64: 370–389.

Siple, P., ed. 1978. *Understanding language through sign language research.* New York: Academic Press.

Siple, P., and S. Fischer, eds. 1991. *Theoretical issues in sign language research: Psychology.* Chicago: University of Chicago Press.

Skutnabb-Kangas, T. 1988. Multilingualism and the education of minority children. In *Minority education: From shame to struggle,* ed. T. Skutnabb-Kangas and J. Cummins, 9–44. Clevedon: Multilingual Matters.

———. 1994. Linguistic human rights: A prerequisite for bilingualism. In *Bilingualism in deaf education,* ed. I. Ahlgren and K. Hyltenstam, 139–159. Hamburg: Signum Press.

———. 2000a. *Linguistic genocide in education—or worldwide diversity and human rights?* Mahwah, NJ: Lawrence Erlbaum Associates.

———. 2000b. Linguistic human rights and teachers of English. In *The sociopolitics of English language teaching,* ed. J. Hall and W. Eggington, 22–44. Clevedon: Multilingual Matters.

Skutnabb-Kangas, T., and R. Phillipson, eds. 1995. *Linguistic human rights: Overcoming linguistic discrimination.* Berlin: Mouton de Gruyter.

Sleeter, C., ed. 1991. *Empowerment through multicultural education.* Albany: State University of New York Press.

———. 2001. Epistemological diversity in research on preservice teacher preparation for historically underserved children. In *Review of research in education: 25,* ed. W. Secada, 209–250. Washington, DC: American Educational Research Association.

Sleeter, C., and C. Grant. 1988. *Making choices for multicultural education: Five approaches to race, class, and gender.* Columbus, OH: Merrill.

———. 1999. *Making choices for multicultural education: Five approaches to race, class, and gender.* 3rd ed. New York: John Wiley & Sons.

Sleeter, C., and P. McLaren, eds. 1995. *Multicultural education, critical pedagogy, and the politics of difference.* Albany: State University of New York Press.

Smit, B. 1993. Language planning for a future South African educational system: The German language scenario—Pedagogical issues. *Journal for Language Teaching* 27: 155–166.

———. 1996. Towards global learning in post-apartheid South Africa. *Journal for Language Teaching* 30: 59–67.

Smit, U. 1994. Investigating language attitudes as a basis for formulating language policies: A case study. *Southern African Journal of Applied Language Studies* 3: 23–35.

Smith, J. 1977. *On teaching classics.* London: Routledge & Kegan Paul.

Smith, N. 2002. *Language, bananas and bonobos: Linguistic problems, puzzles and polemics.* Oxford: Blackwell.

Smitherman, G. 1977. *Talkin and testifyin: The language of Black America.* Detroit, MI: Wayne State University Press.

———. 2000. *Talkin that talk: Language, culture and education in African America.* London: Routledge.

———. 2001. Language and democracy in the USA and the RSA. In *Language ideologies: Critical perspectives on the Official English Movement,* vol. 2, ed. R. González and I. Melis, 316–345. Mahwah, NJ: Lawrence Erlbaum Associates, in conjunction with the National Council of Teachers of English.

Snow, M., M. Met, and F. Genessee. 1989. A conceptual framework for the integration of language and content in second/foreign language instruction. *TESOL Quarterly* 23: 201–217.

Soder, R., ed. 1996. *Democracy, education, and the schools.* San Francisco, CA: Jossey-Bass.

Sokal, A., and J. Bricmont. 1998. *Fashionable nonsense: Postmodern intellectuals' abuse of science.* New York: Picador.

Spener, D. 1991. Transitional bilingual education and the socialization of immigrants. In *Language issues in literacy and bilingual/multicultural education,* ed. M. Minami and B. Kennedy, 424–446. Cambridge, MA: Harvard Educational Review.

Spolsky, B. 1989. *Conditions for second language learning.* New York: Oxford University Press.

Spring, J. 1994. *Deculturalization and the struggle for equality: A brief history of the education of dominated cultures in the United States.* New York: McGraw-Hill.

———. 2000a. *The intersection of cultures: Multicultural education in the United States and the global economy.* 2d ed. Boston: McGraw-Hill.

———. 2000b. *The universal right to education: Justification, definition, and guidelines.* Mahwah, NJ: Lawrence Erlbaum Associates.

Staples, B. 1997. The trap of ethnic identity: How Africa came to Oakland. *The New York Times* (4 January), A–22.

Steedman, P. 1988. Curriculum and knowledge selection. In *The curriculum,* ed. L. Beyer and M. Apple, 119–139. Albany: State University Press of New York.

Steffe, L. 1995. Alternative epistemologies: An educator's perspective. In *Constructivism in education,* ed. L. Steffe and J. Gale, 489–523. Hillsdale, NJ: Lawrence Erlbaum Associates.

Stevenson, P. 1997. *The German-speaking world: A practical introduction to sociolinguistic issues.* London: Routledge.

Steyn, J. 1980. *Tuiste in eie taal.* Cape Town: Tafelberg.

———. 1987. *Trouwe Afrikaners: Aspekte van Afrikaner-nasionalisme en Suid-Afrikaanse taalpolitiek, 1875–1938.* Cape Town: Tafelberg.

———. 1992. Die behoud van Afrikaans as ampstaal. In *Afrikaans ná apartheid,* ed. V. Webb, 201–226. Pretoria: J. L. van Schaik.

———. 1998. Nuwe aktiwiteite rondom Afrikaans: Die totstandkoming van 'n 'Afrikaans oorlegplatform'. *Tydskrif vir Geesteswetenskappe* 38: 253–264.

Stokoe, W., ed. 1980. *Sign and culture: A reader for students of American Sign Language.* Silver Spring, MD: Linstok Press.

———. 1993. *Sign language structures.* Silver Spring, MD: Linstok Press. (Original publication 1960)

Stokoe, W., D. Casterline, and C. Croneberg. 1976. *A dictionary of American Sign Language on linguistic principles* (new ed.). Silver Spring, MD: Linstok Press.

Stotsky, S. 1999. *Losing our language: How multicultural classroom instruction is undermining our children's ability to read, write, and reason.* New York: Free Press.

Strike, K., E. Haller, and J. Soltis. 1988. *The ethics of school administration.* New York: Teachers College Press.

Strike, K., and J. Soltis. 1992. *The ethics of teaching.* 2d ed. New York: Teachers College Press.

Strike, N. 1996. Talking our way out of the laager: Foreign languages in South African education. *Language Matters: Studies in the Languages of Southern Africa* 27: 253–264.

Sumner, W. [1906] 1940. *Folkways.* Boston: Ginn and Company.
Supalla, S. 1992. *The book of name signs: Naming in American Sign Language.* San Diego, CA: DawnSign Press.
Šušnjar, A. 2000. *Croatian-English/English-Croatian dictionary.* New York: Hippocrene.
Suzuki, B. 1984. Curriculum transformation for multicultural education. *Education and Urban Society* 16: 294–322.
Swain, S. 1996. *Hellenism and empire: Language, classicism, and power in the Greek world,* AD *50–250.* Oxford: Clarendon Press.
Swanepoel, P., and H. Pieterse, eds. 1993. *Perspektiewe op taalbeplanning vir Suid-Afrika/Perspectives on language planning for South Africa.* Pretoria: University of South Africa.
Thompson, L. 1985. *The political mythology of apartheid.* New Haven: Yale University Press.
Tikunoff, W., B. Ward, and D. van Broekhuizen. 1991. *A descriptive study of significant features of exemplary special alternative instructional programs: Executive summary.* Los Alamitos, CA: Southwest Regional Educational Laboratory.
Tokuhama-Espinosa, T. 2001. *Raising multilingual children: Foreign language acquisition and children.* Westport, CT: Bergin & Garvey.
Tollefson, J. 1991. *Planning language, planning inequality: Language policy in the community.* London: Longman.
———, ed. 1995. *Power and inequality in language education.* Cambridge: Cambridge University Press.
———. 2000. Policy and ideology in the spread of English. In *The sociopolitics of English language teaching,* ed. J. Hall and W. Eggington, 7–21. Clevedon: Multilingual Matters.
———, ed. 2002. *Language policies in education: Critical issues.* Mahwah, NJ: Lawrence Erlbaum Associates.
Tonkin, H. 2001. Conclusion: La quête d'une stratégie linguistique mondiale. *Terminogramme* 99/100: 391–405.
Trabasso, T., and D. Harrison. 1976. Introduction. In *Black English,* ed. D. Harrison and T. Trabasso, 1–5. Hillsdale, NJ: Lawrence Erlbaum Associates.
Traugott, E. 1976. Pidgins, creoles, and the origins of vernacular Black English. In *Black English,* ed. D. Harrison and T. Trabasso, 57–93. Hillsdale, NJ: Lawrence Erlbaum Associates.
Traupman, J. 1997. *Conversational Latin for oral proficiency.* 2d ed. Wauconda, IL: Bolchazy Carducci Publishers.
Trudgill, P. 1995. *Sociolinguistics: An introduction to language and society.* Rev. ed. Harmondsworth, Middlesex: Penguin.
Trudgill, P., and J. Hannah. 1994. *International English: A guide to the varieties of standard English.* 3rd ed. London: Edward Arnold.
Tutu, D. 1983. *Hope and suffering.* Grand Rapids, MI: William Eerdamans.
Uzicanin, N. 1996. *Bosnian-English/English-Bosnian compact dictionary.* New York: Hippocrene.
Valdés, G. 1981. Pedagogical implications of teaching Spanish to the Spanish-speaking in the United States. In *Teaching Spanish to the Hispanic bilingual,*

ed. G. Valdés, A. Lozano, and R. García-Moya, 3–20. New York: Teachers College Press.

Valdés, G., A. Lozano, and R. García-Moya, eds. 1981. *Teaching Spanish to the Hispanic bilingual: Issues, aims, and methods.* New York: Teachers College Press.

Valdman, A. 2000. Comment gérer la variation dans l'enseignement du français langue étrangère aux Etats-Unis. *The French Review* 73: 648–666.

Valli, C., and C. Lucas. 2001. *Linguistics of American Sign Language: An introduction.* 3rd ed. Washington, DC: Clerc Books, Gallaudet University Press.

van Cleve, J., ed. 1993. *Deaf history unveiled: Interpretations from the new scholarship.* Washington, DC: Gallaudet University Press.

Vandenberg, D. 1998. Rejoinder to Reagan. *Educational Foundations* 12: 83–85.

van Dijk, T. 1995. Discourse analysis as ideology analysis. In *Language and peace,* ed. C. Schäffner and A. Wenden, 17–33. Aldershot: Harwood Academic Publishers.

van Lier, L. 1995. *Introducing language awareness.* London: Penguin English.

van Rensburg, C. 1993. Die demokratisering van Afrikaans. In *Linguistica: Festschrifit E. B. van Wyk,* 141–153. Pretoria: J. L. van Schaik.

———, ed. 1997. *Afrikaans in Afrika.* Pretoria: J. L. van Schaik.

van Uden, A. 1986. *Sign languages of deaf people and psycho-linguistics.* Lisse: Swets & Zeitlinger.

Verhoef, M. 1998a. Funksionele meertaligheid in Suid-Afrika: 'n onbereikbare ideaal? *Liberator* 19: 35–50.

———. 1998b. 'n teoretiese aanloop tot taalgesindheidsbeplanning in Suid-Afrika. *South African Journal of Linguistics* 16: 27–33.

Vernon, M., and J. Andrews. 1990. *The psychology of deafness.* New York: Longman.

Vitas, D. 1998. *Croatian.* Hauppauge, NY: Barron's Educational Series.

Walker, C. 2001. *We can't go home again: An argument about Afrocentrism* . Oxford: Oxford University Press.

Walker, G. 1989. The less commonly taught languages in the context of American pedagogy. In *Northeast Conference on the Teaching of Foreign Languages: Shaping the future,* ed. H. Lepke, 111–137. Middlebury, VT: Northeast Conference on the Teaching of Foreign Languages.

———. 1991. Gaining place: The less commonly taught languages in American schools. *Foreign Language Annals* 24: 131–150.

Wallace, C. 1997. The role of language awareness in critical pedagogy. In *Encyclopedia of language and education, Volume 6: Knowledge about language,* ed. L. van Lier and D. Corson, 241–249. Dordrecht: Kluwer Academic Publishers.

Wallace, D. 1996. *Greek grammar beyond the basics: An exegetical syntax of the New Testament.* Grand Rapids, MI: Zondervan.

———. 2000. *The basics of New Testament syntax: An intermediate Greek grammar.* Grand Rapids, MI: Zondervan.

Wallinger, L. 2000. American Sign Language instruction: Moving from protest to practice. *Northeast Conference on the Teaching of Foreign Languages Review* 48: 27–36.

Wallman, J. 1992. *Aping language.* Cambridge: Cambridge University Press.

Wallraff, B. 2000. What global language? *The Atlantic Monthly* 286: 52–66.

Walter, H. 1994. *French inside out: The worldwide development of the French language in the past, present and the future.* New York: Routledge.

Walton, A. 1992. *Expanding the vision of foreign language education: Enter the less commonly taught languages.* National Foreign Language Center Occasional Papers. Washington, DC: National Foreign Language Center.

Waquet, F. 2001. *Latin, or the empire of a sign.* London: Verso.

Wardhaugh, R. 1999. *Proper English: Myths and misundertandings about language.* Oxford: Blackwell.

Warren, A., and L. McCloskey. 1993. Pragmatics: Language in social context. In *The development of language,* ed. J. Gleason, 195–237. New York: Macmillan.

Webb, V., ed. 1992. *Afrikaans ná apartheid.* Pretoria: J. L. van Schaik.

Weibust, P. 1989. Tradition as process: Creating contemporary tradition in a rural Norwegian school and community. *International Journal of Qualitative Studies in Education* 2: 107–122.

Weinstein, B., ed. 1990. *Language policy and political development.* Norwood, NJ: Ablex Publishing.

Weiss, B., ed. 1982. *American education and the European immigrant, 1840–1940.* Urbana: University of Illinois Press.

Wenham, J. 1965. *The elements of New Testament Greek.* Cambridge: Cambridge University Press.

Whitehead, A. 1949. *The aims of education.* New York: Mentor Books.

Wilcox, P. 2000. *Metaphor in American Sign Language.* Washington, DC: Gallaudet University Press.

Wilcox, S., ed. 1988. *Academic acceptance of American Sign Language: A special issue of Sign Language Studies.* Silver Spring, MD: Linstok Press.

———, ed. 1989. *American deaf culture: An anthology.* Burtonsville, MD: Linstok Press.

———. 1990. The structure of signed and spoken languages. *Sign Language Studies* 67: 141–151.

Wilcox, S., and P. Wilcox. 1997. *Learning to see: American Sign Language as a second language.* 2d ed. Englewood Cliffs, NJ: Prentice Hall.

Williams, G. 1992. *Sociolinguistics: A sociological critique.* London: Routledge.

Williams, M., and R. Burden. 1997. *Psychology for language teachers: A social constructivist approach.* Cambridge: Cambridge University Press.

Wink, J. 2000. *Critical pedagogy: Notes from the real world.* 2d ed. New York: Longman.

Wohl, V. 1996. εὐδεβείας ἕνεκα καὶ φιλοτιμίας: Hegemony and democracy at the Panatheaia. *Classica et Mediaevalia: Revue Danoise de Philologie et d'Histoire* 47: 25–88.

Wolfram, W. 1979. *Speech pathology and dialect differences.* Arlington, VA: Center for Applied Linguistics.

Wolfram, W., and R. Fasold. 1974. *The study of social dialects in American English.* Englewood Cliffs, NJ: Prentice-Hall.

Woodward, A., D. Elliott, and K. Nagel, eds. 1988. *Textbooks in school and society.* New York: Garland.

Yau, S. 1982. Creation d'anthroponymes gestuels par une sourde amérindienne isolée. *Amérindia: Revue d'Éthnolinguistique Amérindienne* 7: 7–22.

———. 1990. Lexical branching in sign language. In *Theoretical issues in sign language research: Linguistics,* ed. S. Fischer and P. Siple, 261–278. Chicago: University of Chicago Press.

Yau, S., and J. He. 1990. How do deaf children get their name signs during their first month in school? In *SLR '87: Papers from the Fourth International Symposium on Sign Language Research,* ed. W. Edmondson and F. Karlsson, 242–254. Hamburg: Signum Press.

Yip Po-Ching, and D. Rimmington. 1997. *Chinese: An essential grammar.* London: Routledge.

Young, N. 2001. *Syntax lists for students of New Testament Greek.* Cambridge: Cambridge University Press.

Zotwana, S. 1991. *Xhosa in context: From novice to intermediate.* Cape Town: Perskor.

Index

About the Author

TIMOTHY REAGAN is Professor of Educational Linguistics, Neag School of Education, University of Connecticut.

DATE DUE